Unbelieva

T. Christian Miller joined ProPublica, the non-profit newsroom for investigative journalism, as a senior reporter in 2008. Before that, he worked for the *Los Angeles Times*, where he covered politics, wars, and was once kidnapped by leftist guerrillas in Colombia. His first book, *Blood Money: Wasted Billions, Lost Lives and Corporate Greed in Iraq*, was called one of the 'indispensable' books on the war. He teaches data journalism at the University of California at Berkeley and was a Knight Fellow at Stanford University.

Ken Armstrong joined ProPublica in 2017. He previously worked at the Marshall Project and *Chicago Tribune*, where his work helped prompt the Illinois governor to suspend executions and empty death row. His first book, *Scoreboard, Baby*, with Nick Perry, won the Edgar Allan Poe Award for Non-Fiction. He has been the McGraw Professor of Writing at Princeton and a Nieman Fellow at Harvard.

Both T. Christian Miller and Ken Armstrong have won numerous awards, including a 2016 Pulitzer Prize for their article 'An Unbelievable Story of Rape', on which *Unbelievable* is based. The rights to the dramatisation of this story have been acquired by Netflix.

Unbelievable

T. CHRISTIAN MILLER
&
KEN ARMSTRONG

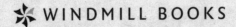 WINDMILL BOOKS

3 5 7 9 10 8 6 4

Windmill Books
20 Vauxhall Bridge Road
London SW1V 2SA

Windmill Books is part of the Penguin Random House group of companies
whose addresses can be found at global.penguinrandomhouse.com

Penguin
Random House
UK

This is an expanded version of 'An Unbelievable Story of Rape'
by T. Christian Miller and Ken Armstrong, which was originally
published on ProPublica (propublica.org) and co-published with
the Marshall Project on 15th December, 2015.

First published by Hutchinson as *A False Report* in 2018
First published in paperback by Windmill Books in 2019

www.penguin.co.uk

A CIP catalogue record for this book is available from the British Library.

ISBN 9781786090072

Book design by Lauren Dong

Printed and bound in Great Britain by Clays Ltd, Elcograf S.p.A.

Contents

DENVER and its suburbs

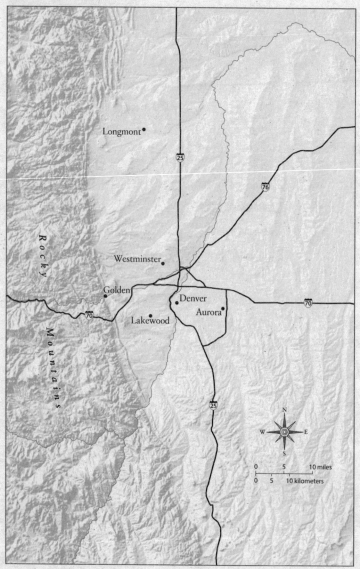

SEATTLE and its suburbs

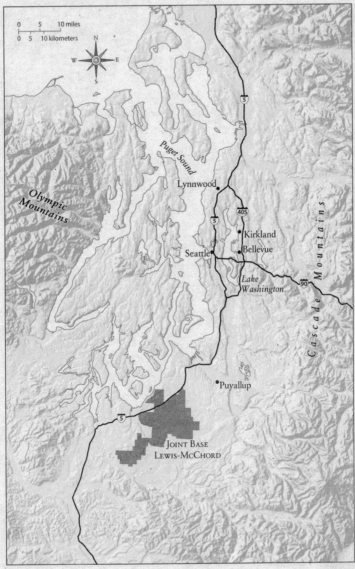

UNBELIEVABLE

1

THE BRIDGE

MARIE LEFT THE INTERVIEW ROOM AND WALKED DOWN the stairs of the police station, accompanied by a detective and a sergeant. She was no longer crying. At the bottom, the police handed her off to the two people who were waiting for her there. Marie belonged to a support program for teenagers aging out of foster care. These two were program managers.

So, one said.

Were you raped?

It had been one week since Marie, an eighteen-year-old with hazel eyes, wavy hair, and braces, had reported being raped by a stranger with a knife who had broken into her apartment and blindfolded, bound, and gagged her. In that week Marie had told the story to police at least five times. She had told them: thin white man, short as five feet six. Blue jeans. Hoodie—gray, maybe white. Eyes—possibly blue. But her story wasn't always the same in the telling. And the police had heard from people in Marie's life who had doubts. And when the police had confronted Marie about those doubts, she had wavered, then buckled, saying she had made the story up—because her foster mom wasn't answering her calls, because her boyfriend was now just a friend, because she wasn't used to being alone.

Because she had wanted attention.

She'd sketched her history for the police detectives. She'd described growing up with something like twenty different foster parents. She'd told them she had been raped when she was seven years old. She'd told them that being on her own for the first time had made her scared. Her story of being raped by an intruder had "turned into a big thing that was never meant to happen," she'd told the police.

Today she had tested whatever patience the police could still summon. She had returned to the station and doubled back, saying she had told the truth the first time, saying she really had been raped. But when pressed in that interview room she had folded once more—admitting, again, that her story was a lie.

No, Marie told the managers at the bottom of the stairs.

No. I was not raped.

The two managers, Jana and Wayne, worked for Project Ladder, a nonprofit program that helped foster kids make the transition to living on their own. Project Ladder taught teenagers—eighteen-year-olds, mostly—the mundane skills of adulthood, from how to shop for groceries to how to manage a credit card. The biggest boost the program provided was financial. Project Ladder subsidized each teen's one-bedroom apartment, making it possible for the kids to get a foothold in the expensive rental market ringing Seattle. Wayne was Marie's case manager. Jana was a program supervisor.

If that's the case, the managers told Marie, if you weren't raped, then there's something you have to do.

Marie dreaded whatever was next. She had seen it on their faces when she'd answered the question. They weren't thrown. They weren't taken aback. They'd doubted her before, just like the others. It occurred to Marie that from now on, people would think she was mentally ill. She, too, wondered if she was broken, if there was something in her that needed to be fixed. Marie realized just how vulnerable she had become. She worried about losing what little she had left. A week ago, she'd had friends, her first job, her first place to call her own, freedom to come and go, a sense of life unfurling. But now that job and that sense of optimism were gone. The place and her freedom were in jeopardy. And friends she could turn to? She was down to one.

Her story had, indeed, turned into a big thing. Last week the television news had been all over it. "A western Washington woman has confessed that she cried wolf," one newscast said. In Seattle the local affiliates for ABC, NBC, and CBS had covered the story. The NBC affiliate, KING 5, zoomed in on Marie's apartment complex—panning up the stairs, lingering on an open window—while Jean Enersen, Seattle's most popular anchor, told viewers: "Police in Lynnwood now say a woman who claimed she was sexually assaulted by a stranger made up the story. . . . Detectives do not know why she made the story up. She could face a charge of false reporting."

Television reporters had pounded on her door, tried to get her to answer questions on camera about why she had lied. To get away she'd snuck out, a sweatshirt over her face.

Her story found its way into remote corners of the Internet. False Rape Society, a blog that focuses on wrongful accusations, posted twice about the Lynnwood case: "Another in a seemingly endless cavalcade of false rape claims. Once again, the accuser is young—a teenager. . . . To underscore how serious this particular kind of lie is, sentencing for false rape claims needs to be tougher. Much tougher. Only then will the liars be deterred." A Londoner who compiles an "international timeline of false rape allegations" going back to 1674 made the Lynnwood case his 1,188th entry, following a Georgia teenager who "had consensual sex with another student then pointed the finger at an imaginary man who was driving a green Chevrolet," and a teen in England who "appears to have withdrawn her consent after texting him to tell him how much she enjoyed it!" "As will be seen from this database," the compiler writes, "some women will cry rape at the drop of a hat, or more often after dropping their knickers then regretting it."

In Washington and beyond, Marie's story became an exhibit in a centuries-long argument about credibility and rape.

The news stories hadn't named her. But the people around Marie knew. A friend from tenth grade called and said: How could you lie about something like that? It was the same question the TV reporters wanted to ask. It was the same question Marie got wherever she turned. She didn't answer her friend. She just listened, then hung up—another friendship, gone. Marie had let another friend borrow her laptop computer—one of those old black IBMs—and now the friend refused to give it back. When Marie confronted her, she told Marie: If you can lie, I can steal. This same friend—or former friend—would call Marie and threaten her, telling her she should die. People held Marie up as the reason no one believed real victims of rape. People called her a bitch and a whore.

The Project Ladder managers told Marie what she had to do. And they told her that if she didn't do it, she would be cast out of the program. She would lose her subsidized apartment. She would be without a home.

The managers took Marie back to her apartment complex and summoned the other teens in Project Ladder—Marie's peers, kids her age with the same kinds of stories to tell about growing up as wards of the state. There were around ten of them. Most were girls. In the front office, near the pool, they gathered in a circle and sat down. Marie stood. She stood and told them—told everyone, including the upstairs neighbor who one week before had made the 911 call to report the rape—that it was all a lie, that they didn't need to worry: There was no rapist out there to be on guard against, no rapist the police needed to be looking for.

She cried as she confessed—the sound magnified by the awkward silence surrounding her. If there was sympathy in the room, Marie sensed it from just one person, a girl sitting to her right. In everyone else's eyes she saw a question—*Why would you do that?*—and a corresponding judgment: *That's messed up.*

In the weeks and months to come, there would be more fallout from Marie's retraction. But for Marie there would be no moment worse than this.

She had one friend left to turn to, and after the meeting, Marie made for Ashley's home. Marie didn't have a driver's license—just a learner's permit—so she walked. On the way there, she came to a bridge. The bridge crossed Interstate 5, the state's busiest road, a north–south highway with a ceaseless current of Subarus and eighteen-wheelers.

Marie thought about how much she wanted to jump.

She took out her phone, called Ashley, and said: Please come get me before I do something stupid.

Then she threw her phone over the side.

2

HUNTERS

January 5, 2011
Golden, Colorado

A LITTLE AFTER 1:00 P.M. ON WEDNESDAY, JANUARY 5, 2011, Detective Stacy Galbraith approached a long row of anonymous apartment buildings that spilled down a low hill. Dirty, half-melted snow covered the ground in patches. Winter-bare trees stood gray against the orange and olive walls of the three-story complex. It was blustery, and biting cold. Galbraith was there to investigate a report of rape.

Uniforms swarmed a ground-floor apartment. Beat cops knocked on neighbors' doors. Crime scene analysts snapped pictures. Paramedics pulled up in an ambulance. Galbraith stood out in the chaotic scene. She was a woman in a swirl mostly of men. Her face was narrow, her hair straight and blond, running past her shoulders. She had a physique like a long-distance runner, lean and coiled. Her eyes were blue.

She walked over to one of the cops. He motioned to a woman in a brown, full-length coat, standing outside the apartment in the thin winter sunlight. She clutched a bag of her belongings in one hand. Galbraith guessed that she was in her twenties, maybe five feet six. She was slight, with dark hair. She looked calm, un-flustered.

The victim.

Galbraith walked up and introduced herself. Want to talk in my car? she asked. It would be warmer there. Safer there. The woman agreed. They slid into the front seat, and Galbraith blasted the heat.

The woman's name was Amber. She was a graduate student at a local college. It was winter break, and her roommate had returned home for the vacation. She had remained at the apartment, luxuriating in the time to herself, staying up late and sleeping all day. Her boyfriend had driven from out of town to visit her. The previous night, though, she spent alone. She cooked herself dinner. She curled up in bed for a marathon of *Desperate Housewives* and *The Big Bang Theory*. It was so late by the time she drifted off that she could hear other people in the complex stirring for work.

She had just fallen asleep when something jolted her awake. In the morning half-light, she saw a shape looming above her. Her senses began to process what was happening. *There was a man in her bedroom*. A black mask covered his face. He wore a gray hoodie. He had on sweatpants. His shoes were black. In his hand, he gripped a gun. It was pointed straight at her.

"Don't scream. Don't call or I'll shoot you," he told her.

Adrenaline raced through her. Her eyes snapped to the gun. She would remember that it was shiny, silver, with black marks.

She pleaded: Don't hurt me. Don't hit me.

She offered him the cash she had in the apartment.

"Fuck you," he told her.

The man terrified her. He was going to hurt her. He was willing to kill her. So she made up her mind: she would not fight. She chose to endure. She would do whatever he told her to do.

He shrugged a green-and-black backpack onto the floor. Inside was everything he needed. He stashed his equipment in clear plastic sandwich bags. They were labeled with neat block letters. GAG. CONDOMS. VIBE. WASTE.

He ordered her to take off her thermal pajamas. Amber watched as he pulled a pair of white, thigh-high stockings from the bag and rolled them up her legs. He asked whether she had high heels. When she said no, he pulled clear plastic high heels from his bag. They had pink ribbons for laces, which he wound up her lower legs. He reached into his bag again, producing pink ponytail holders, and styled her hair into pigtails. Where was her makeup? She retrieved her cosmetic kit from a dresser. His instructions were precise. Eye shadow first. Then lipstick. More. He wanted her lips pinker, he told her. Finally, he ordered her to lie on her mattress. He took a black, silky ribbon from his bag. Put your hands on your back, he said. He tied the ribbon loosely around her wrists.

With a shock, Amber recognized the ribbon. She had bought it with her boyfriend. They had searched for it weeks before, but had not been able to find it. Amber had assumed she had misplaced it. Now, she was confused. How did the rapist have her ribbon?

For the next four hours, the man raped Amber repeatedly. When he would tire, he would rest, dressed only in his shirt, and drink from a bottle of water. When she complained of pain, he applied lubrication. When she said she was cold, he covered her in her pink-and-green comforter. He told her what to do and how to do it. He told her that she was a "good girl." He did not use a condom.

He brought with him a pink digital camera. He posed her on her bed. Move this way, he ordered. Turn that way. When everything was to his liking, he took pictures. He'd stop in the middle of a rape and take more pictures. She had no idea how many photos he had taken, she told Galbraith. Sometimes, he would snap away for twenty minutes at a time. He told her that he would use the photos to convince police the rape was consensual. And he would post them to a porn site on the Internet where everyone could see them—her parents, her friends, her boyfriend.

Amber decided to survive by making herself as human as possible. Every time the man stopped to rest, she asked him questions. Sometimes, he would say nothing. But other times, they would chat for twenty minutes. The man recounted in detail how he had hunted her. It seemed almost to relax him.

He had been watching her through her apartment windows since August, he told her. He knew her full name. He knew her date of birth, her passport number, the license plate of her car. He knew what she was studying and where. He knew that at night, before she went to bed, she would talk to herself in her bathroom mirror.

All of it, Amber told Galbraith, was true. The man wasn't bluffing.

Amber asked about the man's background. He told her that he spoke three foreign languages, Latin, Spanish, and Russian. That he had traveled all over, to Korea, Thailand, the Philippines. That he had attended college and didn't need money. He told her that he was in the military. He said he knew lots of cops.

His world, he told Amber, was "complicated." People were wolves or bravos. The bravos never hurt women or children. But the wolves could do as they pleased.

He was a wolf.

Amber never saw the rapist's face, she told Galbraith. But she had tried to remember as many physical details as possible. He was white. His hair was short and blond; his eyes were hazel. She guessed he was six feet two, about 180 pounds. His gray sweatpants had holes in the knees. His black shoes sported an Adidas logo. He had shaved his pubic area. He was a little chubby.

One detail on his body stood out, she told Galbraith. The man had a brown birthmark on his calf.

When he had finished, it was almost noon. He used wet wipes to clean Amber's face. He ordered Amber into her bathroom and made her brush her teeth. He told her to get into the shower. He watched her soap up, telling her what parts of her body to scrub. When she finished, he told her to remain in the shower for ten more minutes.

Before he left, he told her how he had entered her apartment through the sliding glass door in the back. He told her to put a wooden dowel into the track at the bottom of the door to make sure it was secure. It was much safer, he told her. People like him would not be able to get inside.

He closed the door, and left.

After she got out of the shower, she found that the rapist had ransacked her bedroom, taking the sheets with him, along with her blue silk underwear. He left her pink-and-green comforter bunched on the floor at the foot of her bed.

She found her phone and dialed her boyfriend. She told him she had been raped. He urged her to call the police. She resisted the idea, but he eventually convinced her to call. Amber hung up and dialed 911.

It was 12:31 p.m.

GALBRAITH HAD LISTENED to the woman with alarm. The stalking. The mask. The backpack full of rape tools. The attack was so heinous, the attacker so practiced. There was no time to waste. The investigation would start now, in the front seat of the patrol car.

Galbraith knew that every rape involves three separate crime scenes: the location of the assault, the body of the attacker, and the body of the victim. Each can provide valuable clues. The rapist had already tried to erase himself from one: Amber's body. Galbraith asked Amber if she would allow her to collect DNA evidence using sterile swabs that looked like long, thin Q-tips. As she brushed the swabs across Amber's face, Galbraith could only hope. Perhaps the rapist had failed. Perhaps he had left some small part of himself behind.

Galbraith made another big ask: Did Amber think she could go back into her apartment, to point out anything the rapist might have touched? Again, Amber agreed. Together, the two women walked through the rape. Amber showed Galbraith the pink-and-green comforter on the floor that the attacker had yanked off the bed. She showed her the bathroom that the rapist had used several times during the ordeal. Throughout, Galbraith asked for details. What was the mask like? It wasn't a ski mask, Amber said. It was more like a wrap. He had cinched it tight against his head with safety pins. Could she remember anything about the bottle of water? Yes, the brand was Arrowhead. What did the birthmark look like? Amber drew a picture: a round blot the size of a chicken egg.

When Amber remembered that the man had draped the comforter on her to keep her warm, she called him "gentle."

It puzzled Galbraith. How could anyone, after this happened, describe her attacker as gentle? And it worried her. Maybe the guy came across as normal. Maybe he was a cop. "He's going to be hard to find," she told herself.

After the tour, Galbraith drove Amber to St. Anthony North, some thirty minutes away. It was the nearest hospital with a sexual assault nurse examiner, specially trained to examine rape victims. The nurse would inspect every inch of Amber's body in search of clues. Before they'd left for the exam, Amber turned to Galbraith. The attacker had told her that she was his first victim. Amber thought he was lying.

"I think he's done this before," she said.

On her way back to the crime scene, Galbraith's mind raced. Amber's story seemed almost unbelievable. A rapist dressed all in black? With a backpack stuffed with all the necessities for rape? And the confidence to spend four hours attacking a woman during daylight hours at a busy apartment complex?

It wasn't anything like most rapes that she had handled. Usually, the victim was attacked by somebody she knew, or at least had met: a boyfriend, an old flame, someone at a club. Rapes weren't usually whodunits. They were whathappeneds. Had the woman consented to the sexual act? A national government survey found that about 150,000 men and women reported being raped or sexually assaulted in the United States in 2014—a number equivalent to the population of Fort Lauderdale, Florida. About 85 percent of attacks were classified as acquaintance rape.

Galbraith knew she was dealing with a relatively rare case: stranger rape. These cases could be easier to take to trial, because they often dealt with what prosecutors referred to as a "righteous victim." This was a woman snatched from the street by a stranger brandishing a weapon. The woman fought and screamed, but in the end had no choice but to submit. She was a mother or daughter with a loving family. She had a nice home, a steady job. She dressed modestly. She had not been drinking. She had not been hanging out in some seedy part of town. These were the rapes that prosecutors found easiest to prosecute. They met all the expectations that a jury might have of a violated woman.

Amber fit some of these criteria—but not all. She had been so cool and calm. She had talked with her rapist, referred to him as "gentle." She talked with her boyfriend before calling the police.

None of that bothered Galbraith. She knew that the universe of women who had been raped looked identical to the universe of women. They could be mothers, teens, sex workers. They could live in mansions or in flophouses. They could be homeless or suffer from schizophrenia. They could be black or white or Asian. They could be passed out drunk or completely sober. And they could react to the crime in all kinds of ways. They could be hysterical. Or withdrawn. They could tell a friend, or they could tell no one. They might call the cops right away, or they might wait a week, a month, even years.

Cops took differing approaches to investigating a rape. Though rape was one of the most common forms of violent crime, there was no universal consensus on the best way to solve it. For some detectives, skepticism was paramount. Women could and sometimes did lie about being raped. A cop was supposed to investigate a claim of sexual assault carefully. "Not every complaint is founded or necessarily results in a criminal charge," cautioned one of the leading police manuals on the subject. For other investigators—including advocates concerned by some cops' shoddy treatment of rape victims—the overriding approach was one of trust. "Start by Believing" was the slogan of one campaign by a major police training group dedicated to improving sexual assault investigations.

At the heart of the debate was a question of belief. With most violent crimes, cops face a victim with obvious injuries. But in sex crimes, the injuries are often not as apparent. In a forensic examination, a woman who has had consensual intercourse can appear the same as a woman who was raped at gunpoint. In sexual assault, the victim's credibility is often at issue as much as the accused's.

Galbraith had her own rule when it came to rape cases: listen and verify. "A lot of times people say, 'Believe your victim, believe your victim,'" Galbraith says. "But I don't think that that's the right standpoint. I think it's listen to your victim. And then corroborate or refute based on how things go."

By the time Galbraith returned to the apartment complex, a dozen officers and technicians were swarming the scene. Galbraith, Detective Marcus Williams, Detective Matt Cole, and a crime scene technician, Kali Gipson, stepped through the apartment. Williams dusted for fingerprints and swabbed for DNA samples, while Gipson and her colleagues took 403 pictures— every light switch, every wall, every piece of clothing.

Outside, cops were snapping photographs and digging through garbage bins. Cigarette butts had been found outside the apartment—but Amber didn't smoke. So two officers, Michael Gutke and Frank Barr, scoured the area for every discarded butt they could find: one from an ashtray outside a neighboring apartment, another from between two parked cars, still others in the parking lot. They collected them all and placed them in evidence bags for transport to the police station.

Other officers canvassed the neighborhood. Over two days, Golden officers knocked on every door in the apartment complex, sixty in all, and interviewed twenty-nine people. Like academic researchers conducting a survey, they used a script to ensure consistency: Did you see anyone suspicious in the area? Anyone carrying a backpack or other odd items? Any unusual vehicles in the neighborhood?

Officer Denise Mehnert knocked on thirty doors in three different buildings, starting at the top floor and moving down to the first. At one apartment, a man told her he had seen a "stocky" man a few nights earlier, walking through the complex with a headlamp. A neighbor from a different building remembered a motor home parked over Christmas on a street outside the complex. Another man said he thought he had seen the RV owner. He had worn a wide-brimmed hat and was "middle aged." Nobody could remember seeing anyone matching the rapist's exact description.

Outside Amber's apartment, a Golden patrol officer found footprints on her back patio. One stood out: a single footprint, preserved in a patch of crunchy snow. Gipson tried to make a replica with snow wax, a slippery, spray-on substance designed to lift an impression without melting the snow that formed it. But the wax didn't stick. So she sprayed the print with fluorescent orange paint. The tread suddenly gleamed against the white background, like something left by an astronaut on the moon. It was not much. But it was something.

Galbraith kept driving the investigators forward. Late in the day, an officer suggested a bathroom break.

"Just keep working!" Galbraith insisted.

By the time she left the scene, it was well after dark.

GALBRAITH GREW UP in Arlington, a plain vanilla suburb of Dallas, Texas. Her dad managed restaurants and later worked as a computer programmer. Her mom worked in engineering analysis at an oil company. They divorced when Galbraith was three, and her mother married a tile layer. She remained close with both her biological parents, and their new and growing families.

In school, she was the smart kid who ran with troublemakers. She thought of herself as anti-authority. She played on the basketball team but was once suspended for several games when she was caught smoking cigarettes with some friends. She hadn't done much to conceal the crime: her principal spied her through a pair of binoculars, wearing her team uniform, outside the school gym.

After graduation, Galbraith drifted through college at the University of North Texas. She wanted to try journalism—though she didn't see a future in it for herself. She liked her psychology classes. Murderers, rapists, serial killers—they fascinated her. "I liked to see how people's minds work, and how it affects their actions," she says. Finally, a college counselor suggested she look into criminal justice as a career. She started taking law enforcement classes. She hung out with officers. She liked what she saw. At its core, policing was about helping others. That resonated: "It's the generic answer, but really I like to help. I like to hold people accountable that do bad things, too."

Still, she didn't go into law enforcement straight from graduation. She thought she wasn't the right fit. Too defiant. Too independent. Maybe not even good enough. "I wanted to be a cop, but it was just like, 'Gosh, I probably couldn't cut it,'" she says.

"I sold myself short."

She got married and followed her husband to Colorado, where he had a job lined up at an auto body repair shop. She took a job at a prison. Her fellow guards told her they loved the work. "This is the best job I've ever had," one told her. "You don't have to do anything." Galbraith hated it, precisely because there was nothing to do. She worked the graveyard shift. She counted sleeping inmates. It bored her beyond measure. "This is not for me," she told herself. "I need to do something. I need to do something useful."

Meanwhile, her marriage was falling apart: her husband didn't like the idea of her spending her days with a bunch of other men. They divorced. Galbraith had no regrets. "I don't dwell too long on anything. Just keep going."

Then came one of those out-of-the-blue breaks that can change a life. When she first arrived in Colorado, Galbraith had applied for work as a police officer in Golden, the type of quiet small town where lots of cops get their first jobs. The job at the Department of Corrections had opened up first, so she took it. But after seven weeks, Golden called to make an offer: an entry-level patrol position, working night shift.

Galbraith quit the prison job that day.

GOLDEN WAS BEST known as the home of Coors Brewing Company, founded in 1873. The brewery—the largest on the planet— filled a valley east of town, a massive sprawl of gray, steel, and smokestack that would not have looked out of place in a Dickens novel. Every year, millions of barrels of beer rolled out of the complex, destined for fraternity houses, football games, and two-for-one ladies' nights.

But if Coors was associated with boozy revelry, the town of Golden was not. About nineteen thousand people lived in the historic town nestled in the foothills of the Rockies. Founded in 1859 during the rush for gold on Pikes Peak, the town had once been the territorial capital of Colorado. It retained a Western feel. Big bank buildings and clapboard storefronts lined the downtown. The old state capitol served as city hall. Many residents owned horses. Elk and deer wandered across town streets.

Christmas Day, 2003, was Galbraith's first time in the field on her own, without a training officer. She celebrated the milestone with the man who would later become her husband: David Galbraith, a fellow cop at the Golden Police Department. They cooked prime rib for dinner. Then they headed out to work the late shift.

Galbraith's first call: haul a dead dog off Interstate 70, the 8,541-cars-per-hour highway running through the middle of Denver. As she arrived on the scene, a second dog wandered into traffic to check out the fate of the first. She watched as that dog, too, was pulverized in the high-speed traffic. None of her police training had included dog carcass cleanup. She pulled her car into the middle of the highway and blocked it off. She stuffed the remains into a plastic bag and dragged everything to the side of the highway. She puked up the prime rib.

This is what I have to do. Somehow I've got to do it, she thought to herself.

It became a life motto. Galbraith didn't like to complain. She didn't like excuses. She wanted to get the job done. And she would work ninety hours a week to do it.

In 2007, pregnant with her first child, Galbraith decided to apply for a job as a detective. It was not a large unit, just one supervisor and three investigators. But with David working night shifts, it made sense as a way to juggle family and work. Galbraith was also ambitious. In law enforcement, detectives are often the top of the heap. They get the big cases. They often make more money. They're the straight-A students in the school of street cops. "I had to do it," she says.

She got the spot—and some blowback. Some cops on Golden's force whispered that she had been made detective only because she was pregnant, as a way to keep her on board. The talk upset Galbraith. But she responded the only way she knew how: by getting to work.

In small towns, detectives handle any crimes that come in the door. But Galbraith found herself gravitating toward sexual assault cases. One memorable case involved an accusation that a teenage boy had molested a ten-year-old boy who lived nearby. The two families—the whole neighborhood, really—were close. The wives drank wine together, the kids all played together, the husbands hung out on weekends. The accusation had circulated among some of the families. "That uprooted this whole neighborhood," Galbraith says.

Galbraith and another investigator interviewed the victim.

The boy had specific recollections. He told the detectives that the accused had assaulted him on a couch. He remembered details about the fabric. It was a small thing, but it was enough to convince Galbraith that the boy wasn't inventing a story. And when the family of the accused allowed Galbraith to question their son, he was evasive. As he sat next to his father, the teenager started to cry. Galbraith walked out onto the porch with her partner.

I'm going to arrest him, she said.

You sure you got it? he asked.

I've got probable cause, she said. We'll let a jury decide.

The teenager was convicted at trial. Families in the neighborhood blamed Galbraith. They saw a crusading cop who railroaded a kid with a future. Galbraith saw it as justice: "What if he's done this to other people? What if he continues? If you could stop him now, then we can maybe not have more victims in the future."

Many detectives avoided sex crimes if they could. They weren't as high profile as homicides; nobody came looking to do a movie about a rape case. Where homicides were black and white, rape was filled with grays. And rape victims were alive and hurting. Their pain was always in your face—and you could never, ever look away.

Galbraith's faith got her through the emotional sandblast of rape cases. Both Galbraith and her husband were born-again Christians raised as Baptists. In Colorado, they attended a nondenominational evangelical church. They sometimes even provided security for Sunday services. "I know He gave me certain strengths, so I just have to use them. Even when it's painful," she says.

There was a passage in the Bible that resonated with her. In Isaiah 6:1–8, God appears, surrounded by smoke and seraphim, seeking someone to spread the Word. God asks: "Whom shall I send?" And Isaiah pipes up: "Here *am* I. Send me!" Galbraith saw herself as answering a call. She had gotten into law enforcement to help. And here were victims who needed help in some of their darkest hours. She didn't always know how to make things better for them. But she knew she had to find a way.

"People say, 'Why do you work sex crimes and kid crimes?' I don't enjoy it. But someone's got to do it. And someone's got to do it well."

IT WAS LONG after dark when Galbraith pulled into the driveway of her house. She was exhausted. Her final task had been to find a place for Amber to sleep; she was too terrified to spend the night at the apartment. Galbraith had found an officer to take her to a friend's house.

David had already washed the dishes and put the kids to sleep. His graveyard shift started later that night.

They settled into two couches facing each other in the living room. This was their evening ritual, wedged into the few hours they could find between work and kids. They talked about their days just like any other working couple—it's just that the Galbraiths' stories tended to be a bit darker than most.

And so it was this night. Stacy Galbraith went over the details of the case with her husband. She talked about the masked man. About the four-hour rape. About how he had taken pictures.

And get this, she told him. At the end, he made her take a shower.

David had been holding back. But this was too much. In 2008, he had left the Golden Police Department to take a new job as an officer in Westminster, a nearby suburb. Five months ago, Westminster police had responded to a rape at an apartment complex; David had patrolled the complex looking for suspicious people. He knew that the woman had been raped by a masked man. That the man had taken pictures. And that before leaving, he had made his victim shower.

Call my department first thing in the morning, he told Stacy.

We have one just like that.

3

WAVES AND PEAKS

August 10, 2008
Lynnwood, Washington

I T WASN'T MUCH—A ONE-BEDROOM APARTMENT LIKE ANY other, in an apartment complex like any other. She didn't have a lot of furniture, and some of what there was, was plastic. She propped her two guitars, both acoustic, against a bedroom wall. She kept her computer monitor on the floor, in a corner.

It wasn't much, but it was hers, the first place she could call her own after years of living in other people's homes. Marie was proud of the place. She was proud of *having* a place. She knew that many people who grew up as she did wound up in jail or rehab, or on the streets.

On this Sunday she vacuumed and cleaned. She liked to keep her apartment spotless. She also wanted it tidy, so she walked around, sizing up her stuff, deciding what she could tuck away. Whatever she didn't need she carried outside and stowed in a storage closet on her back porch. Back and forth she went, through a sliding glass door.

She would spend the rest of the day with friends and at church. Other eighteen-year-olds, in their first months of independence, might dedicate the weekend to testing boundaries and chasing adventure. Marie wanted to settle. She took comfort in normalcy, given how little she'd had growing up.

Marie would later be evaluated by Jon Conte, a University of Washington professor who specializes in mental health issues related to child abuse and trauma. Conte interviewed Marie for five hours and wrote a lengthy report, which included a section on her developmental history:

> She met her biological father only once. She reports not knowing much about her biological mother, who she said would often leave her in the care of boyfriends.... She reports entering foster care at age six or seven.

Conte's report continues with the same dry, clinical language, even as it descends into dark terrain. Marie's memory of life before foster care is "mostly of unhappy events," Conte writes.

> She thinks she lived with a grandmother who did not do a very good job of "taking care of us." She remembers being hungry and eating dog food. She has no memories of being cared for by her biological mother. She recalls physical discipline that was abusive (e.g., being hit on the hand with a flyswatter).
>
> She does not know if she attended kindergarten. She thinks she had to repeat second grade and had time outs in school. She said she remembers not liking the police because they took her and her siblings away from their home. She was sexually and physically abused. The sexual abuse happened a lot, she said. She recalls seeing the family dogs beaten by her mother's various boyfriends.
>
> She recalls multiple moves from one state to another before being removed from her home ...

As for Marie's life in foster care, Conte's report forgoes the details:

> Suffice it to say it is fairly typical for children in state care: multiple placements, frequent moving of locations (homes)

and schools, adult caregivers and professionals coming in and then out of her life, some distressing or abusive experiences, and a general lack of permanency.

Marie was the second of her mom's four kids. They were half siblings, but didn't call themselves such. "I have an older brother and younger brother and younger sister," Marie says. Sometimes she'd be in the same foster home as her siblings. Most times they were separated. Whether she has brothers or sisters on her father's side, she can't say.

Marie was medicated from early on for depression. "I was on seven different drugs. And Zoloft is an adult drug. I was on that at eight."

The hardest part, she says, was being kept in the dark about the workings of foster care. Adults wouldn't say why she was being moved. They would just move her. She had "probably ten or eleven" foster families and was placed in a couple of group homes. She preferred to be outside, but sometimes became a shut-in. "When I lived in Bellingham, I played in my room a lot by myself. My stuffed animals."

Switching schools can be daunting. For Marie it was routine. "Start over, make new friends. It was a little bit rough, but I got used to doing it."

The beginning of high school promised an end to all the instability. The first day of school might fill most students with anxiety, but for Marie that day couldn't come soon enough. She was starting tenth grade in Puyallup, some thirty-five miles south of Seattle. She'd landed all the classes she wanted. She'd made lots of new friends. Most important, she was with a new family. She loved the family, and the family loved her. They planned to adopt her.

"It was pretty awesome," Marie says.

Then, at school, on that very first day, Marie got pulled out of class. A support counselor told her: You can't live with this foster family anymore. They've lost their license. The counselor, bound by confidentiality, provided little explanation. Marie simply had to leave—the family, her friends, the school. "I pretty much just cried," she says. "I basically had twenty minutes to pack my stuff and go."

As a short-term placement until something else could be lined up, Marie went to stay with a couple, Shannon and Geno, in Bellevue, a booming high-tech center just east of Seattle, with a skyline all its own. Shannon, a real estate agent and longtime foster mom, had met Marie through meetings for kids with troubled pasts and had sensed a kindred spirit. They were both "kind of goofy," Shannon says. "We could laugh at each other and make fun. We were a lot alike."

The two hit it off. To Shannon, Marie was "real likable"—it was as simple as that. Marie wasn't bitter about all she had been through. And she didn't bristle at all that was ahead. Shannon didn't have to push Marie out the door to school, even with Marie knowing that the school was likely just another way station. Marie could carry on a conversation with adults. She brushed her teeth; she brushed her hair; she was, in a word, easy, or at least "she was a lot easier than a lot of the kids we had." Marie wanted to stay in Bellevue, and Shannon wished she could. But Shannon and her husband had another foster child at the time, a teenage girl who required a great deal of attention. Otherwise, Shannon says, "we'd have taken Marie in a heartbeat."

Marie left Shannon's home after a couple of weeks. She moved in with Peggy, who worked as a children's advocate at a homeless shelter and lived in Lynnwood, a smaller suburb about fifteen miles north of Seattle.

"She was my very first foster child. I was preparing for a baby. I had a crib—and they gave me a sixteen-year-old," Peggy says, with a laugh. "And it was fine. I have a background in mental health and I've been working with kids for a really long time. And I think the agency just thought, 'She can handle it.' So."

The state provided Peggy with hundreds of pages on Marie's

history, chronicling her abuse and the litany of placements. "It was heartbreaking," Peggy says. She read most, but not all, of the file. "In some ways you don't want to know everything. You want to be able to look at a child and not make assumptions about who they are, you know? You don't want to put a label on them. When I meet a child, I want to meet a child as they come to me."

To Peggy's mind, the two got off to a good start. "She was like a little kid. She was walking around and going in the backyard and checking it out and going, 'Oh, wow, this is really cool.' She was very bubbly and full of energy, but she also had her moments when she could be very intense, very emotionally intense." Marie was upset about being taken from the home in Puyallup. Peggy gave Marie phone privileges, so she could stay in touch with friends there. Marie racked up a huge bill. In time, she worked through her frustration. "I was actually surprised at how remarkably well she was coping," Peggy says. "She started a brand-new school. It was amazing, really. She could have just said, 'I'm not going to school.' But she didn't. She went, and she did what she was supposed to do. She did chores around the house. I was very impressed with her resiliency."

But this relationship—a first-time mother paired with a teenage daughter with a history of trauma—figured to be a challenge. And it was. "It was very strained at times," Peggy says. "It was very hard to have a loving bond with somebody who comes to you when sixteen and already angry. I saw my job at that point as guiding her into adulthood. And I tried to be a loving parent, and a caring parent. But it's pretty hard to initiate at age sixteen. And I don't know how she would see it, but—"

Marie saw the relationship as a poor fit. Marie liked dogs. Peggy had cats. Marie liked being in homes with other kids. At Peggy's she was it. "Our personalities didn't match at first either," Marie says. "It was hard to get along."

Marie stayed in touch with several former foster families and remained particularly close with Shannon. Peggy didn't mind. She soon became friends with Shannon herself. The two foster mothers shared insights into Marie—and, in a way, raised her together. Shannon, her hair a whirl of curls, was the fun parent. She and Marie went boating. They took walks in the woods. They dieted together, giving up carbohydrates for weeks. Marie trusted Shannon with her emotions; Shannon was someone she could hug and cry with. Marie would sleep over at her house.

Peggy was the disciplinarian. She was the parent who enforced curfew. To her, Marie could come across as flaunty and outrageous. "Really, really big behavior," Peggy says—like going into a grocery store with friends and riding around on a shopping cart, "getting really silly." Analytical and measured, prone to saying, "Tone it down," Peggy did not mesh with Marie in the way that Shannon did. "We were very different," Peggy says.

For Peggy, it was painful to watch Marie struggle to fit in. When she first moved in with Peggy, Marie was into dark clothes, sort of grungy. But she picked out a feminine white coat with a fur collar, because she thought that's what girls were supposed to wear, then relegated the coat to the closet when she realized it wasn't. Peggy could see that Marie wasn't happy at school. It was "pretty cliquey"—with all the clichés, the cheerleaders and the jocks. Marie was "more of an artist type," into drawing and music, be it Christian, rock, or country.

Together, Peggy and Marie found an alternative school that was a better fit.

And that's when things clicked.

Through friends, Marie met Jordan, a high school student who worked at a McDonald's. "We ended up meeting at a grocery store and then walking around the schoolyard, you know, after hours or something like that," Jordan says of the first time they were alone. They started as friends and, in time, became boyfriend and girlfriend. To Jordan, Marie came off as happy and easygoing, no matter her past. "She was just a nice person to have around. . . . You never had to worry about sharing your emotions with her.

She would never say anything to hurt you. Among her friends and things like that, she was not an attention-seeker. She never did anything openly outgoing or off-the-wall crazy."

That Jordan would see Marie so differently from Peggy doesn't necessarily surprise. Peggy saw Marie wanting attention. Jordan saw her avoiding it. Teens can be one person with their friends, another with their parents. But to Marie there was something more to this disconnect, something she would pick up on as the years passed. "People read me different than I see myself," she says. Marie saw herself as friendly, not flirtatious, as outgoing, not dramatic.

Marie figures her happiest years were when she was sixteen and seventeen, and the happiest day may have been one spent with her best friend, another high school student who was teaching Marie the fine points of photography. "I would spend hours at the beach watching the sunset go down and that was one of my favorite things," Marie says. "There was a particular photo that I really liked that she took. We went to the ocean, it was like seven o'clock at night, I don't know what we were thinking, I got in there and I jumped out and swung my hair back."

Her friend captured the moment. Afterward she did touch-up, darkening parts of the picture. Marie looked like a mermaid emerging from the surf, in the glory of the setting sun.

Marie posted the photo on Myspace and preserved it in an online album on Photobucket.

When Marie was a senior, she opted to quit school and study for her general equivalency diploma. That final year with Peggy was marked by tension, the kind familiar to teens and parents just about everywhere. Marie pushed, staying out late. Peggy pushed back, insisting that rules be followed. "You can't do that," Peggy would say. "You can't tell me what to do," Marie would answer. To Shannon, it was just one of those rebellious stages that can accompany the approach of adulthood: "Wanting to do what she wanted to do. Not wanting to follow the rules. She experimented with different ways to dress, which path she was going to go down. Not unlike a lot of teenagers. Started to smoke, those kinds of things." In the spring of 2008, Marie turned eighteen. She could have stayed with Peggy, provided she abided by Peggy's rules. But Marie wanted to set out on her own.

Peggy, searching online, discovered Project Ladder, a pilot program launched the year before. Funded mostly by a state grant, the program sought to reduce homelessness by helping young adults land stable jobs so they could afford a place to live. Program members would learn self-sufficiency and "financial literacy." Private landlords who housed program members would receive guaranteed rent subsidies and large security deposits. Project Ladder had only fifteen slots for teens transitioning out of foster care, but Marie secured one. She moved into an apartment complex in Lynnwood, allowing her to stay close to Peggy.

In the 1920s, decades before it incorporated and adopted its name, Lynnwood was known for poultry, producing enough eggs in one year that "laid end to end they would stretch from New York to San Francisco." These days people around Seattle know Lynnwood mostly as a shopping mecca. The main attraction is the Alderwood Mall and its 165 shops, from Abercrombie & Fitch to Zumiez. Marie's apartment complex advertised views of the Cascades—and proximity to the mall, just a few blocks away.

Marie thought that when she had her feet under her, she'd like to go to college and study photography. She used a Nikon digital to shoot animals, insects, and most of all landscapes. She'd go to a beach dotted with driftwood and shoot dog prints in the sand, or the sun on the Sound, or beyond the waves the snow-capped peaks of the Olympics. But for now she settled into retail, landing her first job at Costco, the warehouse club known for generous wages and benefits. Marie offered food samples to customers. Six hours on her feet didn't bother her. She enjoyed chatting with people, free from pressure to sell. Working also let her make friends outside the foster-care system.

So Marie had an apartment, an income, and her GED. She had a support system in Project Ladder. She had Peggy nearby. After all she had endured—abuse, instability, hunger—she had made it through. Her greatest goal was a simple one—and it was there, right in front of her. "I just wanted to be normal. When I moved out from being in foster care I wanted to be one of those normal kids who had a normal job, a place to live, just wanted to live my life. Try to be as happy as possible." She didn't want to let the bad things in her past affect the way she was now.

AFTER MARIE FINISHED cleaning her apartment, she went to church with Jordan. They had dated for more than a year, but two months ago went back to being just friends. Jordan had begun studying the Jehovah's Witnesses religion, which condemns pre-marital sex; Jordan feared being a hypocrite if he and Marie kept dating. Still, their friendship was closer than most. They both had insomnia and would keep each other company over the phone, chatting late into the night. They even talked of getting married one day.

In the evening Marie visited Ashley, a friend she had made when both were studying for their GEDs. Marie didn't yet have her driver's license—just a learner's permit—so she snagged a ride home from Ashley's mom. When she arrived home, she real-ized she had left her keys behind; she was always forgetting her keys or her phone. So it was back to Ashley's, then home again.

Before tucking in, Marie visited for a few minutes with her upstairs neighbor, Nattlie, a fellow eighteen-year-old in Project Ladder. Nattlie lived directly above Marie in their three-story building, where each apartment was accessible from the outside. By the time Marie went back downstairs, it was after nine o'clock. She walked inside, locked her front door, and settled in for the night.

Her phone rang at 9:49 p.m. It was Jordan. (In days to come

he would check his call history to provide police with the precise time.) Marie and Jordan talked for about fifteen minutes. Afterward, Marie strummed one of her guitars for a bit before getting into bed.

At 12:30 a.m., Jordan called again. This time, the two stayed on the phone for hours. It was now Monday, August 11, and Marie and Jordan talked until four thirty, the call ending only when the battery on Jordan's phone died.

At 4:58 a.m., Jordan called again.

Marie and Jordan talked until a quarter of six.

Then Marie went to sleep.

4

A VIOLENT ALCHEMY

August 10, 2010
Westminster, Colorado

Eᴀʀʟʏ ᴏɴᴇ ᴍᴏʀɴɪɴɢ ɪɴ Aᴜɢᴜsᴛ, ᴀɴ ᴏʟᴅᴇʀ ᴡᴏᴍᴀɴ sᴀᴛ hunched on a bed in Room 24 of the emergency ward of St. Anthony North in suburban Denver. She was eating yogurt and sipping water from a clear plastic bottle. Her hair was dyed red, the color fading. She wore a white, long-sleeved hoodie with a rainbow splashed across its front. Her thin legs stuck out from a pair of blue shorts.

At 8:04 a.m. there was a knock, and a woman with long blond hair and wide blue eyes entered the room. She wore a blue polo shirt and khaki pants with a police badge resting on her hip. She glanced at the woman on the bed. She thought the older woman looked almost like a lost child, her eyes red, her cheeks streaked. She knelt and introduced herself. Her name was Detective Edna Hendershot. "I know that something terrible has happened to you," she told the woman. "I'm here to find out about it."

Sarah had already told her story to the neighbors she did not know, standing in the cool air outside her apartment in the light of early morning. She had already told the young officer who drove her to the hospital in his squad car. She had already told the other woman sitting quietly with her in the hospital room, a victim's advocate the police had assigned to her for support.

She summoned herself. She would tell her story again.

Sarah had moved into a new apartment at the beginning of the month. After days of sorting and storing, of figuring where to put the couch and how to decorate her bedroom, of unpacking boxes of clothes and shoes and kitchen utensils, she decided to rest. She spent Monday morning dozing by the pool. She walked a trail that circled the apartment buildings. That evening, she had read her Bible in her apartment. At around midnight, she changed into her nightgown and fell asleep to the sound of an oscillating fan.

At around three thirty, she was startled awake. A heavy weight pressed into her back, pushing her hard into the bed. It was a man, straddling her with his legs. He had pinned her arms to her side. She cried out, a sound that seemed to die in her throat. "Just be quiet," the man said. "I won't hurt you if you do everything I say. But I do have a gun and can use it if I have to."

The man wore a white T-shirt and sweatpants, Sarah told Hendershot. A black mask covered his face. He bound her hands behind her and stripped off her underwear. He ordered her onto the bed. He instructed her to pose. He took pictures with a camera. If she didn't do it right, he would correct her. "If you don't do what I say, then these pictures are going to be all over the Internet. Everyone will see them," he told her.

For three hours, he forced Sarah to submit. He would rape her, then rest. Take pictures, then rest. Sarah called them "sessions." She could remember nine of them. She would tell him that he was hurting her. "Just relax," he'd say. At one point, Sarah told Hendershot, she pleaded with the rapist to stop.

"I'm not a bad person," she told him.

"No, you're not a bad person," he answered. "But you left your window open."

When he finished with her, the dawn light was creeping into her jumbled apartment. He set to work eradicating evidence. He cleaned Sarah's body with moist towelettes. He ordered her to brush her teeth and her tongue. He had scooped up some of her bedding. "I'm not leaving any evidence here for the police to find, so I'll have to take some things with me," he told her.

He ordered Sarah into the bathroom. He told her to wash for twenty minutes. Sarah wanted to know when the time was up. She asked him to get her a timer.

Where is it? he asked.

There, on the kitchen counter, she told him. It was a white Sunbeam.

He cranked the dial to twenty minutes and placed it on the counter by the bathroom sink. Then he closed the door and left.

She stood in the shower, the water streaming down her body. She listened to each of the 1,200 seconds tick off, the timer whirring like a cicada in the summer. When it rang at last, she stepped from the shower. She dried herself off. And she began to catalog the damage.

The rapist had stolen a green satin pillow from the bed—the one given to her by her mother as a keepsake.

He had taken $200 from a safe beneath her bed.

He had stolen a camera.

He had changed her life forever.

It was not an easy story to tell. Sarah sobbed throughout the interview. The advocate comforted her. Hendershot comforted her. After thirty minutes, Hendershot decided Sarah had had enough. As she stood, Hendershot told Sarah that a nurse was going to examine her. Perhaps, she said, the rapist had not succeeded in covering his tracks. Perhaps some of his DNA remained inside her.

"I can only hope," Sarah replied.

DRIVING TO SARAH'S apartment complex, Hendershot ticked off the tasks in her head. Sixteen years of police work had burned a crime scene checklist into her. She needed patrol officers to canvass neighbors and search dumpsters. She needed a criminal-ist to search the apartment and the grounds. She needed a crime analyst to start pulling records on everyone who had access to Sarah's apartment.

All hands on deck, she thought to herself.

Hendershot was raised in the sprawling middle-class sub-urbs northwest of Denver. She spent her childhood in Arvada, a close-in suburb of a hundred thousand. Her mother taught music at local elementary schools and played piano and organ for the Presbyterian church. Her father worked in Colorado's state as-sembly building in Denver and got involved in local politics. She was the middle kid, sandwiched between an older and younger brother.

Her parents did their best to make her ladylike. Her mother enrolled her in ballet classes and tried to teach her piano. The pair made regular trips to an arts center just blocks from home. None of it stuck.

"I would go into the living room where the piano was, and my nice mom would be sitting there at the piano wanting me to play the piano. I would just be horrible to her. I know I was really mean about it, but I hated it. I wanted to be outside, running around and playing with my friends. I didn't want to play the dumb piano."

Hendershot was the classic tomboy. She loved sports. She was a swimmer. She excelled at soccer. At a time when girls' athlet-ics was just taking off, Hendershot was already traveling across Colorado on competitive club teams. She competed in high school as starting goalie for Arvada High.

Hendershot could never say exactly what drew her to police work. She didn't have close family who were cops or criminals—the common motivators for many in law enforcement. It was something that was meant to be. "I don't have a storybook an-swer," she'd tell people. "I just always knew that it was what I was supposed to do."

Her career path wasn't straight. After graduating from high

school in 1988, she studied criminal justice at two colleges. But money was tight, so she started working and going to school part-time. She manned the register at a Wendy's. She bussed tables and worked as a waitress for $2.50 an hour and tips at a local Mexican restaurant.

But she was determined to become a cop. In 1990, she got a job as a records clerk at the Adams County sheriff's office, reviewing inmate files from the local jail. A year later, she quit that job to start handling emergency calls as a 911 dispatcher for the Arvada Police Department. She worked nights and took classes during the day, paying her own way through police academy. When she graduated, she didn't stray from home. Westminster, the town next to Arvada, hired her as a patrol officer. She was sworn in on September 19, 1994.

Westminster often gets called a bedroom community of Denver. And in some ways it is, a mostly middle-class, mostly white town of a hundred thousand. Knots of parents cluster each weekend on the sidelines of kids' soccer matches. Big-box stores bunch together at major intersections. Ranch-style houses and apartment complexes sprawl in every direction around the Denver–Boulder Turnpike, which serves as the city's spine. But like many inner suburbs, Westminster defies saccharine characterization. Gangs and drugs plague the neighborhoods that bump against Denver. There was plenty of crime for a young cop who wanted to make a mark.

After five years on the street, Hendershot beat out competitors for a spot on the West Metro Drug Task Force. The elite unit drew cops from around the region to crack down on narcotics and gangs. She was the only woman on the squad. The other cops took to calling her "Ed."

Hendershot learned that her gender could be a kind of superpower. Both colleagues and criminals found her looks striking. When her supervisors were stumped on how to get close to a drug dealer, she'd volunteer for the job. "This sounds arrogant, but they would say, 'Who can get to this guy?' I'd say, 'I can probably do it.' It's disgusting what you can get with a hair flip and a giggle."

She was good at working undercover. She could be the dumb blonde. Or the hot biker chick. Or the stressed-out mother in the middle of a custody dispute. When suspects asked her to do a line, or to take off her clothes, she had an excuse. "I'll go home, and I'll get beat up," she'd say. Or "I've got court tomorrow with social services. I can't be high." Once, she worked a case involving a crooked deputy who was smuggling drugs and weapons to gang members in jail. Hendershot worked her way into the suspect's confidence by befriending a gang member, who made introductions. After the dirty cop was arrested, Hendershot showed up on scene. The gang member—hardened, streetwise—was there, too, in handcuffs. He refused to believe that Hendershot was really a cop. "I took a lot of pride in that," she says. "I was able to be so believable that he bought it."

Hendershot racked up praise. She was selected to serve as a field training officer, a position of trust where she mentored young officers. For twelve years straight, when Hendershot's bosses filled out her performance evaluation, they gave her the highest possible mark for teamwork: "exceptional."

By 2007, things were changing in Hendershot's personal life. She got married again—her first marriage had ended in divorce years before. Her new husband was Mike Hendershot, who had been a police sergeant in Golden and later became a commander at another agency in the Denver suburbs. He proposed to her under the Eiffel Tower. They had found a house big enough for their dog and two cats and moved in together.

Hendershot decided to move out of undercover work—she had spent enough time on the squad that criminals might start to recognize her. But she was nervous about a new assignment. She wondered whether she'd ever be as good at anything else. Okay, great, now what? she thought to herself. I peaked before I'm forty. Yay!

Her new post was in the Crimes Against Persons division. Here, suddenly, was a new world. Her victims were people who had been injured, raped, or killed. When she filled out paperwork as a narcotics cop, the victim was the "State of Colorado" or the "United States of America." Now, she wrote down someone's name. Someone with whom she had sat and talked, someone whose pain she had seen firsthand, someone whose death had sent a family reeling.

It was a little overwhelming.

"I literally had a physical reaction to that. Holy shit. This is a big deal. They are one hundred percent depending on you. It's all you."

AFTER FINISHING THE interview at the hospital, Hendershot drove to Sarah's apartment on the city's west side. It was 10:00 a.m., already hot. The buildings in the apartment complex were three stories tall, with orange panels and brick facades. They shared a pool, a clubhouse, and a trail. The renters were blue collar: health aides, cable installers, fast-food workers.

Outside the apartment, Hendershot met Officer Chris Pyler, who had spent the morning tracking down witnesses. He had spoken with the neighbors who called the police after Sarah banged on their door for help. They, too, were new to the complex. They had listened to Sarah recount the details of the rape. The wife had trouble believing all of them.

For instance, Sarah told the neighbors that the rapist had made her wash her hair. But Sarah's hair had been dry. The wife also thought Sarah made odd remarks. Sarah had told them, "Oh, you just moved in here. This is the last thing you need." The wife didn't think that Sarah was lying, necessarily. She just thought she was behaving strangely.

It's not what I would have done, the wife told Pyler.

The woman's skepticism was not surprising. When it came to

rape, victims frequently encountered doubt—from police, yes, but also from family and friends. There was a sense both in police departments and among the general public that not all reports of rape were true. The problem was, no one knew just how many. Criminologists had spent decades trying to determine how many women lie when they report being raped. The answers were all over the map. A police surgeon in England concluded in a 2006 report that 90 percent of rape allegations were false—a widely criticized figure based on a tiny sample of eighteen cases. The feminist Susan Brownmiller, whose groundbreaking work *Against Our Will: Men, Women and Rape* influenced a generation of activists, pegged the number at 2 percent—though that figure, too, had been sharply questioned.

Researchers who specialized in sexual assault had settled on a range—somewhere between 2 percent and 8 percent of rape allegations were false. But this range was tied to a specific definition: it only counted those rape allegations where police could prove a woman had knowingly lied. In reality, that didn't happen very often. Cops simply dropped cases where they had doubts, conducting no further investigation. The true percentage of false reports proved elusive—obscured by advocacy, different definitions of sexual assault, and the near impossibility of extracting concrete data from a crime shrouded in shame and secrecy.

For her own work, Hendershot needed what she called "definitive" evidence before dismissing a sexual assault allegation as false. There was this guy who had come to an emergency room with a mutilated testicle. It was so badly cut up that doctors had to remove it. The man told the doctors that he had been attacked with a knife and raped. Hendershot spent weeks running down the leads that the man supplied, even driving to Wyoming to search for evidence. But then she found that the man was part of an online pornographic chat room where people engaged in genital mutilation. Hendershot charged him with filing a false report to police—but only after she watched a video of the man maiming himself with a razor and an elastic band usually used to neuter cattle. In other words, she set the bar high.

After talking with Pyler, Hendershot walked into the apartment to check out the crime scene. She was relieved to see an old friend: Katherine Ellis, one of the senior crime scene investigators for the Westminster Police Department. Ellis had been on scene since 7:38 a.m., rushing out after she heard about the rape on a police radio installed in the department's crime laboratory.

The two had met years before, when both worked as dispatchers at a nearby police department. They had advanced upward through their careers together. Ellis's path led her into crime scene investigations long before the field became popular on television. "I was *CSI* before there was *CSI*," she would joke. Over the years, she had built a reputation for thoroughness. She took training courses at the elite FBI Academy in Quantico, Virginia. She had an eidetic memory. Years later, she could recall the case number of a criminal report by heart. She was a realist about her job. "It's not glamorous," she'd say. "It's dumpsters and dismembered children and crawl spaces."

By the time Hendershot arrived, Ellis had already walked through the apartment room by room. Her notes reflected her obsession with capturing every detail of a crime scene:

Unit is a two-bedroom, two-bathroom apartment with a kitchen, dining area, and living room.... The entryway opens into the living room. The living room was located on the south side of the apartment. It was furnished with a piano against the east wall, a leather sofa along the south wall, a round coffee table in front of the sofa, a round end table on the west side of the sofa and a rocker glider. The sofa had a stack of newspapers and a folder for restaurant and grocery coupons on the west cushion, an indentation that could be a foot impression on the middle cushion and a Bible and prayer book open on the east cushion.

Over five hours in the apartment, Ellis dusted for finger-prints on the windowsills, doors, and counters. She deployed cotton swabs across surfaces throughout the home: the living room window, the mattress topper, the bathroom sink and toilet. She took hundreds of photos of the disarray in the master bedroom, the living room, the back porch. She checked the apartment's two outside doors and windows for signs of forced entry. She bagged up evidence—the pale-green flat sheets that the rapist had left behind; purple kitchen gloves found near the sink; a red, orange, and white comforter. She used a special lamp to check the mattress topper for genetic material.

Hendershot told Ellis about the rapist picking up the white Sunbeam timer from Sarah's kitchen. When Ellis got to the bathroom, she found it perched on the edge of the vanity. It was one item in the apartment that she knew the rapist had touched. She collected it as evidence to check for the presence of DNA.

Ellis assumed that a crime occurred as the victim recounted it. But as she examined a scene, she focused on the evidence—whether contradictory or confirmatory. Her job, as she saw it, was to uncover the truth, whatever it was. "We report what the evidence shows us. Not what you're telling us. You want evidence to scream, 'Liar liar.' Not you."

So far, though, Ellis had not found much evidence of anything in Sarah's apartment. She noted that a screen had fallen to the ground under a window near the back door—but that could have happened at any time. On the couch, under a window, there was the depression that looked as if it could have been made by someone stepping on a cushion. But she had found no indication of forced entry. No pry marks on any of the doorframes. No broken windowpanes. She discovered no fingerprints on the windowsills or couch or in the bedroom. Illuminating the apartment had revealed only a small amount of body fluids, restricted to the bed.

One thing, however, did stand out. On the railing surrounding the back porch, Ellis noticed strange impressions—a row of small, hexagonal marks. Like a honeycomb, she thought. She took pictures to make sure they were preserved.

But she was not certain what could have caused them. Maybe a mover's blanket tossed over the railing?

What a weird pattern, she thought to herself.

TWO DAYS AFTER the rape, Hendershot met Sarah at the Westminster police station. They sat across from each other in an interview room, a desk between them. Hendershot turned on her tape recorder. She hoped enough time had passed to allow Sarah to recall additional details. She started slow: What was Sarah's life like in the days and months before the rape?

Sarah told her story. She had divorced late in life, after decades in a loveless, angry marriage. "I just decided I wasn't going to live like that any longer," she said. She found new love with a man twenty years her senior. He had a large family. She had no children. They attended church together. She sang in the choir. They spent nights out at Denny's. They married in October 2009 and moved into an apartment big enough for two. Then, he was diagnosed with cancer. Eight weeks after her wedding, Sarah buried her husband. Her decision to move into a smaller apartment at a new complex was the first step toward acknowledging the reality of widowhood. She signed the lease on July 28, 2010. The rapist had struck thirteen days later.

And what about the rape? Hendershot asked. "We talked about how you were ready for bed and you went to bed about midnight. And then what do you remember happening next?"

"I just remember, um, there was someone on top of me. I was on my back. I mean I was on my stomach, I was on my stomach," Sarah said. She stopped, flustered. "Do we have to go through the whole sequence again?"

Hendershot understood. She had worked more than a hundred rape cases. She knew how difficult it was to talk about rape—so difficult that it stopped many women from reporting at all. One of the top reasons was the fear of not being believed. Younger cops were often puzzled. You want to catch the guy? Why not spill the details?

Hendershot had a standard comeback: "Tell me about the last time you and your wife had sex. Tell me right now," she'd say. Those who didn't let out an embarrassed laugh reacted with shocked silence. They got the message.

In the interview room, Sarah went over the basics again. But she added new details. For instance, she remembered that the attacker had placed thigh-high stockings on her legs. But she couldn't recall their color or where they came from.

"How did they get on you?" Hendershot asked.

Sarah could not describe how.

"And how come you don't see them?" Hendershot asked.

"I think I was, I think I was on my stomach."

Sarah remembered, too, that the rapist had asked whether she had high heels. When she told him no, he came back from her closet with a pair of her own shoes.

"I had this image of what they might have been, but I'm still not sure," she said. She did not know what pair of shoes he had grabbed, nor if he had taken them when he left.

Hendershot was not discouraged. She kept probing. She tried to get Sarah to give her a better description.

"What about by his eyes? Do you remember anything by his eyes?"

"I certainly don't remember anything, really, about his face, I really don't."

"Okay. So no eye color?"

"Um, I couldn't tell."

"Any facial hair?"

Sarah shook her head no. "I could not tell you, I can't."

If Sarah's visual memory was lacking, her aural recollections were precise. She knew that the rapist carried a gym bag because she remembered the noise of zipping. She knew he had gone to the bathroom because she heard him urinating. She couldn't describe the camera he had used, even though he had pointed it directly at her. All she could remember was the sound. *Click. Click. Click.*

But more often, Sarah's story rambled, a jumble of moments and memories, unordered by time. She would struggle to piece together the sequence of events. She told Hendershot that she knew the time that the rapist left because she had seen some little girls playing outside her apartment. She thought for a moment. She had called the cops at around 7:00 a.m. Why would children be outside at that hour? "No, that doesn't make sense," she said, almost to herself.

Sarah grew frustrated at the lacunae of her story. "You know, most of the time my eyes were closed," she told Hendershot. "Part of the time, 'cuz he was forcing me. Part of the time, I just didn't even want to look."

Hendershot reassured her. "If you don't remember, that's okay."

Sarah's fractured world did not alarm Hendershot. She had learned that people who got hurt in traumatic events often had altered memories. Many could no longer recall events in chronological order. Trauma can warp the brain. A car accident. A tree falling close by. Seeing your buddy shot on the battlefield. In those terrifying seconds, the rush of adrenaline and cortisol created a violent alchemy. The mind became an uncertain eyewitness of its own experience. Events were unlinked from the time when they occurred. Memories got buried. Images could arise days, months, even years later, unwanted and unbidden, picture-perfect in clarity, like a landscape suddenly illuminated by lightning.

Rape was a special case. The experience of rape, the feeling of helplessness, impaired memories in ways that seemed almost designed to frustrate investigators. To endure the terrible present of violation, many women looked away from what was happening to them, looked away from their attacker. They focused on a lampshade or a painting on the wall. Or they closed their eyes. That meant women could often not describe the rapist, or what he wore, or the room, the time, the surroundings.

Psychologists have documented the role that a powerful, central detail can play in the formation of memories. At a moment of crisis, the brain fiercely grasps on to something that will help it survive. In some cases, this is the actual threat, like when a cop can describe a weapon pointed at him in extraordinary detail but has trouble recalling the clothing a suspect wore. In other cases, though, the salient detail is not the immediate threat. Indeed, it can be something not tied to the anguish of the rape at all—say, a lamp on a nearby nightstand or a streetlight in the distance. By fixing on such a detail, the mind can shift away from the immediate horror to a cognitively safer place.

Rebecca Campbell, a leading researcher of sexual assault at Michigan State University, says that victims often describe their experience of rape using the metaphor of a jigsaw puzzle. When solving a puzzle, the first thing most people do is flip all the pieces right side up. Next, they sort them into edge pieces, corner pieces, and body pieces. Then, they look at the picture on the box to figure out how to put the pieces together.

But rape victims have no way to solve the puzzle. They don't have all the pieces. They can't sort them in any meaningful way. And who can stand to gaze at such an awful picture, if they can even form the image? "A trauma memory doesn't come together in a nice, neat, orderly memory," says Campbell, who studies trauma's effects on the brain. "It is scattered throughout the brain. Literally."

It was Hendershot's job to help Sarah piece together the puzzle. But at the end of the interview, she felt no closer to connecting a suspect to the crime. The rapist was smart. He had given away few clues to his identity.

As they wrapped up the interview, Hendershot decided to give Sarah some good news. The $200 was gone, but in the apartment, the cops had found the camera Sarah believed had been stolen. Perhaps she had just overlooked it when she surveyed her belongings after the rape.

"But there were two cameras," Sarah said.

"There were two cameras—what do you mean?" Hendershot asked. She had thought there was only one in Sarah's place.

"Well, there was a pink Sony, and then there was a bigger camera, mostly silver."

The cops had found the silver camera, Hendershot knew. Where was the pink Sony? She dispatched police to Westminster's pawnshops, to look for any reports of somebody hocking a pink camera. There were none.

Hendershot was setting up an interview with a Comcast cable guy who had serviced Sarah's apartment complex when she got a call. It was a police sergeant from Aurora, a wealthier suburb thirty miles to the southeast of Westminster.

Through chatter among cops, the sergeant had learned details about the rape in Westminster. One of her detectives had a similar case, she told Hendershot. Perhaps they should compare notes.

Hendershot had just caught her first break.

Two weeks after Sarah's rape, Hendershot sat down in a small conference room at the Westminster Police Department. Across from her was Scott Burgess, a detective from Aurora. Burgess had salt-and-pepper hair. He wore a long-sleeved shirt, pressed slacks, and a tie to work. He was a precise, careful man. On some days, he looped his tie once, twice, three, four times into an Eldredge knot. It was one of the hardest knots to tie. Ties.com gave it five out of five for difficulty.

Aurora's police department had created a specialized sex crimes unit five years earlier. Burgess was one of its pioneers. "I was so lucky to get that draw," he says. Like Hendershot, he loved the idea of helping other people. And Burgess understood victims. "One thing I learned is that there is no right way for a victim to respond to these assaults. I've had victims bring me to tears in an interview where you find out later that they're false reports. I've also had victims that I would think to myself afterward, 'There's no way that this happened. You don't come across like that after something so heinous.' The thing I learned is there is no proper response."

The lesson served him well when he had responded to the rape in Aurora in October 2009. The victim was a woman named Doris, a sixty-five-year-old divorcée who worked as a housemother at a local fraternity. She had been raped at her home in a neighborhood in south Aurora. When Burgess interviewed her the following day, Doris seemed "composed," he told Hendershot. She had "a very matter-of-fact demeanor, was not emotional.

"I don't recall any sort of an outpouring, or a breaking down," he said. "It was just, 'This happened. Now let's see what we can do.'"

With Hendershot listening, Burgess reviewed the bullet points in his report:

- The victim was home sleeping on a Sunday morning at approximately 2:30 a.m.
- The suspect opened the door, straddled her back and shined a flashlight on her.
- The suspect directed her to roll over onto her back. She saw that his face was covered with a black mask or wrap that had a slit for his eyes.
- The suspect was a white male, approximately twenty years old, six feet tall, "big boned," and strong without being

muscular. He had light-colored, or no, body hair and was soft-spoken.

- The suspect told the victim: "I'm not going to hurt you, but I am going to rape you."
- The suspect tied her hands together in front of her. The suspect used a ribbon that was loosely tied.
- The suspect had a large black backpack.
- The suspect assaulted her repeatedly. The suspect took pictures of her and threatened to post them on the Internet if she called the police.
- Afterward, the suspect dressed and stated that he was going to take the sheets.
- In the end, she was made to shower as he stood in the bathroom and directed her on how to wash. He told her to wait twenty minutes before getting out.

Doris had described the rapist as "nice" and "gentle." During the attack, she had told him that she was sixty-five years old, too old to rape. "That's not old," the rapist had responded.

Doris told Burgess that just before the man began to rape her, he removed the pink curlers from her hair.

"I know I'm going to feel bad about this later, but I can't help it," he had told her.

"You should get help," Doris told him.

"It's too late for that," he replied.

Doris said she tried to be sympathetic. He was still young. Maybe he had been abused as a child. It was not too late to change.

The man slapped down the idea. He had never been abused. His parents were loving. He didn't smoke, drink, or do any drugs.

"If they knew what I did, it would kill them," he told her.

He had to rape. It was a "compulsion," he told Doris. He had been fighting it a long time. He had lost again and again.

"I can't help this," he said.

Doris told Burgess that the man had begun to fill the bathtub with water after he ordered her into the bathroom. For a brief second, she imagined the worst.

"I immediately thought he was going to drown me," she said. Instead, he told her to wash herself off.

"Give me twenty minutes because I want to be thorough," he told her.

When she got out, the clock said 3:45 a.m. She was too scared to call the police. She dressed. She made herself a cup of coffee. She sat down at her computer. She browsed the Internet.

Finally, at 6:00 a.m., Doris noticed that she was bleeding from her vagina. She drove herself to an emergency clinic. They told her to keep driving, directing her to the Medical Center of Aurora, which had resources for rape victims. There, a nurse called the police. The hospital performed a three-hour forensic exam to salvage any traces of DNA that might remain on her body.

Burgess told Hendershot that he realized the case would be difficult. Doris recalled many details of the rape. But her memories didn't reveal much about the rapist's identity. "How do I even put this out to the department?" Burgess asked himself at the time. "I can't even tell you really, confidently, what racial or ethnic makeup my suspect might be, because everything was covered." He told Hendershot that he imagined the attacker as a kind of rape expert—"ultra-prepared," as he described it. "This guy was very meticulous."

Burgess's report recounted his efforts. He sent patrol officers to canvass Doris's neighborhood, a cluster of modest homes on a small cul-de-sac off one of Aurora's main east–west thoroughfares. One officer dug through thirty trash cans and three portable toilets at a nearby baseball field. Another officer chased down a man seen walking near the crime scene with a weapon, only to find it was a BB gun. When police pulled over a man for speeding near the scene, they discovered a pink sheet, some towels, and two black bags in his trunk. The officer retrieved the sheets from Doris's house. They didn't match. For good measure, the officer called the man's girlfriend. She backed up his story, explaining that she left the sheets in his trunk after doing laundry.

Burgess's initial suspicion focused on the fraternity house brothers. Doris didn't think so: "It's not one of my guys," she told him, saying that she would recognize the voice. Burgess, however, contacted the police who patrolled the campus to see if they had recorded any similar assaults. A police sergeant directed him to a single case, involving a student who was six feet one and weighed 160 pounds. Police had stopped him for behaving strangely in November 2008. In the trunk of his car, they found police-style equipment—a flashing light that could be mounted on top of a vehicle, a baton, a Breathalyzer, and a 9mm Beretta. But the man had no criminal record. Burgess put the case, and his theory, aside.

Doris had provided a detailed description. But it was a description of a phantom: a masked man dressed in gray. There were no other clues. No eyewitnesses. No video surveillance.

On December 31, 2009, with the year coming to a close, Burgess wrote down the case status in capital letters: INACTIVE.

He wasn't closing the case. There was a possibility that some other clue might trickle in. But he knew, inside, what "inactive" meant. "They're not going to go anywhere."

It was a crushing conclusion for Burgess. The case haunted him. He considered Doris's rape one of the two or three worst cases he had investigated in his career. He would ask himself why she had been targeted. He was glad he could never reach an answer. "If you understand that, that's a bad thing," he'd say to himself.

Burgess left the meeting with Hendershot with new hope. The circumstantial evidence suggested one conclusion: the same person raped both Doris and Sarah. If Hendershot caught a break in her case, maybe he'd catch a break in his. Eight months after archiving Doris's case, Burgess updated the file. The investigation was active again. All it took was one misstep by the rapist. One mistake, two crimes solved.

It was simple math.

IN THE WEEKS after Sarah's rape, Hendershot played coach to a team of detectives, criminalists, crime analysts, and street cops. She had a half dozen cops check every trash can near the apartment in hopes that the rapist had tossed something as he fled. She had them scour the ditches and a retention pond, too. She ran names through Colorado's sex offender registry: the cable guy who had briefly chatted with the victim while setting up her Internet; neighbors throughout the apartment complex; even the garbagemen. No hits.

Leads poured in. One by one, Hendershot knocked them down. Police had arrested Sarah's ex-husband for rape in 1978. But Sarah insisted that she would have recognized her ex, mask or no. Police were investigating another stranger rape in the apartment complex where Sarah had lived with her deceased husband. But the suspect was a Saudi Arabian man who fled the country. One cop called to say he remembered a case from years ago that involved a man who carried a "rape tool kit." That guy turned out to be too old.

Finally, there was the young man with the black backpack who had been spotted wandering along a wooded creek less than two miles from Sarah's apartment complex. He turned out to be a college student with a green streak. Early one morning, he'd gone to the creek to arrange river rocks to improve circulation in stagnant pools of water. He confessed to showing "a little attitude" when cops questioned him. But he wasn't a rapist.

Hendershot knew that rapes—especially stranger attacks— are usually solved in the first week. Each hour, each day, that passed reduced the chance of catching the attacker. She was running out of leads to chase. Other criminal cases were piling up. The trail was growing cold.

By December 2010, Hendershot was feeling déjà vu. She was in the same spot Burgess had been in a year earlier. Actually, it was a worse spot. Because now, the detectives had reason to believe that a serial rapist was on the loose. One who had raped two women for several hours but managed to leave behind no real clues. No eyewitnesses. No description. No fingerprints. And not enough DNA to enter into any database.

What's more, both Hendershot and Burgess believed that the rapist would probably strike again.

All they could do was wait. Wait for a mistake. Or wait for another rape.

The calculations had changed. The math was not so simple.

Who was this guy?

5

A LOSING BATTLE

H E COULD REMEMBER THE MOMENT THE MONSTER WAS born. It was embarrassing, really, to tell people. He was five years old. His parents took him to see *Star Wars: Episode VI— Return of the Jedi*. Early in the film, there is a scene in the den of Jabba the Hutt, the interplanetary gangster who has the hero pilot Han Solo imprisoned in a frozen block. Jabba—an enormous, sybaritic grub—looms on a platform, surrounded by slaves, half-lings, and aliens. Exotic music wails.

The boy and his parents watched Luke Skywalker, mysterious and hooded, sneak into the lair while Jabba slept. There, lying at the base of the platform, is Princess Leia. She is bared, almost naked, in a metallic bikini, revealing her thighs, her stomach, her throat. She is attached to Jabba by a chain, a metal collar around her neck. She starts awake as Luke walks in and jerks uselessly at the chain. She is Jabba's slave.

He would recall that moment often in his later years. At the time, he did not have the words to even describe what he felt. It was alive, it was electric, it was dangerous. It filled him with plea-sure. He knew only that he wanted to have that kind of control over a woman, to totally possess and to own her. He described himself as like a young animal, bonding to the first creature it sees. He had imprinted on fear, on humiliation, on enslavement.

"From then on, I was basically ready to tie up every girl on the block" was how he remembered it.

As he got older, the thrill of the forbidden deepened. When he was eight, he broke into a house with some of his friends and stole cash. It was exciting, being where he wasn't supposed to be. He started breaking into homes just because he could. How many times? He lost track. It was just him having fun. "Something about it—even the act of cracking a window or opening a door, not even stepping in, was just an adrenaline rush," he'd say.

He didn't talk about his obsessions with anyone. Who would understand? His family life was normal enough. "I've had a lot of love in my life," he'd say. He grew up in Tennessee, the oldest of three siblings. His mother and father divorced, but Mom remarried and the new family moved to Longmont, Colorado, a rural town an hour outside of Denver. With a population of about eighty thousand, it was surrounded by farmland, flat fields of corn and alfalfa stretching in every direction. In the background rose the jagged height of Longs Peak, the town's namesake and, at 14,259 feet, the most northern of the soaring heights in the Rockies known as fourteeners.

There, he learned to live two lives. The side that faced the world was fun, gentle. He was a kid with spiky hair and a big toothy grin who loved cats, rollerbladed, and doted on a ferret named Elvis who lived in a habitat that he named Graceland. He picked up the guitar, began playing, and got good. He mastered "Little Wing," the enigmatic tone poem by Jimi Hendrix. He would play it for his mother to song's end, to where a woman "with a thousand smiles" promises relief from some inner turmoil.

> It's all right, she says, it's all right,
> Take anything you want from me, anything.

The other side was that turmoil—internal, dark, confused. He knew that his fantasies about women were sick, pathological, wrong. He knew that voyeurism, that illicit intrusion into the lives of others that he so enjoyed, was abnormal. But, he told himself, these were just thoughts in his head. He could keep them under control. He could keep himself under control. "It's just in my head—my business and no one else's," he'd tell himself.

HE SWITCHED SCHOOLS when he was a sophomore and began attending Olde Columbine High School. It was a low, flat building on the southern end of town, surrounded by an auto parts store, fast-food restaurants, and a mall. He hung out with a small group of friends. On weekends, they would drive out of town, down the long, flat highways that laced the long, flat landscape. They would drink beers by the side of the road. Once, when he was sixteen, he and four buddies were arrested by a Boulder County sheriff's deputy during a sting on underage drinking called Kegger Interdiction. It was 1:30 a.m. on a Saturday. He had sixteen bottles of beer in the back of his car. He paid an eighty-dollar fine.

He graduated from Olde Columbine on May 31, 1995. He moved to Denver and rented a room with a high school friend near Cherry Creek, a posh nightlife district. He worked for a year as a sales rep for one Internet company, then for another year as a tech support guy who would go to people's homes and set up their Internet service. He shot pool with his buddies. He got busted for smoking marijuana, but the prosecutor dropped the charges. He enrolled in the University of Denver, but left after a semester. He moved back in with his parents in Longmont and tended bar at Oskar Blues in nearby Lyons, Colorado, a dark, earthy bar famous on the local brewpub scene. Six years had passed since he graduated from high school. He still wasn't sure what he wanted to do.

Then 9/11 happened. He considered himself a pacifist. He kept his hair long—hippie long, rock-star long. He liked hanging out in Boulder, a lefty outpost in mostly conservative Colorado. He thought people in the military were knuckle-draggers, rednecks, brainwashed. But when he saw the Twin Towers crumple, something stirred in him. He found a calling—a mission that could distract him from the monster.

He walked into the United States Army recruiting station in downtown Denver on January 22, 2002, three months after the United States invaded Afghanistan. At twenty-three, he was a little older than the average Army recruit. He could do thirteen push-ups and seventeen sit-ups, and could run the mile in eight minutes and thirty seconds. He was six feet two but weighed just 155 pounds. It worried the recruiter. The guy would blow over in a strong wind. You can't afford to lose a single pound before basic training, the sergeant warned.

He had a hard time believing that he was entering the armed forces of the United States of America. "I was not exactly the military type," he would write. He stunned his parents, too. "We laughed and thought he was kidding," his mother says. "He really felt in his heart that, you know, he had to go fight and defend what had happened to our country and our people.

"He wanted us to be safe."

He was not sure whether he would fit in. Some Army recruiters divide soldiers into alphas and bravos depending on their scores on the military's entrance exam, the Armed Services Vocational Aptitude Battery. Bravos score lower, but they're considered better soldiers. They tend to be pliable. Willing to follow orders. They rise easily through the ranks. Big Army values obedience over brains. Alphas score higher on the test. They tend to be independent thinkers. But that means they're also more likely to question authority. They can be seen as outsiders, rebels.

He was an alpha. His scores put him in the very top echelon of test takers. He only had a high school diploma, but he qualified for entry into the military's most intellectually and mentally challenging jobs. He had potential to become a geospatial engineer, a criminal investigator, an expert in cryptology—the kind of jobs that usually went to officers and college graduates.

Instead, he signed up to become an infantryman—a grunt, the most atomic unit of the United States military. In 2002 in Afghanistan, the infantry were the guys marching through muddy mountain villages, knocking down doors, and shooting to kill. They were the ones driving across dusty highways in unarmored Humvees, squeezing their butt cheeks together in hopes that a roadside bomb wouldn't send a shank of metal hurtling into their guts. They were the tip of the spear.

But instead of hunting Taliban, he was assigned to Camp Casey, South Korea, a 3,500-acre base ten miles south of the demilitarized frontier with North Korea. His new home was also surrounded by mountains. Now, though, the tallest peak in sight was Mount Kumkang, 5,374 feet high. He was assigned to Company D, 2nd Battalion, of the Army's 9th Infantry Regiment—the Manchus. Their name derived from the unit's legendary courage under fire during the Boxer Rebellion. He had never been out of the country before.

The pacifist distinguished himself as a military man. He quit smoking. He gained weight and added muscle. He excelled in training exercises and learned military tactics. Before a mission, he would do reconnaissance to scope out a target. Before attacking, he would conduct pre-combat inspections, or PCIs, to make sure that he had his gear at hand and his weapon ready.

The Army recognized his work with the usual awards. He was accepted into a special honor guard. He earned medals for good conduct, Army achievement, and service to the national defense. He was recognized for his skill with weapons. He proved himself especially lethal with the M249, a light machine gun, once taking out an opposing infantry team sneaking toward his platoon's outpost during a training exercise. "His maturity has been a contribution in the action of his peers and off duty," one superior wrote. He advanced from private first class to sergeant. He had transformed into a knuckle-dragger. He described himself as "a pretty good soldier."

He wrote his mother frequently, telling her how much he enjoyed his job: He was in charge of training soldiers in South Korea's 2nd Infantry Division who were headed out to Afghanistan and Iraq. His mother thought he was becoming a better person. "He wanted to train those guys as best he could to help them survive because he knew that some of them would not be returning back to their homes," she said. "We really just saw a huge change in him then for the good."

In October 2003, he met a Russian cocktail waitress at a bar near base. Masha* spoke English with a hint of an accent. She had short hair and high bangs. Her face was broad and friendly, her lips full. She kept her nails manicured. She was three years younger. As a foreign national, Masha was not allowed to live on the military base. So each day, he would leave the camp at 4:00 p.m., stay with her until the midnight curfew, then race back to base. After six months of dating, they married on March 11, 2004. He transferred to a base in Seoul, and they moved in together.

They had a typical Army marriage. They hung out with friends, mostly fellow soldiers with their own young wives and girlfriends. They drank at bars at night. They partied at apartments on base. Sometimes they hiked.

He told his new wife nothing of his dark side. He continued to be haunted by images of sexual sadism—women in chains, women subjugated, women terrified as he raped them. He did not ask Masha to fulfill those fantasies. He once filmed them having sex. But she didn't like it, and he never tried again. He didn't even ask to tie her up. He considered their sex life normal, even vanilla. He had a hard time projecting his lust onto women he actually

---

*   Pseudonym

knew, women he liked. It was easier if the women were anonymous, distant.

He had kept his imagination at heel all through his teens and early twenties. The images would rise and then, over time, fade. He would feel normal again. But now, they began to dominate his thoughts, a kind of incessant mental tinnitus. He was constantly fighting his obsessions. It exhausted him, mentally and physically. "I coped the only way I knew how, which was to not tell anybody and to try to control it in my head."

He sought relief away from Masha. He started looking at increasingly violent pornography. He tried going to prostitutes, asking them to play rape victims. Nothing worked to calm him. He was beginning to lose control. He would think about his dilemma, and blame it on his reaction to *Star Wars*. "Where do you go when you're five and you're already thinking about handcuffs?" he thought.

He began to wonder: What if I acted on my desires? How would that change things? Perhaps if he indulged himself one time, he would be at peace. "I convinced myself that if I just did it once then it'd be like an itch that I had scratched and that I could basically get over it and move on with my life," he'd say. What he needed, what the monster needed, was fear. Real fear.

He decided to attack.

OUTSIDE THE HIGH walls of many American bases in South Korea lie districts of narrow, garishly lit streets lined with shoebox nightclubs. The most notorious of these clubs are called "juicy bars," where soldiers buy a ten-dollar glass of juice and quality time with a young Filipina "drinkie girl." At night, the girls flood the streets and side alleys in tight dresses and high heels, unabashed and unafraid.

Perfect targets, he thought.

He began following women at night through the packed streets and labyrinthine byways. He had a mask and gloves, but not much of a plan. He figured he would kidnap a girl, take her someplace—a hotel room, a car parked in the woods, who knew? He'd rape her. And at last, he'd be cured. He wasn't worried about the risk. "What happens in Korea stays in Korea," he told himself.

But it was not as easy as he thought. For months, he tailed girls deep into the night. Each time, after hours in the streets, he'd call it off. At home, his emotions surged, an angry, poisonous sea. He was simultaneously afraid of carrying out his plans and disgusted at his inability to act. But he didn't tell anyone. He always had a story for Masha: he was hanging out with friends; he had to work late. She never suspected anything.

And then, one night, it happened. It was near midnight. He saw a young Korean woman, about his age, wobbling down an alley. She was alone. She looked very, very drunk.

"Fuck it," he told himself. "I just can't sit out here on the fucking street my whole life."

He was in peak shape, 180 pounds, conditioned and muscled. He jumped on the woman and threw her to the ground. She struggled, fighting him back. Screaming in English with a strong accent, she focused on the dark clothes he wore: "Get off me black guy! Go away black guy!"

He burst out laughing. Here was this tiny, drunk girl. And she was trying to fight him off. It was comical. Where was the fear? The terror? Okay, this is not what I expected, he thought.

He pushed himself away. She got to her feet, stood unsteadily, and began to stagger away. She did not run. She walked. He followed behind her for a few steps, laughing. She faced him again. She picked up a rock from the street and threw it at him. "Go away black guy," she screamed again.

It was loud enough that he started to worry that she was attracting attention. He decided to call it off. Again. He was disappointed, confused. The whole thing had been ridiculous. It was theater of the absurd.

He had learned his lesson. "Grabbing someone in an alley isn't for me. It's not going to work," he said to himself.

The next time, he combined his plan to rape with his childhood thrill: breaking into a house. He went on the hunt again, this time through residential neighborhoods. One night, he saw his opportunity. It was a small, ground-floor apartment. The windows were uncovered. He could see everything inside: the kitchen, a small bathroom, and the bedroom. It thrilled him. It was like looking into a dollhouse, each room displayed for his pleasure. In the bed, a woman was sleeping. It was 3:00 a.m. No one else was around.

He glanced at the door, where Koreans leave their shoes upon entering their homes. He saw only women's footwear. If any men lived in the home, they were out, he thought. He tried the door handle. It was unlocked. This was his chance. He put on a ski mask and gloves and slipped inside.

He stopped and looked around. The apartment was tiny. In the kitchen, he saw packages of MREs, the ready-to-eat meals that the Army issues to soldiers in the field. He suddenly worried that the woman was married to an American. He looked around, but saw no other signs of a Westerner's presence. He calmed down. The path to fulfilling his fantasy was clear at last.

As he stood in the kitchen, the angry sea surged again. He was paralyzed, trying to talk himself into the attack, and trying to talk himself out of it. A half hour passed in the strange apartment with the strange woman just lying in bed, feet from him. "What the fuck are you doing?" he asked himself. "You know, just walk out of here and forget this whole thing."

All of a sudden, he heard a noise outside. He exited the kitchen just as an older Korean man flung open the front door. The Korean, unsteady on his feet after a late night at the bar, looked up. A beefy intruder, six feet easy, with hazel eyes framed by a black mask, loomed above him, standing in the middle of his home in the middle of the night. The startled homeowner bolted back outside, slamming the front door shut.

"Shit," he thought. "I'm trapped." He lunged to push the door open and escape, but the Korean man was on the other side, pressing his weight into the door. "I'm going to get locked in," he thought. "Oh fuck, I'm going to get locked in here."

But the next second, the door flung outward. The Korean man had yanked it open. He was standing to one side, like a doorman at a hotel.

He needed no such courtesies. He broke past the Korean man into the street. He sprinted at top speed, flying past houses, through the darkened city, until he reached his home about a mile away. He was gasping. The blood in his veins felt like battery acid. He had almost been caught. He had been an idiot.

He had been the one afraid.

"I can't be making stupid mistakes like that and I definitely can't be impulsive about it," he told himself. "If you don't plan to go to jail, you need to think this through a little bit more."

His enlistment was ending soon. He looked forward to going home, back to the United States.

He could practice there.

6

WHITE MAN, BLUE EYES, GRAY SWEATER

Monday, August 11, 2008
Lynnwood, Washington

THE 911 CALL CAME IN AT 7:55 A.M., THE CALLER'S WORDS leaving no doubt of the urgency. A young woman said her downstairs neighbor had just been raped inside her apartment. The attacker had fled maybe fifteen minutes ago.

The dispatcher kept the neighbor on the line, taking in a flurry of details passed along from the victim—the rapist had a knife; he took pictures; the victim didn't recognize him; he may have been in the apartment all night because he heard a phone conversation she'd been having. At 8:03, the caller reported that the victim had just found the knife in her bedroom; at 8:04, that the victim's mom had just arrived. The apartment complex was about a mile from police headquarters, reachable with a couple of turns. As the dispatcher listened, they were already routing police to the scene, with officers arriving at 8:03, 8:04, 8:05.

An ambulance was called. So was a K-9 unit, in hopes a dog could pick up the attacker's track.

Crime scene technician Anne Miles was the officer who arrived at 8:04, the second on the scene. She pulled up to the complex and made her way to the victim's first-floor apartment. Inside she found an eighteen-year-old with wavy hair and hazel eyes, and asked her what had happened.

This would be Marie's first time telling an officer what took place that morning. But important as the moment was, Marie's memory would erase it. She would remember shaking in a blanket in the corner as police arrived; she would remember talking to the ambulance crew; she would remember moving to the couch and sitting next to Peggy—but she would not remember a woman officer being there, detailed as her account to the officer was.

Marie told Miles that she had awakened to a man with a knife. He pulled away her comforter and sheet and told her to roll over on her stomach. He straddled her, bound her, blindfolded her, gagged her, then ordered her to roll back over. He groped and raped her. It felt like he was wearing gloves. He told her he had worn a condom. She heard clicking and saw some sort of flash. He told her he had taken photographs and would post them online if she went to police. Then he left, through the front door. She heard it shut.

Miles asked Marie if she could describe the man. Marie said she didn't get a good look. Everything had happened so fast. All she could say was he was white. His eyes were blue. His sweater was gray. Miles asked if anything stood out about his voice or smell or anything else, and Marie told Miles again—everything had happened so fast, it was all a blur.

Miles asked how long the attack lasted. Marie said she had no idea.

Marie told Miles that the rapist had dumped her purse out on the floor. She didn't know why.

Miles's job was to collect and process physical evidence, so with Marie, she began walking the apartment. In the bedroom she saw Marie's purse on the floor and wallet on the bed. The wallet was missing Marie's learner's permit. Miles spotted it on the ledge of the bedroom window.

Next to Marie's bed, on top of a plastic storage bin, Miles saw a large knife with a black handle. Marie told Miles that the knife was from her kitchen—and was the one the rapist had threatened her with. On top of the bed Miles saw a shoestring—used, apparently, to tie up Marie. In the bedroom corner, on top of a computer monitor, Miles found a second shoestring, threaded through a pair of women's underwear. "The string tied to the underwear was either used as the blindfold or was placed in [Marie's] mouth so she couldn't scream," Miles would write in a report. Marie told Miles that the laces came from her own tennis shoes, out in the living room.

Miles asked if Marie had locked up the night before. Marie said she wasn't sure. Miles checked the front door and saw no sign of it being forced open. Then she checked the sliding glass door at the rear of the apartment. It was unlocked—and slightly ajar. Miles stepped outside to the back porch and inspected the wood railing. Most of it was covered with dirt, but there was one stretch, about three feet wide, that appeared to have been brushed off, perhaps by someone climbing over.

Miles searched for traces of DNA on the sliding glass door, swabbing the inside and outside handles. She photographed the apartment inside and out. She took at least seventy shots, capturing the details that might illuminate what had happened that morning: the porch railing, the learner's permit on the bedroom window ledge, a knife block in the kitchen with one knife missing, the shoes without laces. The shoes were next to the living room sofa. On top of the sofa, leaning against the wall, were a couple of stuffed animals, a spotted cow and a dog with white paws.

After leaving Marie's apartment, Miles wrote up a two-page report, a simple recitation of the steps she had taken. Her report gave no hint of what she believed or didn't believe; it kept to what she had seen and done.

THE LYNNWOOD POLICE Department had seventy-nine sworn officers, serving a city of about thirty-four thousand people. In 2008, Marie's was one of ten reports of rape the department investigated; with so few cases, the Criminal Investigations Division didn't have a separate sex crimes unit.

On the morning Marie reported being raped, the head of the division, Commander James Nelson, came to the apartment building and pitched in, going door to door to interview potential witnesses. The man in 203 said he hadn't heard or seen anything unusual. He was the only resident Nelson managed to talk to. At apartments 103, 201, 301, 302, 303, and 304, nobody answered the door.

Nelson also tried another apartment building nearby. He interviewed three residents and noted the same response from each: "Did not see or hear anything suspicious." Nelson got no answer at seven other apartments.

At about a quarter after eight, the K-9 unit showed up. The dog "tracked to the south towards [an] office building however it didn't lead to anything," the officer reported. The dog also failed to pick up anything to the north, around a parking area.

Later in the morning a second crime scene technician arrived to help. Like Miles, Detective Josh Kelsey wrote a two-page report. Unlike Miles, he wrote his eleven days later, well after Marie had recanted. Kelsey did a walkthrough and, in his report, recorded his observations: The shoes with the missing laces "were lying next to each other near the end of the couch and the bedroom door, on the soles as if placed there (not disturbed). . . . The bed appeared disturbed, but there was a small fan sitting upright at the head of the bed, next to the two pillows. . . . I did not see any item that would have been used as the blindfold."

Kelsey dusted the sliding door for fingerprints. From the inside glass he managed to lift some partials, which he preserved on a fingerprint card. Although Marie had said the rapist left through the front door, Kelsey made no note of inspecting that door for possible prints or DNA. Neither had Miles during her earlier canvass.

Kelsey inspected the bedroom with an alternate light source, searching for the characteristic glow of body fluids. He didn't spy anything on the comforter or blankets piled on the floor, but he did see two spots on the mattress. On the bed he also saw a couple of hair follicles and some fibers, which he collected.

In all, Kelsey gathered and labeled eighteen items of evidence, removing from Marie's apartment the physical exhibits of her young life, bagging every layer of bedding from pink comforter down to mattress pad, bagging her shoes, wallet, and learner's permit.

SERGEANT JEFFREY MASON, a Lynnwood police detective, arrived at about a quarter till nine. Outside the apartment were Marie's Project Ladder case manager, Wayne, and her upstairs neighbor. Inside, Marie sat on the couch with her foster mother, Peggy. Marie was wrapped in a blanket. She cried off and on.

This investigation would be Mason's to lead. He walked over to Marie and introduced himself.

Mason was thirty-nine years old. He had been promoted to sergeant—and transferred to the Criminal Investigations Division—just six weeks before.

He had spent most of his career in Oregon, where he had begun as a dispatcher for Wasco County and worked his way up to the Oregon State Police. His longest stint was with a small police department in a town called The Dalles, where he served for almost nine years and received a medal of valor.

Over the years he had taken dozens of training courses on all kinds of subjects. He'd gone to sniper school. He'd studied outlaw motorcycle gangs. He'd learned to interrogate suspects and interpret their body language for tells. But there was one subject he knew best, as attested to by the instructional programs listed in his personnel file: Indoor Marijuana Grows; Street Drugs; Polytesting Narcotics Screening & Identification; Reconnaissance and Interdiction Detachment (RAID, for short); Hidden Compartments; Mexican Meth. His courses ranged from aerial spotting— how to spy a pot patch amid other vegetation from hundreds of feet in the sky—to how to keep safe when moving in on a clandestine drug lab. His was a world of undercover buys and informants, in which officers navigated among drug users and dealers.

Mason joined Lynnwood's police department in 2003. Before his recent promotion he had spent four years in patrol and a year as a narcotics detective, earning praise for his dedication and dependability. Superiors appreciated his professionalism, from the quality of his written reports ("thorough and well thought out with few to no mistakes") to his approach to police work ("proactive") to his leadership ("an innate ability to mentor"). "Excellent work habits," wrote one sergeant, who commended Mason's ability to work with minimal supervision.

In his nineteen years in law enforcement, Mason had worked only one or two rape cases. He had received some sexual assault training, but it had been long ago, in the mid-1990s.

When the two met, Marie struck Mason as forthright. "I didn't have a lot of experience dealing with sexual assault victims," he would say later. "But I didn't go in with an expectation of how she might be acting. She wasn't hysterical. She was very matter-of-fact—this is what occurred." Speaking with Mason and a second detective, Marie covered much of the same ground she had gone over with Miles: the unlocked sliding door, the stranger with a knife, the rape in her bedroom. Mason told Marie he would need more details later, but for now, she needed to go to the hospital for a sexual assault examination. After that, he wanted her to come to the police station to give a full statement.

After Marie left, accompanied by her case manager and foster mom, Mason walked the apartment, taking in the emptied purse, the underwear laced with a shoestring, the mattress—askew, about four inches out of line with the box spring. Mason also talked to Nattlie, the eighteen-year-old neighbor who lived directly above Marie. Nattlie said she hadn't heard anything unusual during the night. Then, in the morning, at 7:52, maybe 7:53, she got a call from Marie, screaming, crying, saying someone had broken into her place and raped her. Nattlie grabbed her cell phone, ran down the stairs, and called 911 from Marie's apartment.

Although Mason was the lead investigator on the case, he would receive help from Jerry Rittgarn, another member of the Criminal Investigations Division. Rittgarn had a bachelor's degree in zoology from the University of Washington; he had previously served in the Marine Corps, specializing in helicopter avionics, and worked as a technician in the aerospace industry. He had been with the Lynnwood police for eleven years, the last four as a detective. One of his duties—backgrounding job candidates and recommending whether they be hired—testified to the department's faith in his investigative abilities. In 2006 he had been named Lynnwood's officer of the year.

As was the case for other detectives called to the apartment complex, Rittgarn wrote up his report days later—after Marie had taken back her story. His report said he had looked at Marie's wrists before she left for the hospital, and he hadn't noticed markings on either. When Marie's bedroom was examined with ultraviolet light, he didn't see liquid stains on the sheet or bedding. He searched the apartment—bathroom, toilet, trash cans throughout—for a condom or wrapper, but found neither. He also looked outside, walking the side of a hill, to no avail.

PEGGY AND WAYNE took Marie to Providence Regional Medical Center in nearby Everett. Providence had a center for sexual assault, with victim's advocates and nurses specially trained in collecting evidence.

By August of 2008, the specialized examination of rape victims—often referred to as "rape kits," for the box in which the evidence is placed—had been around for thirty years. They originated by virtue of a victim's advocate, a police microanalyst, and funding from a most unlikely source.

In the mid-1970s, Martha "Marty" Goddard formed a non-profit in Chicago called the Citizens Committee for Victim Assistance. At the time, rape, steeped in stigma, received little attention; what attention it did get often did more damage than good. Goddard, a self-described type A personality—she lived close to the office, worked weekends and holidays, spent hundreds of dollars on a gym membership but never escaped work long enough to go in the door—set out to change that.

Part of her challenge was confronting how people wrote about rape. One of her board members picked up a greeting card in a store, brought it in to Goddard, and, "freaking out," said, "Read this." "*Help stop rape,*" the card's cover said. The note inside was "*Say yes.*" Goddard wrote the card company with her own message: "You guys, I'm sure, think it's funny. But it's not funny." The company, chagrined, pulled the card from shelves. Goddard saw a newspaper story in Chicago about a woman who had reported being raped. The story may not have named her, but with its careless cascading of detail—combining precise physical description with her job (waitress) and the place she worked (the exact restaurant)—it hardly needed to. Identifying her would be easy enough. Goddard went to the newspaper and met with an editor and some of his staff. At first they were defensive. Then they apologized. "And I gotta tell you, they never did it again," Goddard says. For Goddard, such were her days: "One incident by one incident by one incident. It took forever."

Goddard also focused on the enforcement of sexual assault laws. She met with police, prosecutors, and emergency-room doctors and nurses, and discovered a problem in how rape was investigated. The collection of physical evidence was haphazard. If hairs, fibers, blood, semen, fingernail scrapings, clothing, and other evidence were gathered at all, they were often preserved or labeled improperly, jeopardizing their value. Police told Goddard of emergency-room workers rubber-banding two slides together, face to face, contaminating both samples. Sometimes slides wouldn't say where the samples came from. The ER workers were trained to see a rape victim as a patient—not as a patient *and* a crime scene. Often, hospitals didn't have replacement clothes available. Victims, their clothes seized as evidence, might be taken home in a marked police car—and emerge wearing hospital slippers and patient gown, tied in the back. Their neighbors were sure to wonder.

At the Chicago Police Department, Goddard found allies for her cause, most notably Sergeant Louis Vitullo, a microanalyst who was head of the crime lab. Vitullo worked downtown, but lived an hour north of the city. Chicago made him nervous (he didn't let his daughter go there alone until her twenties), which stood to reason, what with the blood and knives coming through his lab. In the sixties he'd worked on the investigation of Richard Speck, the infamous murderer of eight student nurses. Working with Goddard—"The crime lab eventually became my second home, I'm not kidding you," she says—Vitullo devised a blue-and-white cardboard box that standardized the collection of evidence in sexual assault cases. The kit itemized swabs and slides to be gathered and provided labeled folders to be filled and sealed.

So with Vitullo's help, Goddard had a design. What she lacked was the money for parts and assembly. Foundations gave generously to medical research hospitals and symphonies. If they chose to fund women's and girls' programs, they might give to the YWCA or Girl Scouts. But they wanted nothing to do with the subject of rape. "Most of the foundation and corporate people were male," Goddard says. "And they held the big money, so they held the purse strings. And it wasn't loosening up." Ultimately, Goddard turned to a friend, Margaret Standish. Standish ran the Playboy Foundation, the activist arm of Hugh Hefner's publishing empire. The Playboy Foundation provided $10,000—and the use of *Playboy*'s offices as an assembly line, where volunteers, mostly senior citizens, were provided with foldout tables and free coffee and sandwiches while building the first of these revolutionary kits. "I took a lot of flak from the women's movement—but too bad," Goddard says. "If it was *Penthouse* or *Hustler,* no. But *Playboy*? Please, give me a break."

In September of 1978, twenty-six hospitals in the Chicago area began using the kits. The following year, 2,777 kits went to the Chicago crime lab for analysis. In the summer of 1979, prosecutors used one while trying a man accused of raping a Chicago Transit Authority bus driver. The jury voted to convict, after which the judge let Goddard's committee ask jurors if the kit helped them reach a verdict. Nine said it did.

That same year Goddard met a Northwestern University graduate, Susan Irion, who worked in public relations while volunteering with a fledgling group called Rape Victim Advocates. Irion was on call for twelve-hour shifts, during which she could be paged by any of seven emergency rooms to help guide sexual assault victims through medical exams and police interviews. Goddard hired Irion to be assistant director for the Citizens Committee for Victim Assistance. For two and a half years Irion trained hospital workers and police in use of the rape kits and in the complexities of trauma. Don't be hostage to your expectations, she would teach. Sometimes trauma doesn't look the way you think it should.

For expertise Irion turned to Jon Conte, a social work professor in Chicago who would later move on to the University of Washington and evaluate Marie. Irion also incorporated the lessons in *Rape: Crisis and Recovery,* a book published in 1979 by a psychiatric nurse and a sociologist who had provided crisis-intervention services for 146 rape victims admitted to Boston City Hospital. The authors discovered a range of emotional reactions among rape victims. Some were angry or anxious, some composed, some in shock. "I remember doing some strange things after he left such as biting my arm . . . to prove I could feel . . . that I was real," one woman reported. Physical reactions included disrupted sleep patterns and lingering pain. "I am so sore under my ribs," said another victim. "The pain just stays there; it doesn't go away. I guess he really hurt me, although the X-ray didn't show anything." Some victims suffered nightmares, their dreams similar to the rape itself, the victim unable to get away. Some underwent a form of self-imposed isolation, rarely venturing out, missing school or quitting work.

By 1980, 215 hospitals in Illinois were using Goddard and Vitullo's rape kits. From there they became standard issue across the country. The advent of DNA testing in the late 1980s made the kits especially powerful, by pushing forensic science beyond the limitations of blood typing and microscopy.

But valuable as the evidence can be, the collection process—lasting three to six hours—exacts a toll.

At Providence, Marie was joined by Jana, the supervisor with Project Ladder. Jana stayed with Marie during the exam, to help keep her calm. She rubbed Marie's back. She told Marie this wasn't her fault.

The medical team included a nurse who had received special training in these examinations—and was in a position to relate, having suffered sexual abuse herself. A victim's advocate also stayed throughout, to provide psychological support and answer any of Marie's questions. A medical report described Marie as "alert and oriented, and in no acute distress."

A doctor evaluated Marie as the nurse assisted with all that was required.

They asked Marie to describe the assault.

They drew Marie's blood.

They took a urine sample.

They collected vaginal discharge and smeared it on a slide.

They tested Marie for gonorrhea. They tested her for hepatitis, and chlamydia, and syphilis.

They tested her for yeast infection.

They tested her for HIV.

In each case, Marie was told that the test results would not be available until later. She would have to wait to know.

The team's exam also included forensic work, to assist in any criminal investigation.

They collected each item of Marie's clothing, to be inspected later in a crime lab.

They examined Marie, looking for signs of injury. Where injury was noted, they documented it.

"Trauma noted to wrists bilaterally," they wrote in a report. They photographed her wrists and measured the abrasions— length and width, to tenths or even hundredths of a centimeter. The longest abrasion, red and raised, was seven centimeters, or two and three quarters inches.

While searching for genital injury they applied toluidine blue, a staining dye that creates contrast between healthy and injured tissue. "Abrasions to inner aspect labia minora," they wrote in the report.

They swabbed the inside of Marie's cheek to collect DNA. Forensic scientists would need Marie's genetic profile to distinguish it from any other DNA profiles that might turn up in the swabs collected in the rape kit.

They collected four vaginal swabs.

They collected four rectal swabs.

They collected four swabs from the area in between.

The swabs were placed in a drying box, then secured with other evidence in a locker, pending release to the Lynnwood police.

They treated Marie for possible exposure to sexually transmitted diseases, giving her one gram of Zithromax and four hundred milligrams of Suprax.

They provided her with emergency contraception—having her take one pill then, at the hospital, and giving her a second pill to take twelve hours later.

They asked her to let them know if she experienced excessive bleeding. Or unusual vaginal discharge. Or if she stopped menstruating.

They advised her to return to the emergency room if she experienced shortness of breath. Or had trouble swallowing. Or suffered hives. Or thought of killing herself.

Peggy had stayed at the hospital with Marie after driving her there. She watched as they photographed Marie's wrists. She held Marie's hand.

But the exam wound up taking so long that Peggy left. She now had two other foster children—both teenage girls—and after three hours or so, she went home to take care of them.

After the exam, Marie changed into a new set of clothes she had brought with her to the hospital. By the time she left Providence, morning had turned to afternoon.

By 2008, WHEN Marie reported being raped, sex crime specialists had developed investigative protocols with one dominant theme: Evidence trumps assumptions. The year before, End Violence Against Women International, a nonprofit organization that trains police, produced a comprehensive online course on investigating rape. One of its lead creators was Joanne Archambault, a retired police sergeant who for ten years had supervised the San Diego Police Department's sex crimes unit.

Archambault had built her career in policing on challenging assumptions. In the late 1970s she was working at the Educational Cultural Complex in San Diego, helping others find employment. Two police recruiters told Archambault that only men were fit for police work. "They pissed me off," Archambault says—so much so that she applied herself. "I never planned to be a cop. I just planned to show them I could be hired." Her training group at the police academy included 120 recruits; only four were women. To Archambault, the training seemed geared toward weeding women out. The pull-up bar, for example, was too thick for most women's hands. Within a year, Archambault was the only woman left. She was hired by the San Diego Police Department in the spring of 1980, and after a stint as a patrol officer, worked in a half dozen other units, at one point becoming the department's first female gang detective.

For Archambault, her twenty-three years as a cop became a study in the prevalence and corrosiveness of doubt. While investigating child-abuse cases she was stunned at how many mothers did not believe their kids. After joining the sex crimes unit she bristled at the advice she remembered seeing in a 1995 article published by the International Association of Chiefs of Police:

> Generally, the actions and the appearance of a legitimate rape victim leave little doubt that a crime has been committed. Under such circumstances, the victim is highly agitated, emotionally distraught, often in a state of hysteria and may have sustained injuries, cuts, bruises or wounds. The victim's clothing is often ripped or torn off as evidence that it was forcibly removed and if the rape occurs outdoors, the victim is generally thrown to the ground and her outer garments stained and soiled. Questions may reasonably be raised concerning the validity of rape charges in which none or only a few of the above manifestations exist.

Archambault knew that was wrong—utterly, spectacularly wrong. She believed that police departments didn't attach enough importance to solving sex crimes; they didn't give investigators enough training or resources. The police's priorities reflected the public's. People outside of law enforcement didn't want to talk about sexual assault. The public wanted the police to concentrate on gangs and murder.

The online course she helped create cautions that some victims confuse fine points of their story or even recant. Police, the course material says, should not get lost in stereotypes—believing, for example, that an adolescent victim will be less credible than an adult. To interrogate the victim is "totally inappropriate." Nor should police use or threaten to use a polygraph device. That can destroy the victim's trust in law enforcement; plus, a lie-detector test "is known to be unreliable when used with people experiencing crisis."

Archambault has witnessed the impulses that can lead an investigation astray. During training she plays a 911 tape of a woman saying she was just raped in her apartment. In the apartment's background, a stereo blares. The rapist tied her up, the woman says, over the music. When they hear this tape, police officers in Archambault's class usually think it's a hoax. They don't believe that the woman could call with her hands tied. (She dialed with her toes.) And they don't understand the loud music. (The rapist cranked the volume to cover any screams.) But the call was no hoax. The caller was indeed raped. "Research shows the more intimate the crime, the more people focus on the victim's behavior, and of course, there's no crime more intimate than sexual violence," Archambault says.

In 2005, the International Association of Chiefs of Police published a model policy on investigating sexual assaults that dispelled the notions embedded in that article published ten years before. Archambault, at the association's request, wrote the updated policy. Among its signature lines: "The victim's response to the trauma of a sexual assault shall not be used in any way to measure credibility."

AFTER LEAVING THE hospital, Marie went to the Lynnwood police station. Wayne drove. By the time they arrived, it was almost three o'clock in the afternoon.

Sergeant Mason escorted Marie to an interview room, where it was just the two of them. To Mason, Marie looked tired. She told him she'd had less than an hour's sleep last night. She told him she had a headache.

Mason gave Marie some water. He explained why he needed her statement now: It was important to get as detailed an account as possible, as soon as possible. Information Marie provided now might lead to other evidence; other evidence might yield an arrest and protect the public.

Mason asked Marie to recall the past day, with a detailed description of what had happened inside her apartment.

This would be Marie's fourth time describing the attack. She had recounted it to Miles. Later, still at the apartment, she had recounted it to Mason and Rittgarn. She had recounted it to the nurse at the hospital. Now she would be going through it again.

Marie told Mason she had spent much of the night talking on the phone with her friend Jordan. She said she awoke at 6:45 a.m., maybe 7:00, to see a man in her bedroom doorway, holding a knife. She described the man for Mason. Earlier she had told Miles that the man had blue eyes and a gray sweater. Now she told Mason that the man's eyes were possibly blue, and that he wore a hoodie, gray or white.

Marie told Mason that the man appeared to be younger than thirty.

He looked to be five feet six to five feet nine.

He had a thin build.

Marie described being bound, her hands tied behind her back. She described the man lifting her shirt to take pictures. She described the man raping her for what she believed was about five minutes.

Marie recited—step by step—what she did after the rapist left her apartment.

She ran to the front door and locked it.

She ran to the sliding glass door and locked it.

She went to the kitchen, got a knife, and tried cutting the laces off her hands.

Unable to do so, she went to her bedroom and, using her feet, got a pair of scissors from the bottom drawer of a cabinet. With the scissors she cut herself free.

She grabbed her cell phone and tried calling Jordan, but he didn't answer.

She called Peggy, who agreed to come over.

She called her upstairs neighbor, who came down.

As Marie spoke, Mason took handwritten notes. He didn't record her.

When she finished, he handed her a form authorizing the hospital to disclose her medical records to police. She signed the release.

Mason also handed Marie another piece of paper. It was an "Incident Statement Form," with two dozen blank lines that Mason asked Marie to fill in, writing down all that had happened. The form—which included, at bottom, a warning that it is a crime to make false or misleading statements to police—would be Marie's fifth time describing being raped.

Marie told Mason she was worn out. Her head was throbbing. He told her to get some rest—then complete the form, then give him a call.

Before leaving the station Marie met with Josh Kelsey, the crime scene technician who had collected evidence at her apartment that morning. By now at least seven hours had passed since Marie had freed herself from the shoelaces. Kelsey took a dozen photos of Marie's wrists and hands. When he wrote his report more than a week later, he noted marks on both wrists, adding: "The marks were red, but there did not appear to be any abrasions or bruising."

Wayne drove Marie away from the station.

This same day Marie stopped at the apartment complex for a meeting with everyone in Project Ladder. Marie told the others what had happened. She told them they needed to be careful. She said they needed to lock their doors. She was able to speak for only a few minutes before she broke down and cried.

Marie spent the night at a friend's home.

FOR AT LEAST twenty-four hours after the police were summoned, the investigation assumed a normal course. The police made no mention in any report of thinking Marie might be lying. And Marie had no sense that anyone believed as much. She felt supported—by police, by the people at the hospital, by her friends and her extended foster family, by the managers at Project Ladder.

On August 12—a Tuesday, the day after Marie reported being raped—Sergeant Mason faxed a request for Marie's medical records to the hospital where the sexual assault examination had been conducted. That was standard practice.

But on this same day, Mason received a telephone call that would become enveloped in mystery, thanks to the cryptic summary he would later file in his police report. His report didn't identify the caller, although he knew who it was. He summed up in two sentences what proved to be the most pivotal moment in the whole investigation: "I received a call from someone wishing to remain anonymous. The person related that [Marie] had a past history of trying to get attention and the person was questioning whether the 'rape' had occurred."

Mason arranged to meet with the caller in person, in order to learn more.

7

SISTERS

I N HER CUBICLE IN THE WESTMINSTER POLICE STATION, DEtective Edna Hendershot settled in with her Starbucks usual: a venti upside-down skinny caramel macchiato. At 9:07 a.m., an email arrived. It had been posted to a listserv read by detectives throughout the Denver area. The subject line was pleading: "Sex Aslt Similars?"

The email described a rape that had occurred the previous night in Golden. The attacker had bound his victim's hands. He'd made her shower. He'd threatened to post pictures of her on the Internet. At the bottom of the note was a personal plea: "Can Det Hendershot please contact me in reference to this report?" It was from a Golden detective named Stacy Galbraith.

Hendershot did not know Galbraith. But she had an ominous feeling that she knew what the email was about. It had been five months since Sarah's rape, and fifteen months since the attack on Doris. She called Burgess, her counterpart in Aurora, and gave him the news.

It looked like the worst had happened. The rapist had struck again.

Cops can be protective about their cases, fearing that information could be leaked that would jeopardize their investigations. But Hendershot right away recognized the potential in collaborating with Galbraith and Burgess. "Two heads, three heads, four heads sometimes are better than one, right?" she says. So did Galbraith. Her department was small—a little more than forty officers serving a town of about twenty thousand. It only made sense to join forces. "I have no qualms with asking for help," Galbraith says. "Let's do what we can do to catch him."

We need reinforcement, Galbraith told Hendershot. Let's bring in the Colorado Bureau of Investigation. Let's call the Federal Bureau of Investigation. "This is much bigger than little Golden. This is bigger than Jefferson County," she said. Hendershot was more cautious. Her superiors wanted to proceed more slowly. Let's all meet at my station house, she told Galbraith. Me, you, and Burgess. We'll lay out the facts. "We aren't sure of anything," she said. "We have a lot of investigating to do."

A few days later, the three detectives circled up around a table in a conference room at the Westminster Police Department. Each detective carried a file. And each file told a very similar story.

The victims' descriptions of the attacker overlapped. The women estimated his height somewhere between five feet ten and six feet two. They put his weight at around 180 pounds. Amber had gotten the best look at him. He had hazel eyes. His hair was blondish.

The rapist seemed relaxed during the attacks, almost like he was on Xanax. He talked to the victims. He seemed smart, educated. He could be introspective. He knew intimate details about their lives—things that only a close friend or partner would know. Crazy as it was, all the women described him as being, at times, gentlemanly.

The rapist committed his crimes robotically. Each attack was the same, repeated with ruthless efficiency. He wore the black mask that hid everything but his eyes. He tied the women up, but only loosely. He raped the women for hours, in multiple sessions. Afterward, he forced each one to shower.

Hendershot and Burgess described how the rapist had posed

Sarah and Doris for photos, and how he had taken scores of pictures as he raped them. Both women remembered the large black camera with its clicking noise.

Well, there's a difference, Galbraith noted. The attacker had taken pictures of Amber, too. But he had used a pink digital camera.

Immediately, Hendershot flashed back to the conversation she had with Sarah over the second missing camera. A pink Sony. Stolen by the rapist. Who matched the description in Amber's case. Even for Hendershot, it was hard to resist the conclusion: It was the same guy at work.

Together, the detectives bore down. How were the women connected? Did they have something in common that might lead police to the rapist? All shopped at branches of King Soopers, the grocery chain scattered across eastern Colorado and Wyoming. All had links to local colleges. Doris, the victim from Aurora, worked as a housemother at a fraternity. Sarah, the victim from Westminster, had lived in an apartment complex near a community college before relocating to her new home. And Amber was a graduate student.

That was where the similarities ended. Doris was sixty-five and lived in a house in a residential neighborhood. Sarah was fifty-nine and had only recently moved into her new apartment complex. Both were older white women. Both lived alone. But Amber was in her twenties and a woman of color. She had a roommate. And a boyfriend.

The differences—in the women's ages, their races, their physical appearances—ran against a well-established pattern in rape. The study of victim attributes, what the police call "victimology," holds that serial rapists tend to strike similar targets. They could be young or old, teachers or doctors, blondes or brunettes. But they usually had some common unifying trait.

In this instance, the victims were dissimilar enough that the detectives decided they could not rule out the chance that more than one rapist was out prowling. It was possible that the similarity of the attacks was coincidental. But it was easy to imagine more unsettling scenarios. Maybe the rapes were being committed by a group of men coordinating their assaults to throw off the cops. Maybe it was some kind of pornography ring. Maybe Denver's suburbs were under siege by a pair of highly experienced, highly traveled rapists.

The detectives noted another troubling trend. Ten months had passed between the first attack in Aurora in October 2009 and the second attack in Westminster in August 2010. Five months later, in January 2011, Golden happened. In the first two incidents, the rapist had threatened the women with a gun, but he had not displayed a weapon. In Golden, he flashed a handgun. He pointed it directly at Amber. And he threatened to shoot her.

The attacks were getting closer together and becoming more violent. To the detectives, it was a sign that the rapist was growing more confident. It was also an indication that he was getting better at what he did. The cops called it "MO creeping," using the abbreviation for "modus operandi." As a criminal got comfortable with the usual routine, he often pushed new boundaries and took more chances.

Burgess left the meeting burdened by a single question.

"How do we stop him before he rapes someone else?"

GALBRAITH HAD A strong lead. A business across from Amber's apartment had a video surveillance camera that pointed toward one entrance into the complex. The owner turned the footage over to detectives to analyze. The task fell to Matt Cole, Galbraith's partner, another Golden detective who had responded to the scene of the rape.

Cole watched the grainy footage for an entire day. He would play and rewind, play and rewind. He saw a guy on a bike with a dark backpack. Was he staring into Amber's apartment? Why did the silver Chevy Celebrity switch parking spaces?

He counted 261 vehicles coming and going the night of January 4 and the early morning of January 5. One vehicle ghosted across the screen ten times in the predawn hours: a white pickup truck, driving slowly through the snowy parking lot.

Cole marked each appearance down to the second.

12:37:44 a.m.

01:16:25 a.m.

02:30:03 a.m.

05:03:00 a.m.

05:05:26 a.m.

05:14:02 a.m.

05:16:30 a.m.

05:17:14 a.m.

05:19:19 a.m.

05:19:59 a.m.

Could the pickup belong to the rapist? Cole and Galbraith ran the tape again and again, looking for a way to identify the vehicle. They could read "Mazda" on the back. The mirror on the passenger's side looked broken. And it seemed like an older model truck. But the license plate was unreadable. They sent the surveillance tape to an analyst who specialized in video enhancement. The analyst broke down the tape into 1,200 images composed of overlapping, individual frames—a technique called averaging. Nothing. The video was too blurry.

The tape also presented a problem of chronology. The last time the truck was seen on the tape, the time stamp showed that it was 5:20 in the morning. But the attack started two hours later, at about 7:30. By then, the truck was no longer appearing in the video. Maybe it was just some all-nighter student, scrambling out for coffee or snacks. Galbraith gave up. She put the truck out of her mind. It was a dead end, as far as she was concerned.

The Golden Police Department issued a press release with a

rudimentary description of the incident. The assailant was a white male, six feet two, with hazel eyes. There were no further identifying details: "The suspect was wearing a mask so no composite sketch is available," it read. Galbraith made sure the release prominently mentioned the same detail that had drawn Amber's attention. "The suspect does have a distinctive mark or tattoo on the outer area of his lower leg or calf that is about the size and shape of a large chicken egg," it read. Galbraith was taking a leap of faith. Amber's recollection needed to be right.

A few days later, a student at a college near Denver called the police hotline. He sounded shaky on the voicemail. He said he felt obligated to contact the cops. One of his friends had a mark that sounded like the one on the report. The guy's name was Frank Tucker.* He was a fellow student.

With help from the tipster, Galbraith called up Tucker's Facebook page. One photo showed his leg. The image was dark. But maybe there was a birthmark? Galbraith called Amber to come to the station. When she arrived, she peered at a cropped photo that showed Tucker's leg. She couldn't be sure. It seemed like the mark on the rapist had been farther down his leg, she told Galbraith. But it was about the same size and shape as the one on Tucker's leg.

Galbraith ran Tucker's criminal history. Four years earlier, cops at the college had taken a report from a female student. She had gotten drunk at a party. She attached herself to Tucker. After boozy conversation, he ordered her to have sex with him. If she didn't, Tucker threatened to tell everyone that she was a slut. The woman agreed reluctantly. But after they started, she changed her mind. Tucker ignored her. She reported the rape to campus police but had ultimately declined to press charges.

Galbraith was fortunate the woman had come forward. Many women are reluctant to report sexual assault. Only about one-

---
* Pseudonym

fifth of women contact police after they've been raped, according to national surveys. The stigma of the crime remains a serious barrier to speaking out. Women are afraid that friends or family might discover what happened. Or they are afraid of not being taken seriously. Or they don't consider the attack serious enough to merit the involvement of the law. Or they don't want to help the cops imprison a man who may be a boyfriend, a husband, a father to their children.

For Galbraith, the woman's report of rape was enough to make Tucker a suspect. She subpoenaed the phone company for his cell phone records. She banged out a request to place a GPS tracker on Tucker's car. Her concern was clear. She needed to track Tucker's car in order "to identify future victims," she told the judge.

HENDERSHOT FIGURED SHE'D use Amber's case to revisit an evidentiary trail that had so far disappointed.

Television dramas often treat DNA as the key that can unlock every mystery. Investigators find a speck of blood on a weapon or traces of spit on a cigarette butt. They send the sample to a lab. The lab compares the sample against the DNA of a suspect. Boom, there's a hit, and the crime is solved in one hour, minus commercials.

The reality is different. The Federal Bureau of Investigation runs the most comprehensive cold-case database in the country, the Combined DNA Index System, known as CODIS. The database contains the genetic profiles of more than fifteen million people, mostly convicted criminals. The profiles are extracted from DNA samples collected under controlled conditions at some point in the judicial process—for instance, when a suspect is booked into jail and gets the inside of his cheek swabbed. From there, an analyst separates the DNA sample into fragments, which produce a person's profile—a pattern of stripes that appears almost like a bar code on an X-ray filmstrip. The FBI accepts the profile only if it contains genetic material from thirteen separate locations, or loci, of a person's DNA.

The power of the database kicks in when a detective finds some kind of body fluid at a crime scene: blood, semen, saliva. Once the crime scene sample is processed, it can be compared to the millions of stored samples. The FBI will not do the comparison, however, unless the crime scene sample contains genetic material from the same thirteen locations, with some limited exceptions. If the DNA sample is degraded or limited in quantity so that the analysis results in complete information from only five or ten genetic locations, the FBI rejects the sample. By insisting on such "high stringency" matching criteria, the FBI estimates the chances of a false match at one in one billion.

Hendershot figured that the rapist must know something about the process. The police term was "DNA conscious." He was trying to erase his presence down to the molecular level. And so far, he had succeeded.

Burgess had been the first to be disappointed. A few days after the rape in Aurora, Doris had walked through her house with a crime scene investigator named Randy Neri. In each room, Neri asked: "What did you see? Where'd you see him go? What did you see him touch?" When they reached her bedroom, Doris saw the television that sat on a wooden dresser, next to her bed. On top were three teddy bears, two white and one yellow. When Doris saw them, she stopped. The yellow bear, she told Neri. The rapist had knocked the yellow bear onto the floor, and then stooped to pick it up.

Neri swabbed the bear, packed the sample into an evidence bag, and shipped it to the state's crime lab at the Colorado Bureau of Investigation.

The CBI was headquartered in a low brick building, surrounded by pine trees, across a busy intersection from a Hooters restaurant. Much like its federal counterpart, it specialized in using science and technology to solve the toughest crimes. With

250 employees, and offices across the state, the bureau served as a crime lab for local police and sheriffs. It analyzed fingerprints and DNA, conducted toxicology tests, and tracked gun sales. The bureau's crime lab was best known for its Herculean labor in the case of JonBenét Ramsey, the six-year-old beauty queen found murdered in her parents' house in Boulder in 1996. In that case, the bureau's analysts received 2,509 laboratory specimens and conducted 25,520 lab examinations over the course of 3,116 hours. The murder went unsolved. But Colorado cops still held the CBI as the last, best hope for answers in a complicated case.

On December 7, 2009, two months after Doris's rape, CBI analyst Sarah Lewis called Burgess with mixed news. The rapist had been punctilious. But not perfect. Doris's teddy bear had yielded the tiniest trace of him—perhaps no more than seven or eight skin cells, sloughed from his fingertips as he grabbed the bear with gloveless hands. The analysis of touch DNA, as such micro-genetic samples were known, was a revolutionary investigative development. It allowed police to examine minute amounts of genetic material that would have been impossible to analyze with traditional DNA tests. But the new tests had a drawback: The paucity of cells did not render enough information to meet the FBI's standard of thirteen genetic markers.

Lewis had been forced to use a more limited type of DNA exam called a Y-STR analysis. The exam looked for patterns, called short tandem repeats, on the Y chromosome found in male DNA. The results would show nothing in the case of a female suspect. And even for men, they would only reveal a limited amount of information. They could identify a male suspect as coming from a particular family tree. But the results were not unique enough to be a genetic fingerprint. Lewis delivered the news to Burgess: The DNA found on the bear was "either inconclusive or provided no results," she wrote. "This profile does not qualify for entry into the CODIS DNA database."

In Westminster, Hendershot had been excited to learn that

Sarah saw the rapist pick up her white kitchen timer. It was one of the few items police were certain he had touched. Sarah's memory proved correct. CBI analyst Gentry Roth found a trace of genetic material on the timer. But as with the teddy bear in Doris's home, he was able to salvage only enough cells for a Y-STR analysis. "The amount of DNA was not sufficient for a complete DNA profile," Hendershot wrote.

In Golden, Galbraith had managed to capture a few of the rapist's cells when she brushed Amber's face with a swab in the front of her patrol car. But as with Doris's teddy bear and Sarah's kitchen timer, Amber's face did not yield enough of the rapist's genetic material to develop a complete profile. The CBI technicians could only conduct a Y-STR analysis. The magic of DNA had failed Hendershot, Galbraith, and Burgess. The FBI's database could not be tapped for a possible hit.

But a CBI technician pitched an idea to Hendershot. The three samples might not be able to identify a single suspect, but they could still be useful. The CBI could compare the Y-STR profiles with one another. If they were different, detectives would know they were dealing with different suspects. If they matched, detectives would know that a single man—or at least a paternally related set of men—was stalking the suburbs.

They would know they were hunting relatives, instead of strangers.

Hendershot gave the go-ahead to start the work.

THOUGH THEY DID not know each other well, Hendershot's and Galbraith's lives were intertwined. They were members of a sorority within a fraternity. They were female cops.

As a young patrol officer, Galbraith had been inspired by a female detective. One morning, Golden's chief called his officers together to let them know about a drug bust that was going to happen later that day at a local fast-food restaurant. An elite narcotics squad drawn from police departments across the Denver area, the West Metro Drug Task Force, was sweeping in to break up a ring. One of the task force officers in the room for the briefing caught Galbraith's eye. She radiated a quiet intensity. Galbraith had been thinking about applying for a spot on the narcotics squad. At that moment, she knew she would. "She's a chick," Galbraith thought. "If she can do it, I can do it." The detective was Edna Hendershot.

In the United States, female cops have been building on the success of other female cops for more than a hundred years. Once, women were confined to work in police departments as civilian helpers, usually in matters involving children and women. Alice Stebbins Wells helped change that. She became a police officer—or "officeress" as she was then known—when she joined the Los Angeles Police Department on September 12, 1910. Her shield read "Policewoman." The bottom of her gold badge featured her number: 1. She joined the so-called "purity squad," tasked with patrolling penny arcades, dance halls, skating rinks, and other dens of iniquity. Wells "fought for the idea that women, as regular members of municipal police departments, are particularly well-qualified to perform protective and preventative work among juveniles and female criminals," reads her official bio on the International Association of Women Police, a group she founded. Two years after Wells was hired, two other women joined the LAPD.

Wells's argument that women brought special qualities to police work wasn't always enough to win over her male colleagues. But over time, studies have shown that female officers benefit police departments and the communities they serve. Women are less likely to use excessive force than their male counterparts, and are less likely to be involved in lawsuits alleging police abuse. Citizens tend to rank female officers as more empathetic and communicative than their male counterparts. And female officers are more likely to embrace the goals of community policing—a law enforcement philosophy that emphasizes cooperation and interaction with citizens.

Female officers have also been shown to respond more effectively to violence against women. For instance, a 1985 study found that female officers displayed more patience and understanding with domestic-violence victims. A 1998 study of a nationally representative sample of 147 police departments found that female officers were more likely to make arrests in domestic-violence cases than male officers. And a 2006 study of the sixty largest US metropolitan police departments showed that every 1 percent increase in female officers correlated with a 1 percent increase in the number of rapes reported in a jurisdiction.

None of these studies downplays the extraordinary work of the male cops who investigate and arrest thousands of rapists every year. Nor do they suggest that a female officer is automatically better than a male counterpart at responding to gender-based violence. While some female victims prefer to speak with a woman because of a shared gender connection, other victims have said they felt safer and calmer in the presence of a male officer. End Violence Against Women International, the police training organization, has suggested that the most important factor in talking with victims is the engagement of the investigators. "What *is* absolutely clear is that an officer's competence and compassion are far more important than gender in determining their effectiveness at interviewing sexual assault victims," the organization emphasizes.

Despite the benefits of gender diversity, female cops still have a tough time on the job. Some male cops—from patrolmen to police chiefs—remain hostile to hiring women, claiming that they are not strong enough or tough enough to be cops. In studies, between 63 to 68 percent of female officers report suffering some form of sexual harassment or discrimination in the workplace. The most common complaints from female officers involve hostility, a lack of promotion opportunities, and poor policies to deal with pregnancy and other family issues.

But even departments that have put a significant focus on boosting the number of women in their ranks have found it difficult. Many women have little interest in a profession that—at least in popular culture—is all about guns and violence. The result is that no police department in the United States is even close to gender parity. The criminal investigation branch of the Internal Revenue Service may have the highest percentage of female law enforcement agents in the country, with 32 percent. And in some big-city police departments, such as Philadelphia and Los Angeles, women make up about a quarter of sworn officers. But overall, about a hundred thousand female officers fill the ranks of police in the United States—about 11 percent of the total. Police work remains a mostly male field, macho, hierarchical, and militaristic. Officeresses are rare.

BROUGHT TOGETHER BY the hunt for the rapist, Galbraith and Hendershot bonded quickly. Both were outgoing. They cracked fast jokes and smiled fast smiles. Galbraith was younger and crackled with energy. Hendershot's experience complemented Galbraith's enthusiasm.

Both women were at ease working in the testosterone-soaked world of law enforcement. Men accounted for about 90 percent of the sworn officers in Golden and Westminster, but neither Galbraith nor Hendershot felt unwelcome or intimidated. Both had grown up with brothers. Both had few close female friends and tended to get along better with men. Both took pride in being tough. "I don't tolerate drama. If it's drama, I'm like, ugh. If it's emotional, ugh," Galbraith says.

Both also had the same experience breaking into police work. Get your foot in the door, prove yourself, and you were accepted into the brotherhood—just like any other cop. The woman thing didn't matter so much. "It might be at the forefront when you first walk in the door," Hendershot says. "But especially after you've established yourself for a little bit as a patrol officer, it just doesn't come up. It just is."

They reveled in the dark though redemptive humor found in every cop shop, emergency ward, and newsroom. They shared details of crime scenes and traffic accidents. They swore. They swapped stories of disgust: wearing face masks stuffed with dryer sheets to ward off the scent of a rotting corpse, watching a guy masturbate during an undercover drug deal.

"He answers the door, and all he's wearing is a pair of black shorts, no shirt, and an ankle monitor," Hendershot tells Galbraith.

"Cute," Galbraith says.

"The epitome of sexy, let me tell you. Who can resist this?"

Sometimes, they made a point of trying to discomfit their younger male colleagues—a kind of verbal hazing usually involving women's body functions or sex organs.

"It's actually kind of amusing to see how much you can poke it sometimes, I've got to be honest," Hendershot says to Galbraith.

"And then they're walking to HR," Galbraith says.

"Or running."

Both women laugh.

Sometimes, their superiors worried about the male cops saying something offensive. Once, one of Galbraith's superiors pulled her aside when he thought the conversation had crossed a line. He asked whether Galbraith was okay with the chatter. "I'm like, 'God, yes. I started it.'"

They did, of course, have problems as female cops. Galbraith was always having to tie her hair up in a bun to avoid getting it covered in mud or blood. Hendershot could never find a place to conceal her handgun. Neither thought they looked particularly good in a bulletproof vest. "It's not glamorous. I'm not wearing cute shoes. None of it is what society puts forward as to how a female is supposed to look, act, think," Hendershot said.

The women were connected in another way, too. Cops often inhabit an incestuous world, where every officer knows every other, and marriages and friendships stay in the family. Hendershot's second husband, Mike, and Galbraith's second husband, David, had worked together at the Golden Police Department. David wound up working with Hendershot at the Westminster Police Department.

ON JANUARY 18, 2011, the detectives gathered again. The stakes were higher now, and the crowd in the room reflected it. The FBI, the Colorado Bureau of Investigation, the Jefferson County district attorney's office—all sent agents to meet on the second floor of Golden's fire house, off the city's historic district.

One of the new faces was Jonny Grusing, a veteran FBI agent who worked out of the bureau's Denver office. He was tall, thin, and fit, with a dry sense of humor—the consummate G-man. He had been based in Denver for fifteen years—an unusually long time for FBI agents, who rotate frequently through jobs in different cities. For much of his career, Grusing focused on bank robberies. Now, he was assigned to the Safe Streets task force, created after 9/11 to marry the skills of the FBI with the shoe-leather savvy of local cops. He had worked cases with most of the agencies at the table, and those in the room knew he was no bigfoot who would take over an investigation from local lawmen. "I don't know of a department that we walk in or a jurisdiction where we walk in and they go, 'Oh no, it's the FBI,'" Grusing says.

Grusing was in charge of bringing a potentially powerful tool to the hunt for the rapist: an FBI database of thousands of crimes called the Violent Criminal Apprehension Program, or ViCAP. The ViCAP database was designed to catch serial killers and rapists. It was based on the principle that repeat offenders—called serialists by the experts—had signature patterns of behavior nearly as distinctive as a fingerprint or a snippet of DNA. A serial rapist who used a favorite knife in one jurisdiction might use the same knife in another jurisdiction. When local investigators suspected that a serial criminal was at work, they would load as many of the crime's details as possible into the ViCAP database. FBI analysts would then comb through the files of cold cases, hoping to find a match. At its best, the system would connect two agencies together, allowing them to share details as they hunted for the same criminal.

Dawn Tollakson, a crime analyst from Aurora, had already entered details from the three rapes in Colorado into the database. Back in Quantico, analysts had compared Tollakson's reports to thousands of others in the ViCAP database. Now, Grusing held the results: the analysts had found a hit. The Colorado attacker appeared to share many characteristics with a rapist who had terrorized University of Kansas students for almost a decade. He had raped or attacked thirteen young women between 2000 and 2008.

The women had described the attacker as a white male, approximately twenty-six to thirty-five years of age. He was from five feet nine to six feet tall. He attacked in the early morning. He would straddle the women in bed. He used bindings to tie their hands. He dressed in dark clothes. He wore a black mask and gloves. He brandished a handgun.

During the attack, his commands were short and direct. He spoke calmly. He would assault the women orally, vaginally, and anally. He carried a bag with him that contained lubrication and a video camera that he used to film the rapes. Afterward, he would have them shower to remove any evidence from their bodies. He told them to wait twenty minutes before leaving the bathroom.

He attacked his first victim on October 1, 2000. She woke to find him standing in her room. She lunged to hit a panic button, but he pointed a gun at her head and told her to stop. Apparently spooked, he left without raping the woman. As he turned to go, he gave her a warning: "Do me a favor and lock your door next time."

On July 14, 2004, he raped a woman who woke to find him staring at her from the foot of her bed. "I have a gun, don't say anything or I will kill you," he told her. He carried a black bag that contained K-Y Jelly. After he finished, he ordered her into the bathroom. He forced her to brush her teeth.

The last woman was assaulted while her roommate was away on Thanksgiving break. It was more violent than any of the previous rapes. The rapist punched the woman in the face. He shoved a sock in her mouth so she could not scream. He raped her several times. The woman could provide no description of the man. She had been too terrified to open her eyes.

After the final attack, in December 2008, the man had disappeared. Now Grusing raised the question: Had he resurfaced, ten months later, in Aurora, Colorado?

Grusing believed that he had.

"He had warmed up to this level of proficiency. Like someone playing basketball or baseball, you can tell when they've been around and they've handled the ball before," Grusing says.

"We thought this was our guy."

IN TURNING TO ViCAP, the detectives were betting on one of the FBI's most forgotten programs.

Pierce Brooks was the father of ViCAP. A legendary cop, he had a square jaw, high forehead, and dead-serious eyes. During twenty years with the Los Angeles Police Department, he helped send ten men to death row. He served as technical adviser to Jack Webb, who played the fictional Sergeant Joe Friday character in *Dragnet*. And he became famous for tracking down a pair of cop killers, a hunt chronicled in Joseph Wambaugh's 1973 nonfiction best seller, *The Onion Field*. "Brooks's imagination was admired, but his thoroughness was legend," Wambaugh wrote.

In the late 1950s, Brooks was investigating two murder cases. In each, a female model had been raped, slain, and then trussed in rope in a manner that suggested skill with binding. Brooks intuited that the killer might commit other murders. For the next year, he leafed through out-of-town newspapers at a local library. When he read a story about a man arrested while trying to use rope to kidnap a woman, Brooks put the cases together. The man, Harvey Glatman, was sentenced to death, and executed a year later.

The experience convinced Brooks that serial killers often had "signatures"—distinct ways of acting that could help identify them. An early adopter of data-driven policing, Brooks realized that a computer database could be populated with details of unsolved murder cases from across the country, then searched for behavioral matches.

After Brooks had spent years lobbying for such a system, Congress took interest. In July 1983, Brooks told a rapt Senate Judiciary Committee audience about serial killer Ted Bundy, who confessed to killing thirty women in seven states. The ViCAP system could have prevented many of those deaths, he said. "ViCAP, when implemented, would preclude the age-old, but still continuing problem of critically important information being missed, overlooked, or delayed when several police agencies, hundreds or even thousands of miles apart, are involved," Brooks told the lawmakers. By the end of the hearing, Brooks had a letter from the committee that would result in $1 million for the program.

The agency used the money to purchase what was then called the "Cadillac of computers"—an AVAX 11/985 nicknamed the "Superstar." It had 512 kilobytes of memory. The revolutionary computer system took up most of the room in a bomb shelter two floors beneath the cafeteria of the FBI's national academy in Quantico, Virginia. Also housed in the basement was another novel program: the Behavioral Analysis Unit, the profilers who would one day be made famous by Thomas Harris's *The Silence of the Lambs*. At the time, rank-and-file FBI agents saw the unproven unit and its ViCAP computer program as a kind of skunk works. They referred to the oddball collection of psychologists, cops, and administrators as "rejects of the FBI" or the "leper colony." The basement was a dark, moldy warren of desks, bookcases, and file cabinets. "We were ten times deeper than dead people, down there," one agent later recalled.

An FBI agent named Art Meister modified the ViCAP system to hunt serial rapists. To Meister, a former Connecticut state trooper with dark curly hair and glasses, the upgrade only made sense. Research had shown that rapists were far more likely than murderers to be serial offenders. Studies had found that between one-fourth to two-thirds of rapists committed multiple sexual assaults. Only about 1 percent of murderers were considered serial killers.

By the time of the Colorado rapes, ViCAP had amassed an enormous collection of violent and bizarre crimes—enough so that researchers once requested access to the database for an academic paper on cannibalism. (Meister turned them down.) But the program was eking along, a pale, unwanted child that had relocated from the FBI academy's basement into a mini-mall off a two-lane highway in rural Virginia. It was chronically underfunded. The database itself was hard to use—a detective had to fill in ninety-five separate fields of information to input a case. It generated lots of noise: Cops disparaged it for creating a never-ending supply of bad tips. Most significantly, ViCAP had been surpassed by CODIS, the FBI's DNA-matching system. ViCAP's behavioral linkages could never equal the scientific certainty of a genetic match. And CODIS's record of success was indisputable.

It had linked up more than 346,000 crimes over the years. A 1990s review found that ViCAP could claim credit for linking thirty-three crimes in twelve years.

The result was that ViCAP was rarely used. Only about four-teen hundred police agencies out of roughly eighteen thousand in the United States entered information into the database. It con-tained far less than 1 percent of the rapes and murders committed each year. The database was a tragically unfulfilled promise. Only about half of rape cases involved DNA. For the other half, where a serial rapist might wear a certain mask, or speak in a peculiar way, or tie a particular binding knot, ViCAP was the best, and only, nationwide tool to help in the hunt. "The need is vital," said Ritchie Martinez, the former president of the International As-sociation of Law Enforcement Intelligence Analysts. "But ViCAP is not filling it."

HENDERSHOT WAS NO computer expert. But she knew that data could help find a criminal as surely as a snippet of DNA. As Gal-braith and Grusing chased the Kansas connection, she turned to a far more local resource: her department's own crime analyst, Laura Carroll.

Like Ellis, the crime scene investigator, Carroll was one of Hendershot's favorites at the Westminster Police Department. Carroll had stumbled into the profession. She began college want-ing to be a teacher, but ended with a degree in criminology. Being in law enforcement just seemed—well, more interesting. "It's catching the bad guys, being part of the process in order to do good," she'd explain. She wasn't keen on running around in the streets with a gun. That seemed dangerous. So her first jobs were clerical: in police records in nearby Arvada, then as a clerk at Westminster's municipal courts. The work itself wasn't exciting, but she liked feeling like a part of something bigger.

Then, she discovered her true talent. She got a job working in the traffic division of the Westminster Police Department, which required her to take courses in mapping and analytical software. She became a crime analyst, studying long rows of data and computerized maps. She alerted the cops to dangerous intersections, or streets where drivers were ignoring speed limits. She had become part of the crime-fighting team. She loved it.

It was a lonely job, though. Most smaller departments didn't have a crime analyst. Even a large department might have only two or three. Carroll realized it was critical to network with analysts at other agencies, so she began going to monthly meetings of the Colorado Crime Analysis Association. It was a simple affair: a bunch of analysts, most of them women, gathering together in spare conference rooms at different agencies to review cases and data patterns. But the conversations were a revelation. Data combined with collaboration was a powerful tool, she thought. "As analysts, we really try to communicate and work together," Carroll says. "Crime has no borders." She eventually became president of the association.

Hendershot had first contacted Carroll to hunt down possible suspects in Sarah's rape, based on Amber's description of the egg-shaped mark on her rapist. Hendershot figured it might be a tattoo—and she knew that Carroll had access to every tattoo on every criminal who had passed through Westminster's jail. After an arrest, cops would detail each suspect's tattoos—their size, shape, color, position on the body—and enter the information into a database. Carroll found thirty-two guys inked with a collective 124 tattoos on their legs. Two had leg tats that weren't exactly egg-shaped but were close enough for Carroll to pull more reports. One of the guys didn't match the physical description. The other was in prison at the time of Sarah's rape. "Where do we go from here?" Carroll wondered.

A week later, her answer arrived. At the crime analyst association's regular monthly meeting, she laid out the details of the rapist's attacks. Did it sound familiar to anybody? An analyst from nearby Lakewood remembered a burglary call. A man had broken into a woman's house while she was sleeping. He had worn a black mask. The woman managed to escape and the man fled. Worth looking into, she thought.

When Carroll got the report the next morning, she knew she was on the right track. Lakewood detectives had actually classified the incident as an attempted burglary *and* an attempted sexual assault. Their investigation had not turned up much. But Lakewood's crime scene investigator did find footprints and glove prints.

When Carroll showed Hendershot the report, the detective was intrigued. There had been a footprint in the snow outside Amber's apartment in Golden. Hendershot sent a message to Ellis. Could she contact her counterpart at Lakewood and compare the prints?

That afternoon, Ellis was eating lunch at her desk in the crime lab when she got an email from the Lakewood criminalist, an old friend. As the images of the glove prints and shoe prints filled her screen, she jumped up from her seat. She couldn't believe it. She ran toward Hendershot's cubicle. "Where's Ed? Where's Ed?" she shouted. Told that she was at a meeting, Ellis shot Hendershot a text message. It was urgent.

"Call me. 911."

"SOMETHING ABOUT HOW SHE SAID IT"

Tuesday, August 12, 2008
Lynnwood, Washington

SERGEANT MASON REMEMBERED THE WOMAN FROM THE day before.

When he had first walked into Marie's apartment, she had been sitting on the sofa with Marie. She had been one of the first people Marie called for help. She had gone with Marie to the hospital.

Now, a day later, she was sitting with him—in her cozy single-story home on a curvy street with tall evergreens all around—saying she wondered if Marie had made all this up.

Mason's tipster wasn't some alienated friend, whispering to police, nor some ex, nursing a grudge. This was Marie's foster mother.

When she had called Mason earlier today, Peggy identified herself by name but told the detective she wanted to be treated anonymously. She didn't want what she had to say to get back to Marie. Mason, accustomed as he was to the clandestine world of drug investigations, found that request familiar enough and agreed to protect Peggy's identity. He would keep her name out of his report about the telephone call—and for this conversation, the one in person, he would make no record at all.

They talked in Peggy's living room. Peggy chose her words with care. She did not say: Marie is lying. She couldn't say that.

She didn't know that. What Peggy offered was a suspicion, a sense that something was off.

Peggy's skepticism didn't spring from any one source. The roots were deep and tangled, intertwining what she knew about Marie from helping to raise her, what she had seen the day before, and what she had heard from someone else close to Marie.

Peggy had a master's degree in mental health counseling. She had earlier been a foster-care case manager and now worked at a homeless shelter as a children's advocate. In years to come she would work in the schools as an assistant for special-education students. She kept at home a copy of the *DSM*, or *Diagnostic and Statistical Manual of Mental Disorders*, a massive compendium published by the American Psychiatric Association that classifies disorders and is used by clinicians and others. She believed Marie could be found in those hundreds of pages—that her troubled past had given rise to some personality disorder manifesting in shallow relationships and an attraction to drama. "And it's understandable. Her history—that's probably how she had to get attention her whole life," Peggy says. Histrionic personality disorder perhaps? Peggy couldn't say for sure. But some moments made her wonder.

A few days before she had reported being raped, Marie had gone on a picnic with Peggy, Peggy's boyfriend, and the teenage sisters who were now Peggy's foster kids. "And it was a lot of drama," Peggy says. "She was trying to get a lot of attention from me, I felt." Peggy thought maybe Marie was competing, jealous of the new foster kids. And she worried that Marie couldn't see how she was coming across. "There was some guy that was watching her because she was being so outrageously flaunty-flirty. And I tried to have a conversation with her about toning it down a little bit because, 'You're drawing a lot of attention to yourself right now,' I told her. 'First of all, it's really obnoxious. And second of all, there's a guy over here watching you and you don't know what . . .'"

Yesterday, when Marie called and said she'd been attacked, Peggy had been torn. She needed to take it seriously. She knew that. And she did—rushing to Marie's apartment, getting there the same time as the first officers. But on the way over she wrestled with another thought. "There was just another part of me that said—part of her MO is to be really, really outrageous, and to say things that make people react. That's just part of her personality." Even the phone call—the way Marie sounded—contributed to Peggy's speculation. "Her voice was like this little tiny voice, and I couldn't really tell. It didn't sound real to me. It sounded like there was something ... it sounded like a lot of drama, too, in some ways. It was like, 'Oh, boy.'"

At the apartment, Peggy found Marie on the floor, crying. "But it was so strange because I sat down next to her, and she was telling me what happened, and I got this—I'm a big *Law & Order* fan, and I just got this really weird feeling. It was like, I felt like she was telling me the script of a *Law & Order* story." Part of it was what Marie was saying. Why would a rapist use a shoelace to tie her up? That seemed bizarre. Is a shoelace even strong enough to hold someone? Why didn't he bring rope or cuffs? And part of it was how Marie was saying it: "She was detached. Detached. Emotionally detached from what she was saying."

When Marie said the rapist took photos, that also gave Peggy pause. Suspicion turned to supposition. She wondered if Marie had gotten into trouble somehow. Maybe she had let someone take graphic pictures of her—and now those pictures were going to appear on the Internet, so this was a way for Marie to cover up.

Peggy felt horrible about her skepticism. She didn't want to believe that Marie was lying. But whatever her doubts, she had sensed while in Marie's apartment—watching the police work, watching people console Marie—that she was alone in harboring them.

Later she had learned that wasn't so.

FOR SHANNON—MARIE'S other parental figure, the fun mom in Marie's extended foster family—doubt set in from the moment she heard the news.

"I remember exactly," Shannon says. "I was standing on my balcony and she called and said, 'I've been raped.' It was very flat, no emotion."

Marie had called Shannon on Monday, after leaving the hospital. Shannon asked if she was okay, and Marie said yes, she was going to spend the night at a friend's—and that was pretty much it. When Shannon's husband got home, Shannon told him about Marie's call. She also said she didn't know if she believed Marie. "There's something about how she said it that made me question whether or not she'd actually been raped. It was the tone of her voice. There was no emotion. It was like she was telling me she made a sandwich. 'I just made myself a chicken sandwich.'"

Shannon knew Marie to be emotional. She knew her to cry. This stoicism wasn't in character.

And for Shannon, there was another, more personal reason to doubt Marie.

Shannon didn't have to imagine being in Marie's place. She had been there, or at least in a place very much like it. "I was sexually abused as a child," Shannon says. "And sexually assaulted as an adult." In both instances, when she had told someone—nine years afterward, in the case of the child abuse—Shannon was anything but stoic. "I was hysterical. And emotional. And crying. Yeah. Shamed." Shannon and Marie were so much alike. How could Marie be so different now?

Before Peggy called Mason on Tuesday, Shannon and Peggy had talked on the phone—either the night before or the morning of. They were two parents, comparing notes. Peggy told Shannon that not long before Marie reported the rape, she and Marie had argued. Marie had a bike at Peggy's place. She wanted to come over to pick it up, but Peggy said no, she wanted some downtime, and that set Marie off. Peggy told Shannon she didn't want to think this, but maybe, for Marie, this rape story was a way to get the attention she was wanting before.

I don't know what the hell is going on, Peggy told Shannon. I can't tell . . .

Peggy, you're not the only one who doesn't believe her, Shannon said.

The two pondered how Marie seemed to be telling everybody about this horrific thing that had happened—calling one friend after another, saying, I've been raped. Some friends she called had been less than supportive in the past—mean, even. She wasn't treating this as private and personal. She wasn't being selective in sharing. Neither Peggy nor Shannon had known Marie to be a liar—to exaggerate, sure, to want attention, sure—but now, both knew they weren't alone in wondering if Marie had made this up.

Shannon's doubts reinforced Peggy's. Peggy's doubts reinforced Shannon's.

Shannon's misgivings escalated on Tuesday, the same day Peggy was calling the police. Marie and Nattlie, her upstairs neighbor, were assigned new apartments to protect them should the rapist return. Shannon went to Marie's to help her pack for the move. In the kitchen, when Shannon walked in, Marie didn't meet her gaze. "That seemed very strange," Shannon says. "We would always hug and she would look you right in the eye." In the bedroom Marie seemed casual, with nothing to suggest she had been raped there the morning before. "She went about her business like nothing had happened." Some friends of Marie's came over, along with her case manager from Project Ladder, and the group ventured outside. "She was kind of flirting with the guy that ran the program that she was in. She was on the grass, rolling around and giggling and laughing. It was just such strange behavior."

Shannon spent the whole day with Marie, noting all these things that seemed off. The kicker came that evening, when the two went shopping. Marie needed new bedding, because the police had taken hers as evidence. They went to the store where Marie had gotten her old sheets and bedspread—the ones that had been on her bed when she said she'd been raped—and Marie became furious when she couldn't find the same set. It was the only time the entire day that Shannon saw Marie get mad—and to Shannon, it made no sense.

Why would you want to have those same sheets to remind you? Shannon asked Marie.

Because I like them, Marie said.

Shannon was so thrown by Marie's behavior that she tried to call a crisis center to get a better understanding of how someone might react to being raped. She found a number online, but no one answered.

SITTING IN PEGGY's home that Tuesday, Mason was in effect listening to the doubts of both of Marie's foster moms. To Mason, Peggy seemed sincere. Forthright. She expressed concern for Marie, but felt there was information she should pass along. She shared her take on Marie's personality. She shared her speculation about the graphic photographs.

As Marie's last foster mom, Peggy figured to know Marie well. So did the folks at Project Ladder, the program nurturing her to independence. One of the program's managers had mentioned to Mason that before Marie reported being raped, she had been asking to change apartments. The manager didn't come out and say: I think she's lying. I think she made this story up to get her way. Mason didn't even note the manager's aside in a report, suggesting how little it meant to him at the time. But he tucked it away. And now he tacked it on to Peggy's suspicions. Apart, neither was worth much. Together, they took on weight.

When Mason left Peggy's home, he didn't know if Marie was lying. But for him the question had now been planted.

"It was a question that needed answering," he says.

On WEDNESDAY, MARIE returned to the Lynnwood police station and handed Mason her written statement. She had filled in each of the form's twenty-four lines, writing about four hundred words in total about the rape and what she had done afterward.

"After he left I grabbed my phone (which was right next to my head) with my mouth and I tried to call Jordan back."

Jordan didn't answer, Marie wrote. So she called her foster mom.

"I got off the phone with her and tried to untie myself. I tried a kitchen knife but it didn't work so I found scissors and did it."

This sequence caught Mason's eye. It didn't match what Marie had told him before. At the station two days earlier, when she had come in after being examined at the hospital, Marie had said that she cut the laces off first—*then* tried calling Jordan, then called Peggy. Her written statement switched the order, saying she was still bound when she started using the phone.

Mason made a mental note of the inconsistency. He asked Marie a few questions—about her relationship with Jordan (ex-boyfriend, now good friend, Marie said), about the gloves the rapist was wearing (latex, I think, Marie said)—then thanked her for coming in, and said he would be in touch as the investigation continued.

On THURSDAY MORNING, Mason interviewed Jordan at his home. This was August 14, three days after the report of rape.

Jordan told Mason about his relationship with Marie. They were no longer dating, but they were still good friends. He saw her at church study groups once or twice a week. They spoke daily on the phone. They talked about all kinds of things. There was nothing out of the ordinary about their late-night conversation before the attack, Jordan told the detective.

Mason asked if Marie had tried calling Jordan Monday morning—after the attack—but been unable to reach him. Jordan checked his cell phone. There it was, confirmation: a missed call from Marie at 7:43. That tracked: Marie tried Jordan at 7:43, then called Peggy, then called her neighbor. Her neighbor came down and called police at 7:55.

Mason asked if Marie had told Jordan about what happened that morning. Jordan said Marie told him that she had dialed his number using her toes, because she was still tied up. The detective would later note this in his report. If Marie's Monday account was Version 1 (cut laces, then called), and her Wednesday account Version 2 (called, then cut laces), this was like a Version 2(A): called, then cut, but with a new detail about dialing with her toes.

At no point in this interview did Jordan say he thought Marie was lying about being raped. At no point did Mason even ask.

On Thursday afternoon, Mason called Marie, to ask if they could meet. He said he could come and pick her up, to take her to the police station.

"Am I in trouble?" Marie asked the detective.

Mason didn't go alone to pick up Marie. He went with Jerry Rittgarn, his fellow detective.

Mason told Rittgarn he no longer believed Marie. He told him about Marie's question: *Am I in trouble?* In Mason's experience, when someone asked if they were in trouble, they almost always were. Mason also gave other reasons for his conclusion, although Rittgarn's report on their conversation would be maddeningly imprecise: "He told me that, based on subsequent interviews and inconsistencies with [Marie], her foster mother and her friend Jordan, who she had talked with on the phone prior to the report, he believed and others believed that [Marie] had made up the story."

The investigation's focus now shifted. This afternoon Mason and Rittgarn would not be interviewing Marie as a victim. They would be interrogating her as a suspect.

For more than a half century, a particular approach to interrogation has dominated police work in the United States. Like the rape kit, this investigative tool traces to Chicago—and to a cop, John E. Reid, who became renowned for eliciting confessions without force. Reid aimed to extract admissions through words, tells, and expressions of sympathy, rather than with club and electrical wires. He became so identified with this ability that he left the Chicago police force and began training other officers in what became known as the Reid Technique.

In 1962, Reid laid out the fundamentals of his technique for the masses by coauthoring a book, *Criminal Interrogation and Confessions*. From that point forward, his method began gaining followers at a rapid clip, with hundreds of thousands of investigators attending training seminars "across the United States, Canada, Mexico, Europe, South America, and Asia," according to Reid Technique literature. The technique "became a kind of powerful folk wisdom, internalized by generations of police officers," a *Wired* magazine article noted, adding: "Despite its scientific pose, it has almost no science to back it up." Mason and Rittgarn had both received the training, Mason in 1994 while a police officer in Oregon. Mason's instructor, Louis Senese, had taught the technique for decades; during the three-day course he emphasized a tenet of questioning anyone believed to be lying: "Never allow them to give you denials. The key is to shut them up."

A police interview is non-accusatory. It is an act of gathering information. An interrogation is accusatory. It is an act of persuasion. "An interrogation is conducted only when the investigator is reasonably certain of the suspect's guilt," according to *Essentials of the Reid Technique: Criminal Interrogation and Confessions*.

With the Reid Technique, interrogators use provocative questions and are taught to gauge the response. A favorite prompt is: What kind of punishment do you think the person who did this should get? The dodgier the answer—*Well, it depends*—the more likely the guilt. The questioner's tools can include trickery or deceit. A detective might claim that a witness said something he really didn't (*He says he saw you do it*), or that the physical evidence shows something it really doesn't (*We found your prints on the gun*). An innocent person, the assumption goes, will not take the bait. Questioners learn to evaluate verbal behavior. A definitive response? Credible. A qualified response with waffle words like "generally" and "typically"? Not so credible. Staccato is good: I / DID / NOT / DO / IT. Mumbling is bad—that is, suggestive of lying.

The Reid Technique also attaches great value to interpreting body language. Questioners evaluate feet, posture, and eye contact. "Deceptive suspects generally do not look directly at the investigator; they look down at the floor, over to the side, or up at the ceiling as if to beseech some divine guidance when answering questions," *Essentials of the Reid Technique* says. If a suspect's hands go to his face—say, to cover his mouth—that, too, can signal deception: "In this case, the subject, literally, is speaking through his fingers, as if his hand could grab, out of thin air, incriminating words the subject might utter."

Detectives, once convinced of a suspect's guilt, learn to close, much like any salesman. If a suspect starts to deny guilt, the interrogator heads it off—with hand held up, in the universal "stop" gesture, or with head turned away, to suggest disinterest. "The more often a guilty suspect denies involvement in a crime, the less likely it is that he will tell the truth," *Essentials of the Reid Tech-*

nique says. Then the interrogator offers the suspect some face-saving out—*Man, with how little they pay you, who could blame you for pocketing a little extra?*—that minimizes moral culpability. As for legal ramifications of confessing, detectives are trained to avoid discussing that: "It is psychologically improper to mention any consequences or possible negative effects that a suspect may experience if he decides to tell the truth."

And when a suspect confesses? The detectives get it in writing.

MASON AND RITTGARN found Marie outside her apartment, sitting on the grass. It was late afternoon. They picked her up, took her to the station, and escorted her to a conference room.

From what Mason wrote up later, he wasted little time confronting Marie, telling her there were inconsistencies between her statements and accounts from other witnesses. Marie did not immediately push back, at least not in the way the detectives expected from someone telling the truth. She did not "take a stand and demand that she had been raped," Rittgarn later wrote. Marie told the detectives she wasn't aware of any inconsistencies. She went through the story again—only this time, in a way both detectives found telling, saying she believed the rape had happened instead of swearing it.

Tearfully, Marie described her past—the abuse, the instability—and the isolation she now felt being on her own.

From what Marie would remember later, the interrogation's turning point came when the police said two people doubted her.

Peggy doesn't believe your story, the detectives told Marie.

Jordan doesn't believe you either, they said.

For Marie, both names came as a shock. She didn't know what to think.

Why did Jordan say that? she asked.

But all she got was a cagey response: I don't know. You tell me. Rittgarn told Marie that her story and the evidence didn't match. He told her the rape kit didn't support her story. He said he believed she had made the story up—a spur-of-the-moment thing, not something planned out. From what Rittgarn could tell, Marie seemed to be agreeing with him. So he asked her: Is there really a rapist running around that the police should be looking for?

Marie, her voice soft, her eyes down, said no.

"Based on her answers and body language it was apparent that [Marie] was lying about the rape," Rittgarn later wrote.

Without reading Marie her Miranda rights—her right to an attorney, her right to remain silent—the detectives asked her to write out the true story, admitting she had lied, admitting, in effect, that she had committed a crime. She agreed, so they left her alone for a few minutes. On the form, she filled in her name, address, and Social Security number. Then she wrote:

> I was talking to Jordan on the phone that night about his day and just about anything. After I got off the phone with him, I started thinking about all things I was stressed out and I also was scared living on my own. When I went to sleep I dreamed that someone broke in and raped me.

When the detectives returned, they saw that Marie's statement described the rape as a dream, not a lie.

Why didn't you write that you made the story up? Rittgarn asked.

Marie, crying, said she believed the rape really happened.

We already went over this, Rittgarn told her. You already said there's no rapist out there we should be looking for.

Marie pounded the table and said she was "pretty positive" the rape happened.

Mason didn't know what to make of that. Hammered fist. Qualified response. Two different signals entirely.

Pretty positive or actually positive? Rittgarn asked Marie.

Maybe the rape happened and I blacked it out, Marie said.

What do you think should happen to someone who would lie about something like this? Rittgarn asked Marie.

I should get counseling, Marie said.

Mason returned to the evidence. He told Marie that her description of calling Jordan was different from what Jordan had reported. Marie, hands on her face, looked down. Then "her eyes darted back and forth as if she was thinking of a response," Rittgarn later wrote.

The detectives doubled back to what she had said before—about being anxious, about being lonely—and, eventually, Marie appeared to relax. She stopped crying. She even laughed a little. She apologized—and agreed to write another statement, leaving no doubt her story was a lie.

> I have had a lot of stressful things going on and I wanted to hang out with someone and no one was able to so I made up this story and didn't expect it to go as far as it did. . . . It turned into this big thing . . . I don't know why I couldn't have done something different. This was never meant to happen.

This statement satisfied the detectives. "Based on our interview with [Marie] and the inconsistencies found by Sgt. Mason in some of the statements we were confident that [Marie] was now telling us the truth that she had not been raped," Rittgarn later wrote.

To Marie, it seemed the questioning had lasted for hours. She did what she always did when she was under stress. She flipped the switch, as she called it, suppressing the feelings she didn't know what to do with. Before she confessed to making up the story, she couldn't look the two detectives, the two men, in the eye. Afterward, she could. Afterward, she smiled. She went into the bathroom and cleaned up. Flipping the switch was a relief—and would let her leave.

As for Mason, he now had a written recantation, signed and witnessed. He figured this case was closed.

ON FRIDAY, MARIE, shaken, called her case manager at Project Ladder. She told Wayne that she had spoken with police the day before—and the police didn't believe her, they didn't believe she had been raped. She didn't want to go into any more detail on the phone, preferring to talk in person. But she said she wanted a lawyer.

After they finished talking, Wayne called Jana, a Project Ladder supervisor. Jana advised him to call Sergeant Mason.

So that's what Wayne did. He called the sergeant, who told Wayne that the evidence didn't support Marie's story. He told Wayne that Marie had signed a written statement, admitting she'd made the whole thing up.

Wayne shared this with Jana, and suggested she call Mason herself. So she did. Afterward, Jana told Wayne to let Marie stay the weekend with her friends. They would deal with this on Monday.

After her confrontation with the police, Marie also called two other people, to find out what was going on.

You don't believe me? she asked Jordan.

What are you talking about? Jordan answered. What the hell are you talking about? Of course I believe you.

That's not what the detective said.

Of course I believe you. You know that.

When Marie called Peggy, she got a different answer. Peggy said yes, she had doubts about Marie's story. Peggy said that when Marie called her on the morning she reported being attacked, Marie's first words weren't "I've just been raped." Her first words were "I've just been robbed." Marie didn't remember saying that. But her purse had been dumped out on the floor. Marie supposed she might have said something about her learner's permit or wallet. Peggy also brought up the fight over the bike, and how Marie had gotten mad when Peggy wanted quiet time. Maybe this story was a way of striking back.

To Marie, that was hard to hear. *She thinks I made up a story of being raped because of that?*

On Monday, August 18, Jana and Wayne met with Marie in her new apartment, across the street from her old place. It had now been one week since Marie reported being raped.

Jana related what Sergeant Mason had told them about Marie taking her story back. Marie told Jana she had been under duress. The police had kept her in the station for so long, she signed the statement just to get out of there.

So should the police really be looking for a rapist? Jana asked.

Yes, Marie said.

Then you need to tell the police that, Jana told her.

Wayne didn't believe Marie—and would say as much later, in his case notes. Having heard the police's depiction of the evidence, Wayne was now convinced Marie had not been attacked. He told her that if she lied to police about being raped, she would be making a false statement. That would be a crime, grounds for kicking her out of Project Ladder. She would lose her housing.

But Marie didn't back down. So the three set out for Marie to recant her recantation—to tell detectives she had been telling the truth the first time.

At the police station they learned Mason was out for the day. But Rittgarn was there. Rittgarn wanted a second detective in the room, so he hunted up Sergeant Rodney Cohnheim and asked him to sit in. Cohnheim supervised the Crimes Against Persons detectives. He had been out of town, at a training seminar in Dallas, when Marie had reported being raped. Rittgarn briefed

Cohnheim about the case and Marie's recantation four days before. Then they brought Marie to an upstairs conference room while Jana and Wayne stayed downstairs.

Marie told Rittgarn she had been attacked, that she wasn't making the rapist up. She began to cry, saying she kept having a vision of him on top of her.

Rittgarn wasn't moved. Later, when recounting Marie's words in a written report, he would put the word "him" in quotation marks.

Rittgarn said they had already gone over this. Marie had already admitted to wanting not to be alone. She had already admitted to lying. She had already admitted to staging the evidence.

I want to take a lie-detector test, Marie said.

If you take a polygraph and fail it, I will book you into jail, Rittgarn told her.

The threat rocked Marie. Reeling, she pulled back. She said maybe she'd been hypnotized into believing she had been raped.

For Rittgarn, this was too much. He would write in his report: "This is the fourth ridiculous story" Marie had come up with: she was raped, she blacked it out, she dreamt it, she was hypnotized. He told Marie that if the police hooked her up to a polygraph, they wouldn't ask: Did you dream it? Did you black it out? Were you hypnotized? The question would be: Were you raped? And if she answered with a lie, Rittgarn told her, he would not only book her into jail, he would recommend that Project Ladder pull her housing assistance.

This time, Marie backed down.

She said she had lied.

The police took her down the stairs. Wayne and Jana were waiting for her.

So, one said.

Were you raped?

————

LATER THAT WEEK, the state Crime Victims Compensation Program wrote the Lynnwood Police Department to ask for information about Marie's case. The letter requested the offense report, follow-up reports, and anything else that might help determine if Marie was eligible for coverage. "The goal of the Crime Victims Compensation Program is to prevent further hardship and suffering by providing benefits to eligible victims of crime as quickly as possible," the letter said. The program covered everything from mental health counseling to medical expenses and lost wages.

On August 25—two weeks after Marie reported being attacked—the Lynnwood police called the program's law enforcement records coordinator and told her to never mind. This was a case of false reporting, the police said. Marie was not a rape victim. She was a woman who lied about being raped.

FOR MARIE, THESE two weeks had been a spiral. Before she recanted she had quit her job at Costco, unable to stand there, looking at people, lost in her head. She had tried. She'd worked a day or two, offering up free food samples to shoppers. But then she'd walked out, gone home, said she wouldn't be back.

After she recanted, her losses mounted. The normal life she wanted—the freedom from the rules dividing adolescents from adults—faded from reach. Project Ladder gave her a 9:00 p.m. curfew and doubled the number of times she had to meet with staff.

Jordan sat with Marie on her porch and heard the phone calls coming in from Marie's friends and old classmates. With every ring she cried harder. She knew why they were calling. They were calling to say they didn't believe her and couldn't understand why she did what she had done.

When the police announced that Marie had taken her story back, Marie's best friend from high school—the friend who had taught her photography, the friend who had touched up that picture of Marie emerging from the surf—created a web page about Marie and how she had lied about being raped. The police hadn't named Marie. But Marie's friend did. She even posted a picture of Marie, copied from Marie's Myspace page. When Marie saw the web page, she lost it, trashing her apartment. She alerted Peggy, and the two went to the friend's house.

Why did you do that? Marie demanded to know.

I don't know why I did it, the friend told Marie.

The friend took the web page down, then and there. But Marie left as mad as she had come. The least she wanted was a straight answer, not some *I don't know why I did it.* "After that we were no longer friends," Marie says. "Your friend doesn't do that to somebody."

For Marie, there seemed no end to the fallout. Most painful, perhaps, was an edict she received from Shannon. Shannon's home had long provided Marie with an escape or respite. Marie and Shannon would walk in the woods or drift on the water, then, at day's end, crash at Shannon's. Now, fearful he could become the target of a wrongful accusation, Shannon's husband decided it would be best if Marie no longer spent the night. If she could make up one story, what would keep her from making up another? "When you become a foster parent, you're open to that," Shannon says.

It fell to Shannon to break the news: Marie could come over, but not sleep over. Saying it crushed Shannon. Hearing it crushed Marie.

Before August was out, Marie received a letter in the mail.

When she opened it, she realized her spiral wasn't finished. With all she had lost, she now stood to lose more.

THE SHADOW WITHIN

<u>Lakewood, Colorado</u>

H E SIGNED THE LEASE ON JUNE 24, 2009. HE AND MASHA would begin their new lives at 65 Harlan Street, a two-bedroom, two-bath house in Lakewood, Colorado. It was a squat building with gray siding and a low chain-link fence, sitting on a busy street half a block from a gas station, an auto body shop, and a carniceria. Tall trees, summer-lush with leaves, towered above the roof. A beat-down neighborhood of small homes and boxy apartment complexes circled around. The rent was $1,150 a month.

The move, maybe, would turn his life around. His mom and stepdad lived nearby. So did his sister, who worked at a homeless shelter in Denver. He started hanging out with old friends from high school. They shot pool and played guitar together. Masha took a full-time job as a waitress at Olive Garden. He started working out at 24 Hour Fitness. They doted on Arias, their Shar-Pei. They shopped at King Soopers. They planned to have a baby.

But the beast wouldn't rest. It had its own rhythms—he called them cycles. For weeks, months, he would feel normal, be normal. He would lift at the gym. Have dinner with his parents. Take his dog to the vet. But it never lasted. The monster would gather strength. The desire to control, to subjugate, would rise up inside him. His nights turned into treasure hunts, hours spent in his truck or on foot in neighborhoods, peering into homes, patrolling apartment complexes. The cycle would reach a boil. He would break into a house. He would rape. "There's a definite rhythm," he'd say. There's "when I'm normal, and when I'm the rape guy."

It didn't always work out. One night, after weeks at a simmer, he pried open the window of the home of a woman in Golden, Colorado. The bar that secured the window clattered to the ground. He fled as she called police. Another time, he "over-reconned" the home of a divorced mother in Littleton, Colorado. One night, she opened her back door to let out the cat, and caught him lurking in the backyard. "You need to leave," she shouted. By the time he crept back weeks later, she had installed an alarm system.

He was a student of rape. He learned from each failure. He discovered that he could gain useful intelligence from Myspace. He searched women's profiles, seeking clues that they were older and alone. Women like that made easy prey, he thought.

That's how he found Doris. Her profile showed she was sixty-five years old. She was single. She lived alone in a small neighborhood of twenty-six homes just off a busy road in Aurora. Behind her house stretched an apartment complex with long rows of two-story buildings. An alley ran down the middle of the rows. He would hunch down behind a low brick wall that separated the alley from Doris's backyard. There, he watched her.

She didn't come by the place all that often—mostly on weekends. He snuck up to her door once and found a key under the doormat. He figured she had left it for a neighbor. It was so predictable. He made a copy at a hardware store, then set the original back under the mat. She wouldn't be any wiser. He let himself in. He checked to make sure that she didn't have guns in the house. "Unpredictable shit happens," he reminded himself. He learned her name. And which bedroom she slept in.

He raped her on October 4, 2009. Her questions about his family, her pleading for him to get help—they bothered him. He ended the attack earlier than he had planned. When he left, he took a pair of her underwear. He stashed them in the back of a black, fifteen-watt Career guitar amplifier that he kept in his bedroom at 65 Harlan Street. It was a trophy.

Masha was starting to annoy him. She didn't ask too many questions when he'd return after a late night of stalking. But he was always having to make up stories to explain what he was doing. Out drinking. Or hanging with his high school buddies. He wanted total freedom. This wasn't it. One night in February, he told her. "I want to be single. I want to be alone."

Masha worked to save the marriage. She gave him space, flying to Georgia to stay with a friend from their time in South Korea. When she returned a month later, she found a pair of black lace panties stuffed between the cushions of the couch. She confronted him, angry. He told her the truth: He'd had sex with a woman while she was gone.

He just couldn't be married to her anymore.

She stayed for another month. The money from her waitressing job had gone to support him. She needed to save enough to leave. They agreed on terms of the separation. She would take the white 2004 Chrysler Sebring. He got to keep the dog, Arias, and the other car: a 1993 white Mazda pickup.

The deal left him unhappy. The Sebring was an innocuous midsize sedan. Nobody would think twice seeing it parked on a residential street. But his beat-up old pickup? It had clocked more than 178,000 miles. Yellow chunks of stuffing poked out of the front seat. The right mirror was broken. Old scraps of wood filled the back. It was pretty creepy looking.

"The truck is a little more conspicuous," he thought.

On April 16, 2010, Masha returned to Georgia in the Sebring. He was free.

HE ENROLLED IN Red Rocks Community College, a commuter school sitting on a low ridge above US Route 6 in Lakewood. Students walking from the sprawling parking lots that surrounded the low campus buildings heard a constant buzz from the four-lane free-way that carved through the town's center. Inside the classrooms—all cinder-block walls and fluorescent lights—the noise was muted. Red Rocks made no pretension of being an elite school, but it had plenty to offer a military veteran with a high school degree. He considered himself a smart guy. But not educated. He told his professors that he had never read anything longer than a web page.

He plunged into the school's liberal arts curriculum, a fresh-man besotted by new horizons of knowledge. He took history, anthropology, philosophy—anything to explain the human psyche. He read Catholic theologian Thomas Aquinas and Scottish skeptic David Hume, political theorist John Stuart Mill and German ethicist Immanuel Kant, French existentialist Jean-Paul Sartre and American linguist Noam Chomsky. His notes filled hundreds of pages in Mead spiral notebooks that he kept scattered on his desk in the back room of 65 Harlan Street. He planned to major in psychology.

He didn't believe everything the professors at Red Rocks taught him. Some of it seemed woefully ignorant about the way the world really worked. But he loved discovering new things—about the universe, epistemology, himself. He impressed his teachers and his fellow students. A woman who worked with him on a project for psychology class said he was "very smart, probably the best student in the class."

School was an opportunity to redefine himself, he told his English 122 professor. He was struggling to write something grand. But he needed help:

When I reflect upon my previous works, I can't help but cringe a little bit when I realize how vapid and incoherent they were. I have been humbled by great writers as of late, and I can only hope that one day I'll become half the word-smith as the authors that I admire most.

His Anthropology 101 class provided the opportunity to grapple with society and power. Everywhere, he saw faceless, powerful entities exercising dominion over the masses. In one exam, he railed against capitalism.

We are taught through media, education systems, and virtually every institution that material "wealth" is important, and in many cases, "vital" to our survival. Because of all this, all of the systems, whether they be subsistence, social, economic, or political, revolve around the "almighty" dollar, for better or for worse.

But it was Melinda Wilding, his professor for Introduction to Philosophy, who gave him a chance to understand the most mysterious thing in his life: the monster. He held a half-formed belief in the duality of man. Everybody, he thought, had two sides, one public, one private. The idea was a useful philosophy. It helped him comprehend—though not excuse—his own struggle. But Wilding opened him to the writings of a man far more steeped in the human psyche: Swiss psychoanalyst Carl Jung. Here was a man, the eager student thought, who understood the world.

Jung introduced the modern world to the concept of archetypes—universal psychological structures that grew out of what he called the "collective unconscious," shared by all humans. They were abstract ideas of people, situations, and concepts that resonated in the deepest recesses of the psyche. Myths, for instance, trafficked in archetypes: They told stories of the warrior, the trickster, the wise man. Jung dubbed one of the most important archetypes the "shadow"—a dark interior present in all people, though often hidden or denied by the conscious self. Jung believed that the path to self-actualization involved confronting the shadow: acknowledging its existence without embracing its sinister aims.

Jung described the shadow—and the potentially catastrophic effects of ignoring it—in his 1938 classic, *Psychology and Religion*.

> Unfortunately there can be no doubt that man is, on the whole, less good than he imagines himself or wants to be. Everyone carries a shadow, and the less it is embodied in the individual's conscious life, the blacker and denser it is. If an inferiority is conscious, one always has a chance to correct it. Furthermore, it is constantly in contact with other interests, so that it is continually subjected to modifications. But if it is repressed and isolated from consciousness, it never gets corrected, and is liable to burst forth suddenly in a moment of unawareness.

Jung's epistemology sang to him. That's it, he thought. *Repressed. Isolated. Liable to burst forth.*

He had a new project. He would learn everything he could about the monster.

Wilding assigned the class a topic for a paper. What is a shadow in your life? He began his essay by explaining how he joined the Army after the 9/11 attacks despite his liberal politics. The military ignited his "warrior mentality," he wrote. But when he discharged from service, he discovered a surprise.

> I realized that turning on the "warrior mentality" was much easier to do than turning it off. The "old me" would say that I've been brain-washed by the Army. However, the "new me" understands that I am just as much of a free thinker as I ever was; probably even more so. In many respects, I feel the "warrior mentality" has augmented my personality, my individuality and countless other aspects of my life. Nevertheless, I am beginning to discover that this "energy" does not always manifest itself in the most positive of ways.

He didn't really explain his shadow's desires. The blackness of its umbra. The way it controlled him. Only that it kept him in the dark. "Like all personal shadows, it was extremely difficult to discern the negatives, and in some ways I was even fooled into believing that those negatives were actually positives for a very long time," he wrote.

He wanted Wilding to know: He had joined battle with his shadow. He hoped to win. But he couldn't be sure of victory.

Like Jung, I don't believe that a person can fully extinguish their own shadows. Instead, it is best to take 100% responsibility for who we are, and to integrate our shadows into our conscious awareness. Obviously, this is a difficult process and it doesn't happen overnight. But, it is a process that becomes much more obtainable once we learn to start questioning and rejecting the idea that our conscious thoughts and our egos are always in control and always right. Sometimes it's necessary to question the authority within.

Wilding chided him for not providing details about this personal shadow of his. "That is what this assignment called for, but I respect your right to decline," she wrote. Underneath his final sentence about questioning "the authority within," she scrawled "Why? When?" She wanted him to engage that question. She gave him 8.7 out of ten points.

Wilding found her new student interested and eager. He was older than most of the others in his class. But he was intelligent and engaged, joining in conversations.

Years later, when she discovered his past, she would wonder about the lessons she taught him. She found him "bright and insightful" in class. He was one of those students—not always common in community college philosophy classes—who "appeared to want to learn." But had she been providing him insight into who he was? Or just an excuse wrapped in erudite modernist theory, a way to absolve himself of his actions?

"My own personal take is that referencing a Jungian archetype is a way for him to transfer guilt," she would say. "Or, the maneuver is a foil to point to his knowledge of the difference between right and wrong—all the while acting on the desire to prey on women and their fears as well as their bodies."

PAYING FOR SCHOOL was easy. His service in the military entitled him to benefits under the GI Bill. Each semester, the Veterans Benefits Administration sent Red Rocks $3,834.35 for tuition and fees. Each month, the agency sent him an additional check for $1,531 for rent. The amount, based on a housing formula, was more than he was spending to lease 65 Harlan Street. So the United States government also paid for his gym, occasional meals at Hooters, and a subscription to the popular online video game *World of Warcraft.*

When he needed more money, he turned to his shadow.

For years, he had scoured the darkest corners of Internet pornography in search of relief. Porn about bondage and sadomasochism. Porn about rape. Porn about old women. Porn about teenage girls. Porn about dangerously malnourished women, their bones poking from their skin like they were famine victims. He chased the profane, the prurient, the obscene. His computer screen displayed images that were increasingly violent, and disconnected from reality. He masturbated constantly. The hunt for porn consumed him. He called it an "addiction."

His habit did nothing to sate the monster. But he figured out a way to make it pay. He began to build his own pornographic websites.

At night, he would slip into the back room at 65 Harlan Street and get to work. He told his wife and friends that he was a web designer. But really, he spent his evenings trolling the Internet for new obscene images and videos. He would post them to his own websites, with links back to the website where the material originated. When somebody visiting his website clicked a link leading back to the original website, he would get a small commission. It was affiliate marketing, one of the Internet's most basic business models. Each month, he got checks from a German company that served as middleman between him and the affiliate sites. The money was wired in euros to his bank account at the Elevations Credit Union in Boulder. Checks trickled in, $520.57 for one month, $355.78 for another.

He started dreaming bigger. Across the top of a sheet of paper on his desk, he wrote "The Plan." He aimed to boost revenue to $1,000 a month for one of his more popular sites, anilos.com, which featured older women. He hoped to get the flow from one affiliate network up to a constant $2,000 a month. His strategy: Build ever more niche porn sites, at a rate of one per week, to find additional revenue streams. By catering to more and more obscure deviances, he could make real money.

On Myspace, he listed his occupation as "pornographer." He amassed a collection of more than 1.7 million images and videos, some for personal use, some to post on websites. He stored them on the hard drive of his computer in the back room. He downloaded a free software program called TrueCrypt, which he used to encrypt the files with mathematically complex algorithms. The best hackers in the world—including those at the FBI and the National Security Agency—considered TrueCrypt's technology nearly unbreakable. Years before, when he'd taken his aptitude test to get into the Army, he had qualified to study to become a cryptographer. Now he was one.

He built dozens of websites designed to attract kindred shadows. His big moneymakers: skinnyteen.net, abusedteenwhores .com, grannypanties.net, hotteachersex.net. Other sites catered to rape. Still others to incest. The sites featured women in grotesque poses—gagged, humiliated. Older, gray-haired women, splayed on beds or engaged in sex with younger men. Others who looked dangerously young. One site, thinfetish.com, was designed to attract those sexually thrilled by emaciation.

It was never enough. To keep the money flowing, he constantly had to find fresh images to add to his nest of websites. New material attracted new customers and kept old ones coming back. He told one friend that he was tired of "cheesy" porn.

He wanted something more authentic. More real. As real as he could get.

A MONTH AFTER Masha left for Georgia, he plunged into modern romance—the Internet dating scene. Like always, he made sure to prepare. He lined a shelf in his back room with modern-day pickup guides. He was a student of Neil Strauss's *The Game: Penetrating the Secret Society of Pickup Artists* and Erik von Markovik's *The Mystery Method: How to Get Beautiful Women into Bed*. Both books described the transformation of AFCs (average frustrated chumps) into irresistible PUAs (pickup artists), able to bed any SHB (super hot babe). They revealed secret societies where experienced Lotharios met to swap seduction techniques. There was the Tic Tac routine (give her a Tic Tac, describe yourself as an "Indian giver" who wants it back, and then kiss her); the Dryer Lint opening (enter a bar palming a piece of dryer lint, pretend to pick it off her shoulder, then ask, "How long has that been there?"); and the benefits of a glow-in-the-dark necklace (the better to "peacock" and attract attention to yourself).

In the PUA universe, women are "targets." The books contained scripts to help the PUA home in. Some focused on verbal takedowns called "negs." One example:

If your target interrupts you, say, "Hello, I'm talking, jeez," or "Excuse me . . . may I finish my sentence first?" You then say to others in the group, "Is she always like that?" and roll your eyes playfully.

Take the SHB down a notch, in other words, and it might confuse her enough to come on to you. It was practical psychology.

To find women, he prowled online dating services like Ok-Cupid. He browsed the "Casual Encounters" section of Denver's Craigslist—an endless churn of dick pics, amateur porn, and raw cries for sex, mostly from men. When a woman posted an ad looking for a dinner date, he responded with jokes about his humdrum life.

> Was planning on staying in tonight and reading (I know, exciting), but I decided to peruse craigslist and saw your post and thought it might be fun to go have a couple of drinks.
>
> About me:
>
> 32
>
> 6'2" 220 lbs
>
> Divorced
>
> Well-read, well-traveled, confident, funny, and a good conversationalist
>
> Not expecting anything. Just wanting to go out for a bit.
>
> Don't smoke, don't do drugs.

The poster was an amateur photographer. He told her that he would love camera lessons. "I have a Canon Rebel xTi, and I suck at using it haha! Maybe you can give me some pointers." He closed with a smiley emoticon.

Some women found him menacing. He told a twenty-eight-year-old Denver woman that he preferred girls who were petite, dressed in sexy clothes, and wore lots of makeup. "Every girl has a rape fantasy," he told her. He scoffed when a thirty-one-year-old date told him that she liked a sadomasochism club in downtown

Denver called The Sanctuary. The club would host sex parties where men and women could engage in S&M with boundaries. A "Dungeon Master" controlled the level of violence. Everyone was required to have a safe word, which would bring an immediate halt to an uncomfortable act. Bloodletting and scat play were forbidden. "These people here don't know what domination is," he told her.

But he did—and it drove his search for women. "I'd feel them out," he'd say. "I'd grab a girl by the back of the neck, by the hair. If they responded to that, then I knew." A woman he could dominate. He made those dates dress up in high heels and garish lipstick. Sometimes, they begged him to fulfill their rape fantasies. He liked rough sex. "My thing was humiliation and basically degradation," he'd say. But it was always consensual. "The girls I treated with respect. I never abused them—well, other than what they wanted."

These sadomasochistic encounters didn't satisfy him, though. He had gotten to know the women. They were no longer targets. They were real people. "I could do all kinds of crazy stuff with a woman, a good-looking, attractive, intelligent woman that I liked a lot, but that was kind of the problem, too," he'd say. "I liked them and I knew them. For whatever reason, that was a turnoff. I just didn't get the same thing out of it."

Then, while scanning OkCupid one day, he came across a woman named Amy. She was a thirty-three-year-old waitress at a swinger's club in south-central Denver. Dark hair and straight bangs framed a round face with expressive, wide-set eyes. While waiting tables, she wore a schoolgirl outfit or a bikini. In her profile, she listed three adjectives to describe herself: "devious," "curious," and "twisted."

My kind of girl, he thought. He messaged her. "I have to know," he said. "How are you twisted?"

He picked her up at her place for the first date. They shot pool at a bar. She described him as a "perfect gentleman," charming and witty. He left a glowing review of her on OkCupid: "Not only is she gorgeous, she is also a highly sophisticated woman with a mind that moves at warp speed."

"You are one of the few people in the world that I can relate to," he wrote to her in one message.

They did not date long. But they stayed in contact. She had trouble sleeping. He worked late maintaining his porn sites. They traded emails and messages throughout the night. He thought of Amy as a friend in the dark.

She once told him about an incident at her apartment complex. While she was walking down a hallway, a man had jumped out and tried to grab her. She wrestled away. "The guy will come back eventually. He isn't good enough yet. He will come back and succeed," he told her. Under different circumstances, it might even be him. "The only thing that keeps me from being that guy that attacked you is my family and my life," he said.

He told her he was a sadist and that he wanted multiple sex partners. He boasted about his porn sites. He described fantasies about violent, degrading sex. He said that women were masochists who wanted men to hurt and control them. Some women, he told her, enjoyed being raped. "Some women like bruises all over from sex because they like sympathy from it," he told her.

At times, he would apply the techniques he had learned from his pickup books. Once, when Amy didn't respond quickly enough, he sent her a message on Facebook: "If you are open to talking, I'll be keeping my Facebook page up for a little while longer. If not, go fuck yourself with a giant wall-socket-powered vibrator held up with a stack of books, which you probably never read." A good neg—throw her off base, then close with another message revealing emotion and understanding: "When we were together, I told you that I felt as if something was missing in my life. I've finally begun to scratch the surface in finding out what it was. It's complicated. But then again, people like us are complicated beings. Much more than you realize," he wrote.

In August 2010 he began seeing Carla, a twenty-eight-year-old from Denver. One day he took her to Green Mountain Guns, a family-owned shop in a mini-mall. He showed her a pistol he was hoping to buy: a small black-and-silver .380-caliber Ruger.

Later that month, on August 10, he raped Sarah. After leaving Sarah's apartment he pawned his and Masha's wedding bands. He went to the Department of Motor Vehicles and got a new driver's license. Then, he made a final stop: Green Mountain Guns. Using his new license—and paying $328.13 in cash, including the $200 he stole from Sarah and the money from the rings—he bought the Ruger.

When he got home, he stashed a pair of Sarah's underwear in the black guitar amp in his bedroom.

He texted a photo of his new gun to Carla.

He had two trophies.

IN OCTOBER 2010, he got a new roommate to help pay the bills: his younger brother, Michael. Anybody walking down the street could see they were related. He was thirty-two, weighed 220 pounds, stood six feet two, and had blond hair and hazel eyes. Michael was thirty, weighed 230 pounds, stood six feet two, and had sandy blond hair and green eyes. They sometimes got mistaken for the same person.

But the outward similarities concealed deep differences on the inside. They were family. But they weren't close.

Sometimes he found Michael irritating. Michael loved sports. Worshipped the Tennessee Titans. Hung a giant Tennessee football flag in his room. Visited the house's back room at least once a day to check on his fantasy football and basketball teams. He tried to warn Michael: Professional sports were for the weak-minded. They were a waste of time, "made to dumb people down."

That was the thing. Michael was a conventional guy. He'd served in the military after high school. Once out, he wanted to play college basketball. He found an outlet at York College, a small Christian school in a small town rising from the flatlands of south-eastern Nebraska. After graduation, he didn't find much use for his business degree, so he moved back to Colorado and supported himself by delivering furniture. He decided to stake his future on the most regular of regular-guy jobs: He enrolled in barber school at Emily Griffith Technical College in Denver. That was how he thought of himself: just a normal dude. He had a steady girlfriend, a churchgoing woman he knew from high school. They had a big group of friends. They liked going to restaurants and movies. His guiding philosophy was far less complex than his brother's. "I'm just gonna live my life and find what makes me happy."

Michael knew that his brother was different. "Deep, deep guy, very deep," is how he described him. "He's smart as hell." His older brother didn't drink. Didn't smoke. Didn't do drugs. "He doesn't have a lot of friends," Michael would say. "I don't even think he has a best friend." His older sibling pretty much kept to himself, locked away in the back room at 65 Harlan Street with his computer. He never let Michael see what he was doing. He insisted they each maintain separate accounts. "I don't look at his stuff, and I'm pretty sure he doesn't look into mine," Michael would say.

Michael was impressed by his brother's brains. But there was something off about him. He lined the bookshelf with strange books about symbols, ancient religions, secret societies. He'd oc-casionally discuss weird conspiracy theories. His brother, he'd say, just didn't think like regular people think. "As far as like normal society stuff, like normal society way of thinking, he's like way out there."

As an example, he'd point to the new woman his brother began seeing that fall. She was an "out there" woman.

Her name was Calyxa Buckley.* She was thirty-two. She had

---

* Pseudonym

grown up in the San Miguel Basin, a region of broke mining towns and blank prairie in southwestern Colorado. She had joined the Navy when she was eighteen, but hated it, deserting after a year. She returned to Colorado, where she was arrested, accused of burglarizing a drugstore and gas station in the tiny town of Norwood. She wound up living with an older man named Chuck Travers.* They hopscotched through trailer parks and single-story motels in hardly there towns dotting the deserts of Navajo country in eastern Arizona. Chuck got jobs as a mechanic. Calyxa concentrated on writing a manifesto based on Hopi theology. She called it the "Theory of Everything."

Calyxa and Chuck had been together for thirteen years and considered themselves a married couple. They also embraced polyamory; both would regularly date and have sex with other people. So it wasn't strange when Calyxa took an interest in a man from Colorado who contacted her through Craigslist. At first, they conversed by email. Eventually, they switched to the phone. The conversations lasted hours. Movies. Books. Pillow talk. The two became "closer than brothers," Chuck thought.

Calyxa decided to fly to Colorado to meet her new man in person. Chuck, a former Marine, had worked in signals intelligence. He considered himself skilled at vetting people. He had his own phone conversations with the Craigslist stranger. He found him intense, private. His final analysis: The man was "intelligent, well read, a sadist and a megalomaniac." But safe enough for Calyxa to begin dating. In October 2010, Chuck drove her to Sky Harbor International Airport in Phoenix, a six-hour round trip from their room at the Desert Inn just off old Route 66 in Holbrook, Arizona, population 5,053.

He picked her up at the airport in Denver for a two-week stay with him at 65 Harlan Street. She had high, sharp cheekbones, a thin face, and a narrow nose. Her hair was dark, curly, with long

---

* Pseudonym

ringlets falling past her shoulders. Her eyes, which she sometimes lined with dark mascara, could appear almost sunken, menacing. She knew that the world was a complex place, filled with powerful and secret groups that exerted control over the masses. He'd found a woman who understood the world as he did. He felt a thrum of connection. "I like her a lot," he'd say.

His brother, Michael, had the opposite reaction. Calyxa unnerved him. He called her "weird and organic and into conspiracy theories." She held long, hushed conversations on the phone that he overheard. She talked about alchemy and archetypes and the infinite. She hinted that she was a high-ranking member of a powerful secret society. One night, Michael went out with Calyxa and his brother. His brother warned him that they had to be careful. Calyxa was off the grid. Not even the government knew about her—she had no Social Security number. A discreet protective detail shadowed her. They even followed her to Colorado. Michael promised his brother not to reveal anything. "I don't want to end up dead."

From what Michael understood, his brother thought he belonged to an elite, enlightened cadre who knew how the world really worked, and used that truth to dominate the quotidian and the ordinary. Michael knew it sounded crazy. But he believed it. "I'll tell you right now it's not like a bunch of bullshit," he'd tell people who doubted his older sibling's fevered diagrams of hidden societal power structures. "I know it's real from being around him. Like, it's not just a bunch of garbage."

Michael knew, too, that his older brother shared with Calyxa a deep interest in the occult. He consulted *The Magus*, a nineteenth-century grimoire on Kabbalah, the influence of the planets, and the natural magic of unctions, amulets, charms. He considered himself an expert in the *Corpus Hermeticum*, a collection of mystic writings dating from AD 200. He prided himself on being a discerning reader. He didn't much like a Christian Neoplatonic rendering of the *Hermeticum* that he had read, he told one friend.

"I've seen other versions on the web that have—at least in my opinion—better translations from the original Greek."

He was fascinated with numerology. He filled notebooks with scrawls of pagan symbols. He hunted difficult-to-find texts for study: the forty-two *Books of Thoth*, containing the entirety of Egyptian theosophy. He embraced modern science that supported his social theories, like *The Superorganism*, by Bert Hölldobler and Harvard's E. O. Wilson, describing the hierarchical societies of insects. Hypnotism intrigued him.

He wanted to document his insights with a blog. He played around with different names for it. HiveTheory. ThatWhichIs. PrimalMind. TribeTwoZero. His topic, he wrote to a friend, was "spirituality, the occult, philosophy, etc. Pretty much just a regular blog with my thoughts on it."

Calyxa visited 65 Harlan Street again in November. This time, she stayed for a month. He hoped to build their relationship into something more permanent. For the first time since he'd met Masha, he felt an emotional connection. And he still wanted to have kids. "It's been a long, long time . . . since I've been that much into a woman," he'd tell people. When he was with her, he was a different person. It astonished him. He didn't look at pornography. He didn't go out prowling. She kept him calm. The monster never stirred. "Her and I were so compatible and I was so comfortable with her that I didn't even think about it," he said. "I had no reason to think of anything else."

Calyxa, though, had different ideas. She told him she wasn't interested in a deeper relationship. She had her book to write. Her husband abided in his desert solitude. It was time to move on. She turned—suddenly, unexpectedly—into an ex-girlfriend. She left on December 15.

He was alone again.

"She could have helped me," he thought to himself. Instead, she was like the woman in the song he used to play for his mother, "Little Wing."

That's all she ever thinks about,
Riding with the wind.

ON JANUARY 5, he raped Amber.

He hid another pair of panties in the back of his guitar amp.
The cycle began again.

10

GOOD NEIGHBORS

January 25, 2011
Westminster, Colorado

Hendershot and Ellis had worked together a long time. They shared an old joke. In case of a particularly boring meeting—and there were plenty of those in the police business—the trapped person would ask for a favor. "Send a text asking me to leave the meeting. Add '911' to make it seem urgent." It was a mutual escape plan, albeit one they had never actually deployed.

So when Hendershot got Ellis's message—it even included the "911"—Hendershot assumed it was a joke rescue mission. Hendershot had spent the morning at a mandatory training meeting in Westminster's city hall. Funny, Hendershot thought. But the next second, she realized it was no ruse.

Ellis had big news. She told Hendershot she had just received photographs of the glove and shoe prints left at the scene of the attempted rape in Lakewood. The criminalist who uncovered the prints was a friend: Sheri Shimamoto. The pair had bonded at a two-week training course at the FBI Academy in Quantico, Virginia. Shimamoto was part of the blue web—Denver's loose-knit network of law enforcement analysts.

It made perfect sense that Shimamoto had discovered the prints. She had a thing about shoes. She owned fifty pairs—including five sets of Adidas Superstars, the three-herringbone-striped shell toes coveted by sneakerheads around the world. Before she began doing police work, her favorite job had been working retail at Lady Foot Locker. Shimamoto held a degree in mathematics. But her shoephilia had led her to specialize in shoe identification when she became a criminalist.

Shoe prints weren't as good as fingerprints, of course. They weren't unique to a person. But with a little luck, they could tell a story about the bad guy that might help identify him. A shoe print could indicate a particular brand—a Nike or a Merrell. And certain marks—a nick on the heel, a wear pattern on the sole, a high arch—could leave behind impressions that a crime scene technician could link to an individual pair of shoes. To determine the origin of a shoe print at a crime scene, Shimamoto would spend hours on Zappos.com, the Internet shoe superstore that featured lovingly detailed images of the soles, uppers, and sides of thousands of shoes. Or she would go to the local mall and hang out at shoe stores. It was all research to get her closer to the perpetrator.

Shimamoto had searched for shoe prints when she arrived at the scene in Lakewood, dusting the floor around the bedroom and kitchen with a bichromatic powder that revealed traces of oil or dirt left by fingers or shoes. She found four distinct impressions that looked like they were made by a tennis shoe. She found another similar shoe print in the wet dirt outside the bedroom window. When she dusted the window to look for fingerprints, she found instead what she thought was a glove print.

A glove with a honeycomb pattern on the palm.

As soon as Ellis pulled up the images that Shimamoto sent her, she recognized the pattern. It matched the size and shape of the strange honeycomb marks that she had discovered on the railing behind Sarah's apartment. At the time, she wasn't sure what had made the marks. Now, she told Shimamoto, she knew. Shimamoto was so excited that she raced out to a Dick's Sporting Goods store, where she discovered a pair of soft, black Under Armour gloves. The fingers and palm featured a raised grip in the shape of a honeycomb.

Next step: the shoes. Ellis examined the photo that her fellow criminalist Kali Gipson had taken after spray-painting the foot-print behind Amber's apartment in Golden. They looked nearly identical to the ones that Shimamoto had lifted from the mud be-neath the bedroom window in Lakewood. Matt Cole, Galbraith's partner, shipped an image of the prints to a shoe-identification website for law enforcement. A match came back: The prints were from a pair of Adidas ZX 700 mesh shoes. They first started sell-ing in stores after March 2005.

When Hendershot saw everything that the two criminalists had linked together, she knew: The man who attacked the woman in Lakewood on July 6, 2010, had to be the same person who had raped Doris and Sarah.

Hendershot put in an immediate call to the Lakewood Police Department.

It was the strangest case that Lakewood detective Aaron Hassell had ever been assigned. He had been called out to an at-tempted rape at a home in a nicer neighborhood. The caller, a woman named Lilly, reported that a man in a black mask had at-tacked her while she was sleeping. When she called out for help, the man had gone to another room to check if anyone was home. Lilly seized the chance to escape. She dove out a window above her bed. She fell seven feet and landed headfirst, cracking her ribs, breaking a vertebra in her back. In intense pain, she'd staggered next door to her neighbors' house and banged on a door to wake them.

When police arrived, though, they found no signs of forced entry at the house. No pry marks on the doors. No windowpanes smashed. The doors were all locked. So, too, the windows. Has-sell talked with four neighbors, none of whom had seen or heard anything unusual. Technicians recovered no DNA. "There's no evidence anywhere," Hassell thought.

That wasn't quite true. Shimamoto had turned up the shoe and glove prints. They didn't match anything that belonged to Lilly. But neither did they point to any suspects—or even confirm that an attack had taken place. A gardener took care of Lilly's yard. Workmen came to the house every now and again. And she had an elderly male friend who occasionally stayed at the home. Any of them could have left the prints.

Lilly presented her own mystery. She was a free spirit. She made all sorts of unusual requests. She called Hassell to report that since the attempted rape, her cat had scratched at people wearing black boots. Perhaps the police should be looking for someone with black boots. "She felt this was information that could be useful to the investigation," he wrote. She had a Russian artist friend draw a sketch of the attacker based on her description and asked Hassell to distribute it to the press. The drawing was of a man with a mask covering his face, except for a slit showing blue eyes and blond eyebrows. There were no other features that would help a person recognize the man in the sketch. Hassell declined to hand it out. On another occasion, she asked Hassell to canvass gyms around Denver in search of a well-built, six-foot-tall white man with blue eyes. "That's going to be a lot of guys," he told her. More than two months after calling police, she suddenly remembered that a strange wireless network had popped up on her computer before the attack. It was named "Pure Evil," she said.

Finally, she asked Hassell for a hypnotist to interview her in a trance state. Hassell contacted an investigator for the Jefferson County district attorney's office who was a licensed hypnotherapist. The trio met on a windy day in October at the Lakewood police station, some three months after the attack. The investigator began the session with a common technique to induce hypnosis. Imagine you're in an elevator, he told Lilly. You're going down, down, down.

She stopped him. No, I'm not, she told him. She had her own technique. I'm walking through a meadow, she said. She asked the investigator to allow her to act as a medium. She could speak for the cats, the squirrels, and the trees who witnessed the attack. Under hypnosis, Lilly described scenes she had not previously recounted, nor could have witnessed. She reported seeing how the attacker had snuck into her house through the garage. How he had stood and watched her through her windows.

Lilly's trance-induced insights did not impress Hassell, nor the investigator. The investigator "told me he did not feel it was a productive session," Hassell wrote in his report. Lilly wasn't hurting the investigation. But to Hassell's mind, she sure wasn't helping.

Lilly was frustrated, too. She didn't put much faith in cops in general. A few months before the attack, she'd had a bad experience with the police in Lakewood. She liked to worship in front of a towering tree at a neighbor's house. When new owners moved in, they called police at the sight of a strange woman chanting and dancing in their new yard. The cops told Lilly to leave. She filed a complaint against them for harassing her.

On another occasion, after the break-in, she heard a sound at 3:30 in the morning outside the home where she was staying. She called police. A Denver officer responded to the call. When he knocked on the door, he lifted up his flashlight by his shoulder. Lilly thought he was holding the light in the same way in which the attacker had held his knife. She refused to let the officer in. The next day, she asked Hassell to investigate him as a possible suspect in the crime. Hassell declined.

She was frustrated with Hassell. He was always telling her no. When she asked for a police artist to sketch her attacker, he refused. That's why she had turned to her Russian friend. The police weren't taking her seriously. "It's not that important. It's not that big of a deal," she recalled them telling her.

"It is a big deal," Lilly protested. "I know what he looks like. I know how he moves. I know a lot about him. I saw his eyes. I saw his body. I'm an artist. I'll help you."

About a month after the attack, she was gardening. She spotted a wood-handled knife stuck in the ground, near her back fence. She recognized it as coming from her own kitchen, a knife that she usually used to cut open watermelons. It must have been the knife the rapist had held. He must have stabbed it into the ground before he fled. Why hadn't police found it before she did? Why did she have to call to alert them to such an important clue? She complained about Hassell's "lack of response."

Lilly's parents weren't happy with Hassell, either. They hired a private investigator to sleuth around. The PI, a retired Denver police detective, turned up what looked like a scuff mark on top of the six-foot-high wooden fence surrounding Lilly's backyard, but not much else. Nonetheless, the find was a clear signal to Lilly and her parents: Hassell wasn't doing his job. One day, Lilly's mother came down to the station. She confronted Hassell.

Tell me the truth, she said. Do you believe my daughter?

It was a tough question to answer.

Hassell had grown up as a conservative Christian in a military household. His father, an Air Force veteran, repaired appliances. His mom was a schoolteacher. He'd gone to Cedarville College, a small Baptist school outside of Dayton, Ohio. Students at Cedarville were required to minor in Bible studies. Instructors taught creationism. The school's motto was alliterative and unambiguous about its mission: "For the crown and covenant of Christ." There was not much room on campus for people who believed in telepathy and tree spirits.

Hassell also knew that women could lie about being raped. Early in his career, he had responded to an apartment where a woman said she'd been attacked. She fought the man off, she said, by dousing him with pepper spray. Hassell found pepper spray all over the woman's bedroom. But other things bothered him. The woman said the man had ripped off her pants. But he found the jeans curled in a pile, as though someone had pulled them down and stepped out. Then he found a receipt indicating that the woman had purchased the pepper spray on the previous day. When he questioned her about his discoveries, the woman folded. She acknowledged that she made up the incident. Hassell also discovered that she had complained to neighbors about being attacked by a different man a few weeks earlier. He figured she had an "insatiable need for attention." He cited her for filing a false police report.

And yet, Hassell knew enough to know he didn't know everything. Just seven miles up the road from Cedarville sat another private school that offered an education in what seemed like an alternate universe. Antioch College was the quintessential small liberal arts school. It stressed democracy, student governance, and social justice. Students were required to work in the community. Instructors did not give just grades; they delivered narrative evaluations. Antioch's motto: "Be ashamed to die until you have won some victory for humanity." Hassell had plenty of opportunity to hang out with Antioch students. He realized that you could be different without being deranged. It made him hesitant to judge Lilly. "A lot of people that I worked with said, 'She's nuts.' I didn't think she was. I thought she had unusual beliefs."

With experience, he had also learned the dangers of calling a possible victim a liar. He didn't feel like he had made the wrong decision at the start of his career—false reports took up time and energy. But now that he was a detective, he realized that informants might not feel comfortable sharing tips if they feared being arrested for lying. Lakewood's top brass, in fact, discouraged arresting people for making a false report, except in extreme cases.

And then there were the risks specific to sexual assault. Rape is already an underreported crime. Charging someone who has come forward—and not been believed—threatens to chill reporting further, allowing rapists to get away, maybe to rape again. It would fuel the myth that many women lie about being raped. In its training literature for police, End Violence Against Women International notes that false claims of rape often stem from "serious psychological and emotional problems. . . . They are probably best handled with appropriate referrals for social services rather than prosecution for filing a false report."

Hassell developed a theory about what had happened in Lilly's case. Lilly told him that she had drunk an herbal tea before falling asleep. He had done research online and found information to suggest that strong doses of the tea had been linked to vivid dreams. The way he figured it, it was possible that she had awoken from a powerful vision and dove from the window before coming to. It was a way to reconcile the lack of evidence with Lilly's statements, without calling her a liar.

He wavered though. The mystery footprints and glove prints couldn't be easily explained away. And Lilly's injuries were serious. Perhaps some monster had entered her home. Perhaps he was still out there. He had a hard time making up his mind.

Still, with little evidence to go on, Hassell felt he had done everything he could.

In October 2010, he stopped actively investigating the crime, but kept the file open, just in case new information surfaced later.

His final entry: "No viable leads."

SHARON WHELAN WAS a good neighbor. She and her husband, Gary, had lived in the Lakewood neighborhood of Applewood for fifteen years. She taught arts and drama at local schools. He worked as a geologist. They raised three kids in their big five-bedroom home a block from the lake. They knew just about everybody. When a restaurant abutting the neighborhood tried to expand its size, they had helped lead the opposition. "It's a tight place" was how she described her community.

She kept special watch on her neighbor directly across the street, eighty-nine-year-old Kathleen Estes, a widow. Late one summer Monday, on June 14, 2010, Whelan looked up and saw a white pickup parked by the side of the road in front of Estes's

house. It struck her as odd. It was too late for workmen. And most
people in the neighborhood parked their cars in garages or drive-
ways.

She called Estes. "There's a truck sitting out front. Is somebody visiting you?"

Estes hadn't noticed the truck. Maybe it was somebody at another neighbor's house? They had teenagers. Their friends were
coming and going all the time. "I'll watch it, too," she told Whelan.

A half hour later, Whelan was getting ready for bed. She
glanced at the clock. It was 10:49 p.m. The truck was still in front
of Estes's house. But now, she saw a man in the cab. He seemed to
be just sitting there, doing nothing. Her husband wrote down the
license plate number. When Whelan called again, Estes decided
to contact the police. She gave the dispatcher the plate number
that Whelan's husband had written down: 935-VHX.

When a Lakewood cop arrived a few minutes later, the truck
was still there. But the man was gone. The officer walked around
the pickup. It was a white Mazda. Nothing seemed unusual. He
ran the license plate number. It came back clean. The officer
knocked on Estes's door. He hadn't found anything wrong, he told
her. Back at the police station, he created a brief entry about the
encounter called a field interview report. He labeled it "suspicious
vehicle."

Early the next morning, Whelan happened to look out her
window. She noticed that the truck was gone. She stopped worry-
ing about it. So did Estes.

The neighborhood was back to normal again. And Whelan
wouldn't think about the white pickup until she saw a local news
broadcast eight months later.

In early February 2011, a Lakewood police detective walked
over to a cubicle belonging to Danelle DiGiosio, one of Lakewood's crime analysts. He had been brought into the case to find

more links between the attack on Lilly and the other rape cases. At a briefing, he learned that the rapist had stalked the women and taken underwear from their homes. He knew that DiGiosio had all sorts of databases she could tap. Could she look for any burglaries where someone reported stolen underwear? he wondered. And could she do it by tomorrow? The task force was having a big meeting to review all the evidence in the case.

DiGiosio almost laughed out loud. There were many things she could find using her data sets. But this wasn't one of them. "If I found my favorite underwear missing, I'd say it must be stuck in a pant leg somewhere, or the washing machine ate it. Not in a million years would I think to report it to the police," she told the detective.

DiGiosio was used to being asked to do the impossible. She had grown up in a small town in the undulating, agricultural plains near Greeley, Colorado. It was a quiet, safe place. She played volleyball and basketball and ran track for the Valley High School Vikings in Gilcrest, Colorado. But she had her heart set on joining the FBI. She enrolled at the University of Denver, hoping to get a degree in criminal justice. But a professor told her she needed an edge to get into the agency, and suggested statistics. The FBI had started investing heavily in data analysis.

Math was not DiGiosio's strongest subject. "I was really good at English. I liked music," she says. But she wanted a shot at law enforcement. If she had to study statistics, she'd study statistics. "I made myself like math," she says. And she was intrigued by the power of statistics to solve problems in the real world. She called it "math with a purpose." She graduated in 1999, but never applied for an FBI job. Instead, she got a job training other police officers in how to use maps for crime analysis. She got married, had kids, and decided that she preferred stability over teaching and traveling. By 2008, she was working at Lakewood—one of the few criminal analysts in Colorado with a full degree in statistics.

At Lakewood, she filled her desk with computer monitors,

pictures of her kids, and a coffee pot. Across the room was an enormous printer that produced city maps on rolls that looked almost like butcher paper. The printer was her weapon of choice. She used it to plot out car burglaries and convenience store robberies, helping cops figure out how to stop them. She might not have a database to examine underwear theft, she told the inquiring detective. But she could use her mapping software to help pull every report of every suspicious vehicle and person logged within a quarter mile of Lilly's house.

"It's like finding a needle in a needle stack," she said. "But that's something I can do."

By the end of the day, she'd found her needle: a record of the call Estes had made eight months earlier, when she reported the suspicious white truck parked in front of her home. The location and timing of the report stood out to DiGiosio. The date, June 14, was only three weeks before the rapist struck Lilly's house. And Estes's home was only a few blocks from Lilly's home.

"Hmmm," she wondered. "Why are you there at this time of night? You don't belong there."

The next morning, February 9, 2011, Hassell and DiGiosio drove to the Westminster Police Department. When they walked into the room, DiGiosio was surprised. Some two dozen cops and FBI agents were gathered around a long conference table on the second floor of the station. Hendershot and Galbraith were there. So, too, Burgess and Grusing. It had been thirty-five days since Amber's rape.

The news was not great. Galbraith had pulled the cell phone records for her chief suspect, Frank Tucker, the college student who had been accused of sexual assault. He turned out to have been skiing in Vail when Amber was raped. And when he was brought in for questioning, he showed off the splotch on his calf that Amber had thought might be the birthmark she saw on her rapist. It turned out to be a circular, blue flame tattoo.

The FBI's ViCAP program had also failed to deliver. Grusing

and Galbraith had talked with detectives in Lawrence, Kansas, who had investigated the chain of rapes that had plagued the college town. The possibility of a connection was tantalizing. But the Kansas investigators had run into the same problem now facing the roomful of cops in Colorado. They were able to connect the rapes, but they had not identified a suspect.

Lewis, the analyst from the Colorado Bureau of Investigation, reported on the results of the testing that Hendershot had requested—comparing Westminster's DNA sample to Aurora's and Golden's. They had only one shot. The testing procedures had destroyed the few cells that had been recovered. But they found that the DNA samples were, indeed, linked. The evidence wouldn't be useful in identifying a single individual. But now, the detectives had concrete proof of what they all suspected. The same man—or men from the same family—had raped Doris, Sarah, and Amber.

Sergeant Trevor Materasso, the Westminster cop in charge of dealing with the media, realized that he was going to have to tell a crowd of reporters about a serial rapist loose in Denver's suburbs. And he would have to admit that the police had no clue as to his identity. Thoughts raced through his head. How should police tell the public? What clues could they give that might help narrow down a suspect? What would he tell reporters when they asked the inevitable question: Did police think the rapist would strike again?

DiGiosio listened as officers shared whatever evidence they had. She wasn't sure she wanted to chime in with her own discovery. After all, it was just a report of a white truck parked near Lilly's house. She hadn't even bothered to tell Hassell about it as they drove to the meeting. She didn't want to look foolish. Maybe the investigators would dismiss her because she was a crime analyst, not a street cop. Some might look down on her because she was a woman. Law enforcement was a man's world. And even though Hendershot and Galbraith were there, the room was mostly tall white guys with short haircuts. "You have to be a different kind of female to be able to hold your own in this profession," she says. "You have to be strong enough to hold your own, but not so strong that people call you a bitch. You have to find your place. You still have to be you."

Before the meeting, DiGiosio hadn't realized how brutal the rapist was, nor how many women he had attacked. "It was news to me." Now the meeting was starting to break up. Some of the cops stood talking in small groups. Others were leaving the room.

DiGiosio decided to speak up.

"I looked at suspicious vehicles and suspicious calls," she told the cops at the long table. "I don't know if this is a big deal or not. I found this one call. It was a person in a white truck."

Galbraith was talking with another police officer. She stopped mid-sentence. What had DiGiosio said? "White truck." Galbraith flashed to the white truck from the videotape, circling Amber's apartment complex on the night of the rape.

"Do you have any details," Galbraith said, getting to her feet.

DiGiosio brought her laptop over to Galbraith. The license plate traced back to a 1993 white Mazda pickup truck.

The truck on the videotape was a Mazda.

Who's the registered owner? Galbraith asked, her eyes racing across the screen, seeking an answer.

DiGiosio had researched that, too. She brought up another file. It was an image of the driver's license of the man who owned the white truck.

At the top was a name.

11

A GROSS MISDEMEANOR

IT LOOKED LIKE A TRAFFIC TICKET. IT WAS EVEN ON THE same form used for traffic offenses—a one-page, fill-in-the-blank citation, with one box at the top labeled "Traffic," another labeled "Non-Traffic." On the page Marie held in her hand, the Non-Traffic box was marked with an *X*.

The envelope came in the mail in late August, less than three weeks after she had reported being raped. When she opened it, she discovered she was being charged with a crime. "False Reporting," the citation said, the two words written by hand in all capital letters. The form didn't say what kind of charge this was—a misdemeanor? a felony?—nor what the penalty might be. But the citation listed the state statute she stood accused of violating, RCW 9A.84.040. With that and Google, she could answer her questions. False reporting was a gross misdemeanor, the most serious charge short of a felony. A conviction could land her in jail for up to a year.

The text of the statute reads:

A person is guilty of false reporting if with knowledge that the information reported, conveyed, or circulated is false, he or she initiates or circulates a false report or warning of an alleged occurrence or impending occurrence of a fire, explosion, crime, catastrophe, or emergency knowing that such false report is likely to cause evacuation of a building, place of assembly, or transportation facility, or to cause public inconvenience or alarm.

Boiled down, Marie stood accused of creating a false scare, claiming she was raped when she knew she wasn't.

The news devastated Marie. She had given the police what they wanted—given them a written statement, given up her demand for a polygraph. And now this: Now any hope of moving on, of getting past it, was gone. She didn't know the court system; she had no idea how long this prosecution would take or how it would turn out. But she knew she'd probably find out alone. Her friends were now few. They wouldn't be lining up to accompany her to the courthouse.

Marie needed to appear in Lynnwood Municipal Court to enter a plea. If she failed to show for her arraignment, she could be arrested.

A fill-in-the-blank form dropped in the mail seems a casual way to alert someone to the threat of a year in jail. But the means of notifying Marie was in keeping with how the decision had been reached. There had been nothing complicated about the charging process—no mandatory review within the police department, no sign-off by a prosecuting attorney. Sergeant Mason filled in the citation and signed at the bottom. It was his decision alone to charge Marie—and for Mason, the decision had been easy.

Mason had no doubt Marie had lied. The law said her lie was a crime. Where there is a crime and a culprit, there follows a charge. "It was that straightforward," Mason says.

Penalties for false reporting can be severe. Research by Lisa Avalos, a University of Arkansas law professor, shows that while forty-two states, including Washington, treat false reporting as a misdemeanor, eight make it a felony. In Illinois and Wyoming, it carries a sentence of up to five years in prison. It's six years in Arkansas. False reporting is also a felony on the federal level, where it can lead to a five-year sentence and a maximum fine of $250,000. And the United States seems downright lenient compared to the United Kingdom. There, the crime, called "perverting the course of justice," carries a maximum sentence of life in prison.

For the police, it stands to reason that the punishment could be stiff. A false report wastes resources. In Marie's case, patrol officers, crime scene technicians, detectives, a police commander, and an ambulance crew scrambled to the apartment complex, diverting them from other duties or calls. Later, at the hospital, a doctor and a specially trained nurse conducted a lengthy examination of Marie, which kept them from other patients. Mason and his colleagues had devoted more time to the case in the days that followed. And then there was the effect the case had on the public at large. Marie's story of rape had been broadcast widely in the Seattle metropolitan area: A stranger had broken into a home and attacked a woman at knifepoint. That no doubt caused alarm, and the people who shared her apartment building and housing program would have been particularly rattled.

In Marie's case, the police had no suspect. But if they had, an innocent person could have been put through the crucible of being questioned by police. The suspect's family might have been questioned. Maybe coworkers. Maybe neighbors. Worse, an innocent person could have been charged, even convicted. False accusations can produce waves of publicity, imperiling reputations. In 2006, three Duke lacrosse players were accused of raping an exotic dancer. They weren't cleared until the following year; the case's prosecutor, found to have withheld exculpatory DNA evidence, wound up being disbarred and jailed for a day. In 2014, *Rolling Stone* would publish an explosive story in which a student described being gang-raped by members of a fraternity at the University of Virginia. The student's account was soon discredited by other media and the police—and the following year, the magazine retracted the story in its entirety. One journalism institute

named the story "Error of the Year." *Rolling Stone* wound up settling defamation lawsuits filed by both the fraternity and a university administrator who alleged that the story wrongly turned her
"into the face of institutional indifference."

Marie's case in Lynnwood had a recent parallel, just a few
miles south. In March of 2008—five months before Marie reported being raped—a woman in King County, Washington, had
pleaded guilty to false reporting and been sentenced to eight days
in jail. But her story had done more harm than Marie's. She had
accused a specific person—a college professor—of rape, and had
gone so far as to alter email messages from him, making it appear
he had professed romantic interest and promised a higher grade if
she met "a few conditions." The professor had been arrested and
spent nine days in jail before being cleared.

For the Lynnwood police, the formal determination that
Marie had made a false report meant the rape investigation was
over: There was nothing to investigate. No more evidence would
be gathered. The neighborhood canvass would go unfinished.
At the apartments where no one had answered—six in Marie's
old building, seven in the building nearby—no officer would go
back and try again. The evidence that had already been collected
would now be disposed of according to department protocol.
Once enough time passed, Marie's bedding would be destroyed.
So would the hairs and fibers from her bed, and the DNA swabs
from the sliding glass door. So, too, would the rape kit.

Even Marie's account—the very story itself—would disap-
pear from the official record. Every year the FBI collects crime
data from police departments around the country. Law enforcement uses the data to plan budgets, researchers to study trends,
legislators to draft crime bills. In its annual filing sent to the FBI,
Lynnwood designated Marie's rape claim as unfounded—the
catchall tag for any reported crime deemed baseless or false. In
all, ten rapes were reported to the Lynnwood police in 2008. The
police labeled four as unfounded.

On September 11, the day of her arraignment, Marie didn't show up in court. Failure to appear is a crime, so the prosecutor asked the judge to issue a warrant for Marie's arrest. The judge agreed. Now, Marie was looking at two potential charges—and the possibility of being arrested, handcuffed, and booked into jail the next time she came across a police officer.

Lynnwood Municipal Court can be a confusing place. It's busy, for one thing. In 2008 Marie's was one of 4,859 misdemeanor cases. The court also handled 13,450 infractions, mostly traffic-related. For those charged or ticketed, the court can be a vertiginous hive, a swarm of suits coming and going. Key functions get farmed out. A private law office, Zachor & Thomas, prosecutes the cases. Another contractor, nCourt, handles payments made online or over the phone, charging extra for the convenience. As a case moves forward, fines, fees, and other legal obligations can multiply. Defendants like Marie are usually required to attend each hearing, even if that hearing proves to consist entirely of entering a postponement and scheduling the next hearing, at which the defendant might show up to learn that the matter is being postponed yet again.

In a message posted online, the court's judge, Stephen E. Moore, says the court's goal "is to correct behavior—to make Lynnwood a better, safer, healthier place to live, work, shop and visit." The court's "overriding value . . . is customer service. It is sometimes difficult for people who've been issued a traffic ticket or charged with a crime to think of themselves as 'customers' but they are." Everyone—victim, witness, juror, or defendant—"may expect to be treated with professionalism and respect," the judge writes.

On September 12, Marie showed up at the counter at Lynnwood Municipal Court to ask about her case. She knew nothing of the hearing scheduled the day before. She had no idea there was a warrant out for her arrest. A clerk rooted through the paperwork and discovered that the hearing notice had, for some reason, been sent to an address in Seattle, not to Marie's home in Lynnwood. So the court rescheduled the arraignment—and canceled the arrest warrant. But if not for Marie's diligence—checking in, to see what was up—she could have been hauled in and spent the night in jail.

When the arraignment was held, on September 25, Marie was represented by a public defender, James Feldman. Like the prosecutor, Feldman worked in Lynnwood's court part-time, under a contract. He managed a small, private firm that did criminal and civil cases, fielding everything from domestic violence and DUIs to dog bites and slip-and-falls.

When he reviewed Marie's case, Feldman, who had thirty-four years of experience, was surprised she had been charged. Her story hadn't hurt anyone—no suspect had been arrested, or even questioned. His guess was that the police felt used. They don't appreciate having their time wasted.

At the hearing, Marie pleaded not guilty. Her next court date was set for six weeks later, on November 10.

ON OCTOBER 6, 2008, a sixty-three-year-old woman in Kirkland, Washington, reported being sexually assaulted.

Kirkland is just east of Seattle. Abutting Lake Washington, the suburb is dotted with art galleries, bronze sculptures, and marinas. The woman, a grandmother, lived alone in a ground-floor condominium in a two-story building. Her complex was a sun-dappled, forested enclave with towering trees, splashes of pink and purple rhododendrons, and trails covered with leaves, bark, and small pinecones. She told police she awoke at about four in the morning to find a man, his face covered by black mesh, holding a gloved hand over her mouth. His other hand held a knife to her throat. Don't scream, he told her. He tied her hands, using the laces from one of her pink tennis shoes. He groped her. He took photographs. He placed the knife's tip under one of her eyes and said he could cut it out. When she struggled, the knife sliced the web of her hand, between thumb and index finger. When she asked him why he was doing this, he laughed. He told her not to call the police. He said he would know if she did.

The woman said the man had "white, white skin," sloping shoulders, smooth hands, and bad breath. As for age, she couldn't say. "He might have been forty. He could have been fifteen. I don't know," she told police. Nor could she distinguish his size. "His build was pretty average," she said. "He wasn't big. He wasn't muscular. He wasn't tiny. He wasn't skinny."

The Kirkland Police Department assigned two detectives to the case, Corporal Jack Keesee and Audra Weber. The crime struck both as unusual, beginning with its level of cruelty and calculation. "You know, it's Kirkland. You don't expect those kinds of things to happen," Keesee says. "We often refer to ourselves as Beverly Hills North."

For Weber, the case had elements of a locked-room mystery, the kind written by Edgar Allan Poe or Ellery Queen. The grandmother had taken pains to safeguard her home. A metal bar secured her front door. She placed rods in the tracks of her rear sliding glass door and bedroom window. How did the attacker get in? Weber wondered. The grandmother offered one possibility. She had been tired the night before and had fallen asleep with the TV on. Maybe when she woke up and turned off the TV, she'd gone to bed without remembering to lock the sliding door.

For two to three months before the attack, the grandmother told police, she'd felt as if someone had been following her. Afterward, she had called 911 only to startle at the dispatcher's voice. The voice seemed to be her attacker's. He must have intercepted her call to police, she thought. He must have been telling the truth when he said he would know. She was so convinced of this that she refused to answer any of the dispatcher's questions.

Keesee conducted a long interview with the grandmother. At times, her answers went in unexpected directions.

"Do you ever get a weird feeling about anybody?" Keesee asked.

"Yeah."

"And share that with me?"

"Um, there are raccoons."

"Uh-huh."

"There are people that let their dogs out. They go back and forth."

"Uh-huh."

"You know, there are small animals and chipmunks. Um, a couple times I've felt just creepy."

At the police station, Keesee heard skepticism from some of his fellow officers. They couldn't believe this crime—so malevolent and serpentine as to be a candidate for one of those A&E crime shows—could have been committed in their placid suburb. "I had several people coming by my desk, saying, 'Ah, come on. This didn't happen.' And my response was, 'I don't know that it didn't happen.' . . . It's human nature, I guess. Or maybe that's just what happens in the cop world. Everybody lies. Everybody lies to cops." But at no time did anyone tell him to stop pursuing the case. "It was just office talk that you get from time to time."

The detectives on the case wrestled with some doubts of their own. But ultimately the grandmother's idiosyncrasies didn't throw Keesee, who had ample experience with trauma as a domestic-violence detective and as a hostage negotiator. "Nobody acts the same," he says. "I've done a countless number of death notifications. I've seen every possible reaction that you can imagine. The same goes with rape victims, sexual assault victims." Nor was he thrown by any inconsistencies in her description of what happened. "Most victims will . . . the core issue, they're firm on. It's the stuff that happens around that they'll deviate from. And that's not unusual.

"Until I found some reason not to believe her, I believed her," Keesee says.

———

SHANNON, SITTING AT home with her husband, learned about the Kirkland attack while watching the television news.

Oh my God, she thought. I was wrong. The police were wrong. Marie must have really been raped.

The Kirkland attack took place two months after and thirteen miles away from the one Marie had reported in Lynnwood. Shannon seized on the parallels—the breaking in, the binding of hands, the taking of photographs. She wasted no time. Shannon's father had been the chief of police in Kent, south of Seattle. She grew up with police, trusted police, knew how the police worked. She went to her computer, looked up the telephone number, and called—immediately—to alert the Kirkland police to Marie's story and all the similarities. The detective she reached said Kirkland would check into it.

After that, Shannon called Marie. She told Marie about the newscast and urged her to call the Kirkland police herself, to share what she had reported in Lynnwood, to make sure that any possible connection would be investigated.

Marie refused. She'd been through enough already—and, with the pending criminal charge, was facing more ahead. She couldn't bring herself to reach out to the police—any police—to say anything more. But she did go online and look up what had happened to the grandmother in Kirkland. And when she read the story, she cried.

For a detective, tying one unsolved crime to another can revive an investigation. Evidence multiplies. Patterns emerge. Detective Weber called the Lynnwood police not once but twice, to see if there might be a link. Both times Lynnwood told her: We have no crime to connect. Our victim was no victim. She admitted to making her story up. So Weber let it go: "I just kind of trusted their judgment, in terms of it's their case, they know the details and I don't." Still, she was "kind of shocked" to learn they had charged Marie. She hung up the phone and thought: "Okay, I hope that works out for you guys."

"That's so extreme to do that," Weber says. She figured there must be some backstory; perhaps the woman in Lynnwood had a history of lying and wasting the police's time. Keesee, Weber's partner on the Kirkland case, also called the Lynnwood police and was told the same thing. He had the same reaction as Weber. Oh, that's not good, he thought, upon hearing of the false-reporting charge. "Just because it's on the books doesn't mean you have to charge somebody with it," he says.

One of the Kirkland detectives got back to Shannon, to share what their department had learned. Lynnwood's case was closed, so Kirkland was dropping Shannon's lead. Shannon suggested the Kirkland police go talk to Marie for themselves. But the detectives never did. "That was the end," Shannon says.

Shannon was now more confused than ever. The way she had latched on to the Kirkland story made her realize: Maybe she hadn't been so sure after all that Marie was a liar. "I did want to believe her," Shannon says. "I loved her."

But Marie's reluctance to follow up and reassert her innocence brought all the doubts back. The Kirkland case had given Marie a second chance to talk to police—different police, not the detectives in Lynnwood—and to insist she had been raped, to insist her case be reopened and connected to Kirkland's. That Marie wouldn't do it convinced Shannon anew. Marie had lied. She hadn't been raped. Shannon was left to wonder, once again, what really happened inside Marie's apartment.

IN NOVEMBER, MARIE went back to court. Sitting there, waiting her turn, she had no idea what the people next to her had been accused of. It could have been speeding or shoplifting. It could have been a hit-and-run or domestic violence. When Marie's case was called, Feldman, her public defender, told the judge that the defense had no pretrial motions to offer. And that was pretty much it for the day. Marie was told to come back next month.

When she returned in December, her case was pushed back to January. She returned in January, to learn her case was being postponed until February. In February, the case was continued until March.

Finally, the prosecution made Marie an offer. Called a "pretrial diversion agreement," the deal amounted to this: If Marie met certain conditions for the next year, the false-reporting charge would be dropped. She would need to get mental health counseling for her lying. She would need to go on supervised probation. She would need to keep straight, breaking no more laws. And she would have to pay $500 to cover the court's costs.

To Feldman, this was a good offer. If Marie met the terms of the agreement, she could walk away without a record.

Marie wanted this behind her.

So in March she went to court, accompanied only by her lawyer, for what was her sixth appearance—and took the deal.

In Kirkland, Corporal Keesee worked the case. He went from condo to condo in the victim's complex and in another complex nearby, asking if anyone saw or heard anything. He sought out maintenance workers and questioned them. He interviewed one neighbor who had been inside the grandmother's home, helping her hook up a television two or three months before the attack. He interviewed another who reported that someone had tried breaking into her own home. He went to nearby businesses—a grocery store, a gas station, a drugstore—to track down surveillance video from the morning of the assault. He rounded up information on other attacks—in Seattle, in the nearby towns of Shoreline, Kenmore, and SeaTac—to see if there might be any connection.

But after two months, with all those leads exhausted, Keesee had to give up the case. He was being rotated back to patrol. Any follow-up would be Weber's to handle. Between Christmas and New Year's, the two detectives reviewed the investigation while going over the handoff. They concluded there was one last hope: DNA.

The investigation had produced a decent suspect. On the morning the grandmother had reported being attacked, a Kirkland officer, responding to the call, had pulled into the condominium complex at about five thirty. In the parking lot he spotted a man in the passenger seat of a Toyota, its engine running. When the officer walked up and tapped the window, the man gave his name, along with his date of birth. The officer called the information in to dispatch to run a computer check.

The man told the officer he lived in one of the units with a friend. He worked as a machinist. His roommate worked at the same shop. This morning he was grabbing a cigarette while waiting for his roommate to come out and drive them to work. The officer thanked the machinist for his time and began walking away. Then he heard back from dispatch. The machinist had a warrant out for his arrest. The warrant had been issued in June—for indecent exposure.

So the machinist was in the area and had a criminal sheet with a sex offense. He also wore a sweatshirt that fit what the police were looking for.

But the machinist said it wasn't him. He said he had been in his condo since two o'clock the afternoon before. And when the police drove the grandmother by to eyeball him, she said she didn't think he was the attacker, although she couldn't be sure. Plus, he was six feet four, 240 pounds, hardly an average build. Nonetheless, he remained a suspect, unless and until he could be excluded.

At the Washington State Patrol crime lab, an analyst swabbed the shoelace that had been used to tie up the grandmother and detected male DNA. The sample wasn't sufficient to develop a full genetic profile. But it would allow for Y-STR analysis, the testing that can narrow in on a paternal family line. The state didn't do that kind of analysis, but some private labs did.

Weber asked the machinist if he would provide a DNA sample for comparison purposes. He agreed, allowing the detective to swab the inside of his cheek.

In July 2009, Weber sent those cheek swabs and the shoelaces to a private lab. Then she waited.

Given its limitations, the analysis would not be able to determine, for sure, that the machinist was a match. But it could say for sure if he wasn't.

Six weeks later, on the last day of August, Weber heard back. The machinist was ruled out. The DNA belonged to someone else.

For Weber, that was it. There was nothing else to do. On September 2 she designated the case as inactive, and moved on.

MARIE'S PLEA DEAL removed the threat of jail. But her sense of loss lingered. The months and years following that morning in Lynnwood hollowed her out.

She stopped going to church. "I was mad at God," she says. With her withdrawal from church, her relationship with Jordan withered. "We stayed friends, but we didn't talk like we used to."

She lost interest in photography. She stayed in her apartment and watched a lot of television.

She shelved thoughts of college. She took jobs that made few demands. "I hurt so bad, this deep dark hole I was in. It was hard for me to do much." She worked at a clothing store, handling the cash register, tagging, stocking. She worked at a collection agency, taking messages, doing data entry. She did sales at a store that sold discount items for parties.

The learner's permit that the police had found in her apartment was supposed to be temporary—a step along her path to independence. But she never took the next step, never got her license. She took the bus to work.

Self-esteem gave way to self-loathing. She started smoking, drinking, gaining weight. She made bad choices, taking up with troubled people who stole her money.

She felt like everyone shunned her—and she wasn't alone in sensing this; Shannon saw it, too. "All the people in her circle of friends and support people just didn't want to have anything to do with her," Shannon says.

Marie suffered from depression and post-traumatic stress disorder. That was the diagnosis she received from a specialist she consulted as part of her plea deal. Some days she'd declare herself happy as could be. Other days she was tired, dead to the world, unable to shake the thought that she had given up everything, that the normalcy she craved would never be hers.

As ordered by the court, Marie saw a counselor for a year. She dreaded it at first. Then she settled in. "In counseling, you're not judged. It felt nice to tell my story when I'm not shut down." The two were supposed to work through Marie's life, building up to the lie she had told. But "a year was not long enough," Marie says. Once she had covered everything else, Marie had time to talk just once about what happened that summer morning in Lynnwood.

"I gave her the whole story," Marie says.

She couldn't tell if the counselor believed her or not.

12

MARKS

M ARC PATRICK O'LEARY.

That was the name on the driver's license displayed on the laptop screen in front of Galbraith. O'Leary was just over six feet tall. He weighed 220 pounds. His hair was blond. His eyes were hazel. His face seemed square, heavy, like a clay doll. His lips were thick, his hair short. He had a prominent brow. He lived at 65 Harlan Street, in Lakewood. His birthdate: June 22, 1978. Galbraith did the math. He was thirty-two years old.

"*It's him,*" she thought.

Galbraith felt a pang of regret. She hadn't told her fellow investigators about the white truck because she didn't consider it a strong lead. It was luck, just pure luck, that DiGiosio had found it. But sometimes, that's what it took. Galbraith quickly explained the connection to the other cops around the table in the Westminster conference room.

A white Mazda in the vicinity of two of the victims.

The victims' description of the attacker matched O'Leary's driver's license.

The cops in the room—Hendershot, Galbraith, Burgess, and Hassell—had lived blurred days in the month since Amber's rape. They had dug in dumpsters and ditches, questioned college kids and cable guys, created a task force on the fly, and collaborated with each other's crime scene investigators and crime analysts.

They had exhausted themselves, certain that a serial rapist was loose. Now, with a suspect finally identified, they would work even harder. The conference room in the Westminster Police Department cleared out. The cops raced back to their offices to dig into one question.

Who was this guy?

Galbraith checked the National Crime Information Center, which showed no criminal record—not even a traffic ticket. She enlisted her husband, David, to search the Internet. Once again, they sat across from each other on their living room couches, each armed with a laptop. David got the first hit. Marc P. O'Leary had registered a porn site called teensexhub.net. The rapist had threatened to post photos of the victims online. As soon as David saw the link, he figured he wouldn't be seeing much of his wife anymore. "Stacy's a very driven person when she gets a major case. She'll work thirty to forty hours straight to get ahead of it."

Grusing contacted his counterparts in the investigative arm of the Defense Department to find out whether O'Leary had been in the armed services—something both Amber and Lilly had suspected. He got a quick response, but with little detail. O'Leary had enlisted in the Army. He had risen to the rank of sergeant. He had been honorably discharged from active duty.

DiGiosio continued her digging. The Lakewood Police Department, like more than 70 percent of law enforcement agencies in the United States, had invested in a crime-fighting tool called a license plate reader, or LPR. The small, high-speed cameras—they can take 1,800 photos a minute—are affixed to the front of patrol cars. As cops drive around, the readers snap pictures of every license plate passed. The information on the license plate—in addition to the date, time, and location of the photo—is automatically fed into a database. Over time, the database had proven far more useful than any log of stolen underwear.

As it turned out, one of the vehicles with a reader was driven by a cop who passed 65 Harlan Street on his way to work. So when DiGiosio typed in the license plate number, she got three hits. One picture captured O'Leary standing next to the white Mazda in his driveway. Another showed the right passenger-side mirror—bent just like the mirror of the white Mazda pickup in the surveillance video from Golden.

Later, Hendershot pored over DiGiosio's discoveries at her cubicle in Westminster. One of the LPR photos captured the Mazda driving through Lakewood on August 10, 2010. That was the same day Sarah had been raped, Hendershot realized. She looked at the time stamp: 8:49:05 a.m. Only two hours after the rapist had fled the apartment. Then Hendershot found something even more astonishing. Colorado Department of Motor Vehicles records showed that O'Leary had his picture taken for a new license at 11:13 a.m. on the same day. In the picture, he wore a white T-shirt. Sarah had described her attacker as wearing a white T-shirt. It was an astounding chain of events. But Hendershot was still cautious. Who knew what more they were going to find out?

"I want the right guy to go to prison forever, you know what I mean? But you can't be narrow in focus. You can have that bit of excitement, but there's still so much more work to do. I can't imagine how horrible it would be to jump to the conclusion and convict the wrong person, right? I'm excited . . . but there's still so much work to be done," Hendershot said.

IT HAD BEEN a chilly morning for the two FBI agents on the stakeout. They sat in their car, parked down the street from O'Leary's home at 65 Harlan Street. Cars whizzed past. The temperature hovered just above freezing. The sky was clear. It was Friday, February 11, 2011.

At 12:13 p.m., a man and a woman stepped out of the house. He was about six feet one, blond hair, maybe two hundred pounds. She had dark hair, looked to be about twenty. O'Leary and who? A girlfriend? The pair got into a Toyota Corolla and drove off. The agents followed. They were hoping that O'Leary would go for a sweaty workout. Or spit on the ground. Or do anything, really, that might result in his leaving body fluid in a public place. Such remnants were called "abandoned DNA"—genetic material left in the open. Even though the Fourth Amendment required a warrant to gather a suspect's genetic signature from his home or body, the courts had ruled abandoned DNA fair game for police. The agents could collect it; the state crime lab could analyze it. If O'Leary's DNA matched the partial profile from the rapist, they would know that the two men were at least related, if not the same man.

O'Leary and the woman drove a half mile to the Lookin' Good Restaurant and Lounge, a Greek, American, and Mexican diner. The agents waited outside as the couple ate for an hour and a half. When they left, an agent rushed in. He stopped the busboy, who was collecting dishes from the table. After a quick talk with the restaurant manager, the agent walked out with the coffee mug that O'Leary had used. It would have plenty of abandoned DNA on its rim.

While the surveillance agents watched O'Leary, Grusing and a local cop ventured to the front door of 65 Harlan Street. They were dressed like civilians, slacks and shirts. They planned to install a surveillance camera to watch the house and wanted to make sure nobody was home. But when Grusing knocked, a man answered. Grusing recognized him immediately.

It was Marc O'Leary.

Holy shit. Grusing had prepared for the possibility of someone being home. But he hadn't expected it to be the suspect he thought had just left. He fell back on the ruse he had practiced. His partner explained they were cops. Grusing pulled a police sketch from his pocket and showed it to O'Leary.

There's been a bunch of burglaries in the neighborhood, Grusing said. Seen anybody who looks like this?

In reality, the sketch was from an FBI murder case. Grusing watched O'Leary closely. Did he suspect? O'Leary held the sketch and examined it. If he were the rapist, Grusing thought, he sure didn't show it. He seemed to be thinking. But he didn't seem panicked.

"No, I haven't seen that guy," O'Leary told Grusing. He handed back the sketch.

Can I get your name and birthdate? Grusing asked. O'Leary provided them. Still no signs of panic.

Anyone else live here? Grusing asked.

Just my brother, Michael, O'Leary said. He promised to share the news about the burglaries.

As Grusing walked away, he felt like the trick had worked. He had studied bad guys. He knew how they thought. Every cop they saw, every patrol car that passed, was a source of paranoia. "The bad guys always think somebody's after them," he said.

He knew, too, how they compensated. They simply got used to it. O'Leary would be suspicious of him. But it would be the same distrust he held of every cop who looked too closely at him. He would rationalize it as another close call. He would have no idea how close.

It didn't take long to sort things out. The surveillance agents had been following Michael O'Leary and his girlfriend. Michael's DNA was on the coffee mug. Could they use Michael's DNA to compare to the rapist's DNA? Grusing called the director of the state crime lab. Yes—it didn't matter which male relative provided a sample to compare to the rapist's DNA. They could do the analysis overnight, the director told Grusing.

The next day, at 2:15 p.m. on February 12, Galbraith got the results. The rapist's DNA—the few dozen cells found on Doris's teddy bear, Sarah's white kitchen timer, and Amber's face—matched the cells on the rim of Michael O'Leary's coffee mug. The chance of such a match happening at random was one in 4,114 for white males. If you were a gambler, you'd bet that the rapist was an O'Leary man.

During the investigation, Grusing and Galbraith met regularly at his office in a turn-of-the-century red-brick building in the middle of Denver's dusty stockyards. It had once housed the Denver Union Stockyard Company and had the feel of a bank, with Ionic columns, wide staircases, and aged wood paneling. The FBI office on the top floor felt more like a men's club. The agents had decorated the inside with taxidermy of illegally caught game seized by the US Fish and Wildlife Service—a javelina here, an elk head there. The men's bathroom featured a white porcelain urinal the size of a small refrigerator. The metal venetian blinds behind Grusing's desk were bent—the victim of an impromptu interoffice football game.

Now, the two discussed a new set of facts. A day before, they hadn't known that Michael O'Leary existed. Now, they knew he was almost Marc's twin. The two men looked alike—they were almost the same height, and were maybe ten pounds apart. Since the rapist wore a mask, the victims would have a hard time picking between them in a lineup. And Michael was military, too. He had served in the Army. What if Michael had been driving Marc's pickup to commit the rapes? Or what if they were working together, taking turns?

They still believed that Marc O'Leary was the rapist. But they both knew that a good lawyer would have no trouble making a case for reasonable doubt. *Ladies and gentlemen of the jury. None of the victims can say for sure which man assaulted her. And neither can modern science. Our legal system says it is better to let ten guilty men go free, than to convict an innocent man. You must acquit.*

They needed more.

That evening, Galbraith wrote an affidavit asking a judge for a warrant to search 65 Harlan Street. She listed all the evidence that pointed to Marc O'Leary: his physical appearance, his time in the military, the DNA match. She cataloged the crimes and the lives ripped apart. Using the dry language of a legal document, she wrote down all the things that she hoped to find in the house to prove his guilt:

- Items missing from the victims in the cases described above: Pink Sony Cybershot camera, nightgown with blue and yellow floral pattern, women's panties, green satin pillowcases, green sheets, a solid pink fitted sheet and two matching pillowcases, a pair of white "granny panties," hot pink sheet, snowflake pajamas, black silk-like bindings.
- White T-shirt (possibly with coloring on the front), gray sweatpants with holes in the knees, greenish khaki pants, gray hoodie, black mask, cap or combination thereof, gloves or other item with a honeycomb pattern or imprint, black Adidas shoes with white stripes.
- Zippered bag or backpack, items of rope, string, twine or other material that could be fashioned as a ligature; dildo, personal/sexual lubricant, water bottle, wet wipes, thigh high nylons or stockings, vibrator, black camera.

Galbraith finished late that evening. The on-duty judge didn't want to read the affidavit in an email. He insisted on a facsimile. Galbraith raced around town until she found one store open late, a Safeway, that had a fax machine. The judge signed the warrant at ten o'clock on Saturday night. The raid was set for the next morning.

Galbraith knew that finding the evidence at O'Leary's house would help the prosecutors build their case. But she needed only one thing to be certain that Marc O'Leary was the rapist.

She emailed a crime analyst at another police department: "I so want to see this guy's leg! BAD."

———

AT 8:15 A.M. on Sunday, February 13, Galbraith knocked on the side door of 65 Harlan Street. It was a clear, cold morning. Snow covered the yard. The circling trees stood winter-bare.

"Police. Search warrant. Open the door!" she shouted. Grusing and six officers from Golden and Lakewood stood behind her, pressed against the south side of the house. They wore bulletproof vests and khaki pants. They had guns drawn.

Galbraith heard noises from inside the house. The door swung open. Marc O'Leary stood in the frame. His dog, Arias, and Michael's dog, a pit bull, tumbled out ahead of him. Seeing the cops, O'Leary started to kneel.

Outside, outside! Galbraith ordered.

He looked dazed as he stepped out into the slanting midwinter sun. He wore a gray hoodie, baggy gray sweatpants, and slip-on house shoes. He told Galbraith that his brother, Michael, had gone out last night and hadn't returned. He was alone.

Galbraith pulled him to the side. She patted him down. She knelt down and raised his pants legs.

There it was, on O'Leary's left calf: a dark birthmark the size of a large egg.

It was him. He was the rapist.

Galbraith turned to Grusing. Thumbs up.

We have a warrant to search the house, Grusing explained to O'Leary. O'Leary said he wanted a lawyer. At that moment, Galbraith walked up behind him.

"You're under arrest for burglary and sexual assault, which occurred in the City of Golden on January 5, 2011," she told him. At 8:35 a.m., Galbraith handcuffed O'Leary. She watched as another officer drove him away for booking in the Jefferson County jail. He was fingerprinted. A technician ran cotton swabs against the inside of his cheeks to obtain a complete DNA profile. In a photo room, he stripped naked so that a police photographer could take photos of every part of his body. At his first court appearance, on February 14, 2011, O'Leary was charged with sexual assault, kidnapping, burglary, and menacing. Bail was set at $5 million. The judge worried that O'Leary was "an extreme danger."

Galbraith was wearing new boots the morning of the arrest. Whenever she looked at them in the future, she would remember catching O'Leary. She had wanted to make the arrest herself. "I wanted to see the look on his face . . . and for him to know that we figured you out."

Golden crime scene investigator Amanda Montano led a team of eleven cops, FBI agents, and criminalists in the search of the house. Westminster's Katherine Ellis had volunteered to help. So had Detective Aaron Hassell from Lakewood, and Detective Marcus Williams and criminalist Kali Gipson, both from Golden. They dressed in white jumpsuits with hoods, and wore blue surgical gloves and white booties. They looked like a biohazard team swarming the scene of a toxic wasteland.

Room by room, the team combed the house. Marc O'Leary's bedroom was in the northeast corner. Black curtains covered the windows. The bed was pushed against one wall, beige sheets bundled in the middle. The floor was clean. There was a dresser with a television set on top. Inside the drawers, everything was neat, orderly, in its place. His shirts and pants were stacked, three piles to a drawer. On the floor of the closet, several pairs of shoes were positioned side by side. Montano noticed that one pair were black sneakers with three distinctive white stripes. They were Adidas ZX 700 shoes. Just like the website said, Montano thought.

She moved to the computer room in back of the house. Maroon curtains covered a window that normally offered a view of the Rockies. An L-shaped brown desk sat in one corner. On top were a computer, spiral notebooks, and an iPhone. Above the computer, hanging on the wall, was a framed clock with a military coat of arms. Underneath was an engraving, thanking Private First Class Marc Patrick O'Leary for his dedicated service to the 3rd Platoon "Cocks," A-Company of the 503rd Air Assault Infantry Regiment—one of the units he had served in while in

Korea. Military, just like the victims had suspected, Montano thought.

Bookshelves rose above the desk. Montano wrote down the titles. *A Brief History of Time* by Stephen Hawking. *Ethics* by Benedict de Spinoza. *The Ethical Slut* by Dossie Easton and Janet Hardy. A biography of Sigmund Freud. *The Only Astrology Book You'll Ever Need*. The Bible. *Sexy Origins and Intimate Things*.

A stack of CD-ROMs in blue plastic cases sat on another shelf. On top of the pile: a pink Sony Cyber-shot camera.

That's almost too perfect, Montano thought.

Throughout the day, Montano and the rest of the team sifted through O'Leary's life. In the bathroom hamper, they found a black piece of cloth, knotted to form a kind of mask. In the kitchen, sitting in a basket, they discovered a pair of Under Armour gloves with a honeycomb pattern. Under the mattress, they found a black Ruger .380-caliber handgun. The magazine contained six rounds. A black-and-green Eagle Creek backpack hung in a closet in the computer room. It was stuffed with bags. One held a pair of clear, plastic high heels with pink ribbons. Another was a clear plastic Ziploc bag. Neat block letters, scrawled with a black Sharpie, revealed the contents. STOCKINGS. CLAMPS. DILDO. GAG.

In the back of the closet, Williams noticed a small black guitar amp. He turned it around. Two plastic Ziploc bags peeked out of the back. Williams pulled them out. Montano placed the bags on the floor. Inside, she saw women's underwear. Peach-and-white striped, bright pink, white, light pink, brown, silky baby blue, and white with colored flowers. There were ten pairs in all.

His trophies.

The abundance of evidence astonished every cop on the scene. It was like finishing a jigsaw puzzle. The jagged pieces formed a clear picture: Marc O'Leary.

"As a detective, you serve search warrants all the time. Sometimes you find good stuff. Sometimes, you find a little bit. But you don't usually find almost every single thing that ties a case to every other case," Hassell says. "There was so much stuff, you're like, this is silly."

After the arrest, Galbraith drove over to Amber's new apartment. It had been thirty-nine days since the rape. She wanted to break the news.

Amber met her outside in the parking lot. Galbraith told her that the man's name was Marc O'Leary. That he'd raped other women before her. That Amber had helped to solve the case. Her attention to detail. Her ability to draw him into conversation. Her instincts on his background. Her phone call to police. Galbraith rarely got emotional. But now, she felt overwhelmed—with relief, with satisfaction, with happiness. She began to tear up. *I did this for you,* she thought.

Amber showed no emotion. She thanked Galbraith. She gave her a quick hug. And then she went back inside the apartment. Galbraith had wanted more of a reaction, even though she knew better. It wasn't her emotion to have. A victim's experience of rape was intensely personal.

Hendershot called Sarah. They needed to meet, Hendershot told her. Sarah said she was busy running errands. She didn't know if she had time to get together.

"Well it's really, really important," Hendershot told her. "I'll go anywhere you are. I don't care where you're at, I'll go anywhere."

That evening, Hendershot drove to meet her at a Denny's restaurant. Hendershot saw her in a back corner, eating alone. Sarah had no family nearby. Her husband had died. She had suffered, over and over.

Hendershot sat down, and broke the news.

"It's over. It's over. We have him," she told Sarah.

Both women sat in the booth, tears running down their faces.

"That's where I got my happy moment, if you will, was when I got to sit in front of her, and tell her that after all this, after everything that you've been through, you'll never, ever have to worry about him again," Hendershot says.

MICHAEL O'LEARY COULD not understand what was happening. He had driven up to the house at 65 Harlan Street and found it swarming with cops. A crowd ringed the police tape. News crews stood outside, the reporters speaking into cameras. He got out of his car and identified himself to a cop. He was handcuffed and placed into the back of a squad car.

Now, he was sitting in a room in the headquarters of the Colorado Bureau of Investigation. Two detectives sat in front of him. One introduced himself as Scott Burgess. The other identified herself as Edna Hendershot.

"So do you have any idea what this might be about?" Burgess asked.

"Heck no. I have zero idea," Michael replied. He knew that his brother had been arrested. But he didn't know why. He'd seen a story on TV about a guy in Arizona arrested for shooting a bunch of people. The guy had reminded him of his brother: a loner, off-the-grid type. Had Marc been building a bomb or something?

"You don't get this kind of treatment for a traffic ticket," Burgess told him.

Burgess and Hendershot fired questions. How did he spend his days?

He went to barber school each morning at eight, and worked at a furniture-delivery store in the afternoons.

Had he ever driven Marc's pickup anywhere?

Yeah, once. He had used the truck to drop off a television stand somewhere in the Denver suburbs.

Did he use the computer in the back room?

Sure. But he had his own account with his own password. He checked fantasy football scores. Sometimes, he perused a dating website called Plenty of Fish.

Had he ever been to Aurora? Or Westminster? Or Golden?

No. Yes. No.

"Do you have any cousins that live in the Denver area, male cousins?" Hendershot asked.

Nope. There was just his dad. And he lived in Arizona.

Burgess asked a final question. Could he pull up his pants legs?

Michael showed him a scar on his calf. It had come from a bicycle accident when he was a kid. What did that have to do with anything?

"Are you guys gonna tell me what he's been arrested for or what?" Michael asked.

Burgess hesitated a second. It was a heck of a thing, telling this guy. He literally had no idea. Several women had been raped, Burgess told him. They had described their attacker as six feet tall, about 225 pounds. DNA had tied the rapist to the O'Leary family. And one woman had seen a birthmark on the rapist's leg.

"I'm sorry to tell you that and I'm sorry to say that this is going to be something that is going to be difficult, I would imagine, for a family to deal with here," he told Michael. "But we are very confident that Marc, unfortunately, is our suspect."

Michael said nothing. Burgess and Hendershot continued to ask questions, but Michael stopped answering. Minutes passed in silence as the two cops waited for him to speak.

Finally, he found his voice.

"This is just gonna kill my mom," he said.

"She's not gonna be able to handle this, I guarantee you that, like, she's done. Her life is over. This is just gonna eat her alive forever. It doesn't matter, there's nothing I can do about it, nothing anybody can do about it," he said.

He pressed Burgess. Were they sure they had the right guy? Maybe he was being framed?

Burgess told him no. They'd found plenty of evidence at the house. "In my mind, it's overwhelming," he told Michael.

Michael didn't want to be disloyal to his brother. Blood thicker than water and all that. But this—this was too much.

"I actually looked up to him and thought he was doing good. I don't know what to think anymore. I'm just, I'm embarrassed like, I'm embarrassed to even show my face.

"He might as well be dead. He's gonna be gone forever," Michael said. "I wish I could just like shoot him."

He told the detectives that his brother was involved in occult stuff. Astrology. Alchemy. Secret societies. His brother and his friends subscribed to strange beliefs about the world's social order, he told the detectives. There were only two kinds of people: those at the top, and the rest in their thrall.

"In their world, everything is broken down, like with alphas and bravos," he said.

The words resonated with Burgess. The rapist had made a cryptic reference to Amber about wolves and bravos. Now, the rapist's brother was using similar words. Imagine laying that coincidence out for a jury. *Could it be two different guys with the same secret philosophy? What are the chances?* Here was a chance to fit another puzzle piece into place.

Burgess asked, "Have you ever heard the term 'wolves and bravos'?"

"Yeah, wolves and bravos," Michael said.

"What's wolves and bravos?"

"The wolves are basically like alphas and the bravos are just like the majority masses of the people. They're not physically fit, they're not mentally fit, they're not anything. They're just on the next level down. That's how they break it down, the same way wolves do, because that's how wolves break down."

"Is that how he regarded himself? Was that the kind of stuff he was studying?"

"They basically classified him as alpha and that alpha males in that society basically can have sex with multiple women, they don't have to be tied down," Michael said. "I don't see how that ties into frickin' going out and raping and stuff like that but I mean it's just all way too deep to even try to think about, you know?

"The dude's fucking psycho," Michael said.

As Montano stepped through O'Leary's house, she was followed by another man—John Evans, a fifty-year-old computer expert. A civilian investigator with CBI, Evans knew that the rapist had threatened to post the victims' pictures on the Internet. And that O'Leary owned pornographic websites. Evans's job was to scoop up all the computers, hard drives, and cell phones in the house. Montano was searching for physical signs of O'Leary's guilt. Evans was seeking digital ones.

Evans had a long history with computers. As a young man, he had purchased one of the first computers made to use in the home, a Commodore 64. That was back in the 1980s. It couldn't do much. Add numbers. Print HELLO. Show blocky graphics. But he fell in love with the machine with the clunky brown keyboard and glowing screen. At the time, it seemed like magic.

He turned his hobby into a career. After serving in the Navy—he had worked in Antarctica for three years, wowed by the polar nights and then days without end—Evans moved to Colorado. He got a job as an animal-control officer—a dogcatcher, as they were once called—and then joined the Golden Police Department as an evidence clerk and a crime scene technician. Working mostly alone, in an office lined with shelves, he logged fingerprint cards and DNA swabs, pistols and photographs, bedsheets and torn clothes. His fascination with electronics led him to take classes in computer and video forensics, the analysis of digital media to use in court cases. He became a certified computer forensic examiner—the first in Golden and one of the few in the Denver region.

Evans's reputation as a computer whisperer spread. Other agencies began sending him their computer crimes. At first it was mostly around Golden. But soon, cops from around Colorado were asking him for help. Did your case have blurry surveillance video? Evans could enhance it. Need to crack open a hard drive? Evans could do that, too. Encrypted emails? Evans was the man to call.

This was how Evans learned that computers contained black magic, too. Many of the cases he worked involved child pornography. That meant he had to spend long hours looking at the most disturbing images possible. He got to know the canon—the standard set of tens of thousands of photos and videos of sexually abused children that circulated on the Internet among the world's perverts. It was never easy. Never normal. But he got used to it, like cops with dead bodies. "You build an immunity to it after a while. It was rough. At times, I just had to get up and walk away," he says. Evans kept his eyes alert for new images. Ones he had never seen before. Those were the children he might still be able to save.

In the back room, Evans inventoried each component of O'Leary's computer setup. There were two computers, one on his desk and one stored in the closet with the backpack and the guitar amp. There was an iPhone. Two thumb drives on the bookshelves. The CD-ROMs. And two SSD memory cards in O'Leary's cameras—the stolen pink Sony Cyber-shot and the Canon Rebel XTi, the same model he had mentioned in his exchange with the woman on Craigslist.

Evans transported everything back to the Rocky Mountain Regional Computer Forensics Laboratory, located in an uninspiring office park in Centennial, one of Denver's most southern suburbs. Funded by the FBI, the lab brought together federal agents and Colorado investigators to serve as a local crime lab for all things related to computer forensics. State law enforcement agencies would bring encrypted files, half-erased accounting records, Internet IP logs in hopes of turning up evidence of a crime. Evans, on permanent loan from the Golden Police Department as part of the FBI program, enjoyed the collaboration. "You try to help everybody out," he says.

At his desk in a long floor filled with cubicles, Evans had seven computers—PCs and Macs—each with two screens. They whirred away, unearthing digitized secrets. Evans looked like a stockbroker on the floor of the Wall Street exchange, but his fourteen screens showed losses, never gains.

"We're all looking at really bad stuff, all day long, every day."

O'Leary's computer yielded evidence almost immediately. Evans found a backup of O'Leary's iPhone that contained the notes he had taken while he stalked Amber. The notes dated back to September 28—more than three months before the rape. On that day, he recorded several entries over five hours spent outside the apartment. The last one was at 2:30 a.m. Amber "comes home, strips to undies and takes a really long time in the bathroom, sits down at her desk and starts writing," he wrote. On November 10, he described watching Amber and her boyfriend. Amber "comes home with white BF about 10:30 to 10:45, BF in PJs, game over." On January 3, he worried that Amber might be moving out. He could see boxes being packed in her house. He picked the lock on the door that night, to prepare for slipping into her apartment. "Got here about one, home alone," he wrote one day before the rape.

On the same iPhone, the investigators found evidence that O'Leary had been stalking another woman—a divorcée from Littleton. There was no sign that he had actually struck. Just that he was planning to.

The iPhone also divulged O'Leary's contacts. He didn't have many. There was his brother, Michael. His mother and stepfather. Some local friends. And one number with a 602 area code. It was a woman from Arizona. Her name was Calyxa.

Evans forwarded everything he found to Galbraith or Hendershot. He'd write a quick, familiar note: "Here's a couple of interesting things found today." Evans's best friend was Mike Hendershot, Edna's husband. They'd met at the Golden Police Department—where Evans had also met Galbraith. Evans, too, was part of the blue web.

Among the files that O'Leary had downloaded, Evans found an electronic copy of a book on police techniques: the *Rape Investigation Handbook*. It had been written by two streetwise cops who spent decades investigating sexual assault: John O. Savino, an ex–NYPD officer, and Brent E. Turvey, a criminal profiler. The handbook was written in a folksy style, with lots of anecdotes. Many of them were profiles of rapists and their crimes. But the book also described investigative techniques. The analysis of touch DNA. The use of ViCAP. The characteristics of serial rapists. It seemed to Evans that O'Leary might have studied the book.

He was a student of rape.

One day, Evans stumbled onto a strange file stored on the hard drive of the computer that had been on O'Leary's desk. It had a suggestive name: "Wretch." It was enormous—nearly seventy-five gigabytes, big enough to store all the books on a library floor, big enough to store tens of thousands of high-quality photos and videos. And it was sealed tight. Evans discovered that O'Leary had used the software program TrueCrypt to protect the file from prying eyes—eyes like his.

Evans became obsessed with discovering the secrets of the Wretch.

Though encrypted, the Wretch provided clues. O'Leary had transferred images into the Wretch for storage. That act, the moving of a folder of photos, left behind a record. Evans found that O'Leary had named one folder "girls." Within it were more folders—each one with a woman's name. Evans found Amber's name and Sarah's name. He found Doris's name mentioned 1,422 times on 211 different files.

He found eight other names, too, names he didn't recognize.

He put them aside. They might help investigators track down other victims.

"If you saw how meticulous he was, even with his underwear drawer, it was easy to understand" why he labeled the folders with the women's names, Evans says. "He was really careful about everything he did."

Evans dedicated one of his computers entirely to hacking into the Wretch. As he waited, he applied his tools to the smallest things he had taken from 65 Harlan Street: the two memory cards from O'Leary's cameras. Each was the size of a stamp.

There, he found the evidence he was seeking.

The photos of the victims.

O'Leary had attempted to hide them. As far as Evans could figure out, O'Leary had transferred the photos from the camera into the Wretch. Then, with the images copied and stored in the safety of the Wretch, O'Leary deleted everything from the photo cards. Only he hadn't succeeded. The names of the files of the images had vanished. But the electronic bits that formed the images themselves remained on the card until permanently overwritten by another photo. The most careful of rapists had again left behind traces—digital ones.

Using software to recover deleted files, Evans rescued more than four hundred images of Amber, posed and photographed, her face a mask of fear. There were more than a hundred images of Sarah, forced to lie sprawled on her bed, her hands tied behind her back. There could be no mistake. The man in the photos was O'Leary. And he was raping the women in exactly the way they had described.

As he scrolled through the photos, Evans sometimes had to stop. He would go outside for a cigarette break. He estimated he had seen millions of pornographic images—many violent, many involving children—in his twenty-five years in law enforcement. But the people pictured in them had been anonymous and unknown. Now, he knew the names of the terrified faces staring at him on his computer screen. "You couldn't sit there and go through it all," he says. "It just gets to be a little overwhelming. It is real. You know you have a real victim out there."

When Evans called Galbraith and Hendershot to deliver the news, they raced over to the lab to view the files and immediately identified their victims.

Hendershot's succinct assessment: "I can't think of a more vile human being."

Hendershot noticed one picture where Sarah was wearing a pair of chunky red sandals. She recalled seeing them in a box when she had searched Sarah's apartment. Sarah had said the rapist put shoes on her. But she couldn't remember what they were. Hendershot decided to try one more time. She called Sarah. After chatting a few minutes, Hendershot asked her the same question she had asked before. Any chance that Sarah could remember the shoes?

As a matter of fact, she could. Sarah told her that she had been looking at a photo album a few weeks ago and saw a picture of herself wearing red sandals. Her memory suddenly flashed: Those were the shoes the rapist had grabbed.

Hendershot was amazed. Six months after the rape, Sarah's traumatized brain had recovered a lost image. Her memory was still finding puzzle pieces, still fitting them together.

Evans continued to unearth files that O'Leary thought he had deleted. He found eight photos that had been taken years before. They had been part of a bigger set, but most of the images had been overwritten as O'Leary had raped more women and taken more pictures. One more attack, and the eight images would have shared the same fate, vanishing forever.

Instead, Evans managed to recover them. He reviewed the photos with Galbraith. They were pictures of a young woman. She wore a pink T-shirt. She had the same look of terror as the other women.

Galbraith's heart sank. Another O'Leary victim. But how would she find her?

The last photo provided the answer. Marc O'Leary had placed the woman's learner's permit on her torso. Click.

The image clearly showed her name. And her address.

Lynnwood, Washington.

13

LOOKING INTO A FISH TANK

H E ARRIVED IN THE PREDAWN HOURS, THEN WAITED OUT-side her apartment, outside her bedroom, listening to her talk on the phone. The night was dry, letting him settle in. The wall was thin, letting him hear her voice.

He liked trees, for the cover they provided, and this complex had plenty of them. Apartments didn't offer him the privacy of a house, but still, there were advantages. All those sliding glass doors, for one thing—ridiculously easy to pick, when they weren't left unlocked, which so often they were. And then there were the windows. There were times he could dwell in the dark and run his eyes across a building, every blind open, every light on. It was like looking into a fish tank.

He'd spotted her a couple of weeks before. He'd been out driving, scoping out apartment complexes, looking for ones that fit his criteria. He wanted a complex that offered opportunities for concealment, ways to duck for cover. If the outside was open and bright, he'd be exposed. He wanted bedroom windows he could look through. He wanted the apartment to offer multiple escape routes. He didn't want to get boxed in. Sometimes, appraising a complex, he'd go into an empty apartment, maybe a model unit, to study the layout and mark exactly what was where.

He also wanted the complex to be at least a mile from his

home. You don't shit where you eat, he'd say. Her complex was four miles away, a ten-minute drive. And he found himself in Lynnwood a lot—to shop, like everyone else. Circuit City, Fred Meyer, Best Buy, Walmart. He ate here at Olive Garden and Taco Bell, and sat in the dark, smoky interior of Secret Garden, a local Korean barbecue restaurant. Just last week he'd been at the Alderwood Mall, shopping at Barnes & Noble.

Lynnwood had plenty of neighborhoods that were mostly houses. And houses had their appeal. In addition to greater privacy, they offered greater predictability. With people in houses, there tended to be less coming and going. There were fewer people to account for. But an apartment complex was easier to prowl, easier to drive through or walk past or just stand in front of without being conspicuous. There, he could blend in. Still, he knew he couldn't stay in one place for too long, even in a complex like this. So a couple of times he left his position outside her bedroom and walked around—just for a while, lest he raise suspicion.

Then he returned, and listened. He knew she was on the phone because no other voice responded to her. He waited for her to fall asleep.

She was eighteen years old. His preference was eighteen to maybe thirty. Monstrous as he was, there were limits to his depravity, or at least that's what he told himself. Eighteen was as young as he'd go. He also avoided homes with children, because he didn't want them caught up in this. His preference was single women, living alone. He also avoided places with dogs, because dogs barked. Dogs were worse than security alarms.

Aside from her age, she wasn't his type, not really. He'd realized that before, while peeping into her bedroom. But he spent so much time hunting (that's what he called it, hunting), hundreds of hours, maybe even a thousand, that he had conditioned himself to incorporate into his fantasies as many kinds of women as possible.

He had been in Washington for two and a half years now. After leaving Korea he had moved here and joined the Army Reserve, tasked with training ROTC cadets. He reported to Fort Lewis but lived in Mountlake Terrace, north of Seattle.

In Washington his early attempts were often as pathetic as those two in Korea. He couldn't say for sure how many times he had failed.

"I don't even know," he'd say.

"Quite a few," he'd say.

"At least seven or eight," he'd say, if pushed.

One of those times, he went into a woman's bedroom, knife in hand—and when she saw him, she ran right past him. Just like that. And he let her go. If he grabbed her, he might cut her, and he didn't want to do that. All the work he had done, all the preparation, ran out the door with her, into the night. It was foolish, what she did. But a part of him respected it.

Another time, he was prowling a condominium and saw a woman who looked to be in her sixties. But he couldn't see her well. The backyard was exposed, so he watched her from behind a fence, in some woods maybe ten to fifteen yards away. He waited, then went into her home. She had the television on. He went into her bedroom and saw her asleep. She looked pretty old, enough to make him wonder. I don't know about this, he thought to himself. He spent fifteen or twenty minutes debating. Then he went to the bed and covered her mouth to keep her from screaming. She looked so terrified that he worried she might have a heart attack. He pulled down the covers and realized he couldn't do it. She was too old. He covered her back up. He told her, I made a mistake coming here. I'm not going to steal anything. I'm not going to hurt you. I'm sorry I scared you. Please don't call the cops. I'm going to walk out the back door.

And he did.

But then he stewed. In the days and weeks after, he chastised himself: You're wasting your life; you spend night after night prowling, preparing, and then, if a woman doesn't fit your fantasy, you walk away. So he committed himself to expanding his fantasy realm. He sought out pornography featuring older women, then watched and watched. He made sure the next time his wiring would be different. The next time, his work would not be wasted.

Her phone call went on and on.

As she spoke with Jordan, Marie noticed something in the dark. But she didn't think much of it.

"It was outside my window. Just a shadow."

Maybe someone walking by, she thought. The shadow was there, then gone.

By the time her voice died out, it was fifteen minutes before sunrise. He climbed over the railing, brushing the surface. On the back porch there was a storage closet. He walked past it to the sliding glass door. The door was unlocked. He went into the living room.

He knew the apartment's 644 square feet, the living room that opened into the small dining area that led to the bedroom door. Since spotting her two weeks back, he had broken into her home a couple of times so he could check the place out. He'd gone through her papers and searched the drawers in her bedroom to make sure she would have no weapon within reach.

There was a learning curve to what he did. He put it this way: "As you become more proficient, you make fewer mistakes." That's a word he would use—"proficient." He had an entire vocabulary for rape; his words dehumanized and often mimicked military lingo. A nest of apartment buildings was a "target-rich environment." While conducting "surveillance" he wanted "multiple potentials to pursue." He called his final prep—on the night of, when he would be just outside, inventorying mask, bindings, gloves—"pre-combat inspection."

By this time he was maybe halfway around that learning curve. He'd slipped up before, catching the attention of police. In April of 2007 an officer in Mountlake Terrace had stopped him at five in the morning. The cop didn't arrest him, but he took his name and wrote a report: "Subject prowling around apts and residences wearing dark clothing." He gave the cop some bullshit story about his car breaking down and knocking on doors to use someone's phone. But for the next couple of weeks he noticed cops driving by his home, going slow, eyeballing. Shit, he thought to himself. I'm on their radar. After that he shut down for a while.

He knew that his fixations and his creeping about had also given people around him reason to wonder. He'd come home in the morning to Masha, his clothes dirty, as though he'd been crawling through something. He took classes at the Art Institute of Seattle, where he paid a fellow student, a photographer, to take pictures for a website. The student showed up to discover a photo studio with fetish gear and a metal cage with latch and padlock. Three women modeled naked. They were, in the photographer's words, "dangerously skinny." His marriage was unraveling. It was so bad he had asked for an open marriage. It was so bad she had agreed. Masha had worked to support them while he sat at his computer for hours on end pretending to do web design, while really he was beginning his foray into the porn business.

Between the websites and the prowling, his obligations to the military suffered. He had become a no-show at battle assembly, the Army Reserve's monthly training drills. It had been a year since he even made contact with his commanders.

In the living room, just on the other side of the sliding glass door, he saw a pair of black tennis shoes—hers. He removed the laces and placed the shoes back down. A police detective would later note how precisely the shoes had been arranged, as though something in the tidiness didn't square.

He was just being neat, the way he was with everything.

He threaded one of the shoelaces through a pair of her underwear. The other lace he planned to use for binding.

He didn't pack the same equipment every time. Sometimes he brought handcuffs or blindfolds; other times he made do with what he could find. Sometimes he brought a gun. On this occasion he would use a weapon he had spotted in one of his earlier canvasses of the apartment. As his fantasies evolved, so did his packing list. Tonight he planned a first for him. Tonight he brought a camera.

Inside the apartment, he spent a half hour getting ready, maybe longer. Part of it was mental—talking himself over the cliff, to use his words.

In the kitchen, he went to the knife block and removed a black-handled blade from the top row, far left.

Then he walked to the bedroom.

Around seven in the morning, maybe a quarter till, he stood in her bedroom doorway, the knife raised in his left hand.

He watched as she awoke.

Turn away, he told Marie—and she did. Roll over onto your stomach, he told her. When she did he straddled her, putting the knife near her face.

Put your hands behind your back, he told her. He bound her wrists and covered her eyes. He stuffed cloth into her mouth to muffle any sound.

That was an interesting conversation you were having, he told her, letting her know he had been there, listening and waiting.

You should know better than to leave the door unlocked, he told her.

Roll back over, he told her—and she did, and then he raped her, and while he raped her he ran his gloved hands over her.

He found her purse, dumped it out, picked up her learner's permit, put it on her chest, and took pictures.

Marie heard the rustling, but couldn't make sense of it. She recognized the click of a camera, a sound she knew well. Unable to speak, unable to scream, she prayed. She prayed that she would live.

When he was finished, he said that if she told the police, he would post the photos online so that her kids, when she had kids, could see them.

He took out the gag and removed the blindfold, telling her to avert her eyes and keep her head in the pillow.

One of the last things he said was that he was sorry. He said he felt stupid, that it had looked better in his head.

He left the room, walked to the front door, and was gone.

ON AUGUST 14, 2008—THE same day Marie was taken to the Lynnwood police station and interrogated, pressed into saying she had made up her story—Marc O'Leary dropped into Lynnwood Gun & Ammunition, a store off Highway 99. He bought four boxes of ammo and a rifle.

The following month he registered five more pornographic websites, including teensexhub.net and porninjector.com. The month after that he was in Kirkland, east of Seattle, raping another woman, sixty-three years old, his modus operandi almost identical to the rape in Lynnwood, right down to using the victim's own shoelaces as binding.

The next year he was discharged from the Army Reserve. While he had received an honorable discharge from active duty, for the Reserve the conditions were "other than honorable." On a list of values—the rating binary, yes or no—he received a no on everything: loyalty, duty, respect, selfless service, honor, integrity, personal courage. His evaluation report said: "cannot be counted on to accomplish any task, even those assigned to lower skill levels." He had been unaccounted for for about two years.

In the summer of 2009 O'Leary got on Interstate 90 and left western Washington. He drove east and south, going over the mountains to Yakima. Then he picked up Interstate 84 to Baker City, Oregon; Burley, Idaho; Ogden, Utah, and caught I-80 to Rock Springs, Wyoming. He continued east through Wyoming, almost to Nebraska, then turned south—home, to Colorado, where he would settle in the outskirts of Denver and begin anew.

14

A CHECK FOR $500

For Detective Galbraith, this was a call to look forward to. She would be helping another police department tie up a major case, extending a hand from four states away: *Hey, look what I have for you.* Or at least that's what she figured.

When she called the Lynnwood police—it was Thursday, March 3—Galbraith identified herself, then provided Marie's name and asked if the department had any case reports involving her. Told yes, Galbraith asked for a copy.

Fax us your request on letterhead, the Lynnwood police said. They wanted to confirm that Galbraith was a cop. So Galbraith grabbed some stationery emblazoned with her department's police shield and typed: "Please forward this CR to my attention at your earliest convenience. We have 4 similars with a person in custody. Thanks in advance!—Stacy."

About twenty minutes later, Galbraith received a fax from Lynnwood's records department. She looked at the cover page— and looked again, seizing at what was scrawled across the bottom. There, written by hand, were the last words she expected to see:

Vic was charged w/ false reporting in our case.

False reporting. The woman in the photo. "Vic was charged." Galbraith startled at the words.

Her heart sank. Then she let out a curse, knowing just how wrong the charge was.

Galbraith told the officers around her: *Hey, listen to this.* Then she went through the file. The investigations in Colorado had generated thousands of pages of records, documenting leads chased, lab work conducted, canvasses completed. The fax from Lynnwood included only forty-four pages. Galbraith pored over what little there was. She read what Marie had told police that first day about being attacked; Galbraith knew—because of O'Leary's photos—that Marie's account was true. The images matched Marie's words.

She wouldn't be helping fellow investigators solve an open case, Galbraith realized. She would be notifying them of an unthinkable mistake, about the worst any detective could make. As she reviewed Lynnwood's investigation—seeing where the doubts started, how they spread, how Marie had buckled when challenged and even taken a plea deal—Galbraith could only imagine what the woman in the photo had gone through. And she could only imagine the days ahead for the Lynnwood police.

SERGEANT MASON WAS heading to work when he got the telephone call letting him know.

Two months before, he had been transferred from the Criminal Investigations Division to the Narcotics Task Force, the field he knew best. He was still picking up classes outside of work. He was wrapping up a course in criminal justice procedure at Skagit Valley College, earning an A to go with all the other As lining his college transcripts.

It had been two and a half years since he had closed Marie's case, and in that time he had not once second-guessed himself: "I had no indication that how the investigation concluded was anything but 100 percent correct."

Mason's investigation had gone sideways with a call from

Peggy, saying she suspected Marie was lying. Now a call from Rodney Cohnheim, a fellow Lynnwood sergeant, informed Mason that Marie had been telling the truth. She had been raped. The man who raped her had been arrested. The police who arrested him had found photographs that verified Marie's story.

Her unbelievable story.

He had confronted a woman who had been assaulted at knife-point, convinced her to recant, and charged her with a crime. In his car, alone, he absorbed the news. The shock was so profound it reduced the surrounding details to fuzz. Most likely he pulled off the road, although he doesn't remember: "It's the law. I'm sure I did." Most likely Cohnheim offered support: "I'm sure he did. But it didn't register."

He went into the station and met with higher-ups. Everyone around talked about reopening the investigation and extraditing O'Leary and notifying Marie and reimbursing her costs and expunging her record—and for Mason it was all but a hum, everyone around feeling horrible, not sure what to say to the detective in the middle of it all.

As his colleagues set to work, Mason thought about the case, retracing the steps he took, mulling where he lost his way. The phone call from Peggy. The Project Ladder manager saying Marie wanted to change apartments. Marie, when asked to come in, saying: *Am I in trouble?* None, alone, meant much. But at the time they seemed to add up. He'd been a cop for more than twenty years now, and for the first time, he questioned whether he was qualified for the job. Like every cop, he'd experienced trauma; he had seen death, faced danger. And he had acquitted himself. He had pulled through and moved on. This was different. And though in this moment he thought about himself and all he had to answer to, he thought more about Marie. If he could get something like this so wrong, should he keep doing what he was doing? Maybe it was time for him to quit.

THE INVESTIGATORS IN Colorado not only helped solve the Lynnwood case from thirteen hundred miles away, they also helped close the case in Kirkland, Washington—with an assist from the Naval Criminal Investigative Service, or NCIS.

In 2004, the NCIS created the Law Enforcement Information Exchange—LInX, for short. To protect Navy assets, this program aimed to gather investigative records from law enforcement agencies at the federal, state, county, and municipal levels. A search of those records could illuminate patterns or connect cases across jurisdictions. By 2011, at least 275 agencies participated in the Northwest alone, sharing more than thirteen million narratives of criminal investigations. That enthusiastic participation allowed the LInX program to achieve a power that the FBI's ViCAP program never realized.

After linking O'Leary to the rape in Lynnwood, Galbraith used this database to search for other unsolved cases in Washington State with similar markers. Up popped the case in Kirkland, where the sixty-three-year-old grandmother had been assaulted two months after Marie. From there, everything fell together. A search of O'Leary's computer produced a hit on the Kirkland victim's name. O'Leary's DNA was compared to the genetic profile recovered from the grandmother's shoelace. It matched.

Before filing charges in the Kirkland case, a prosecutor in King County, Washington, wrote to Galbraith, asking her to review a prepared summary of the evidence for accuracy. Galbraith marked up the document and wrote back:

> FILE FILE FILE!!! Way BAD DUDE!
> Have a great weekend.

AT THE LYNNWOOD Police Department, the task of cleanup went to Commander Steve Rider and to Cohnheim, the sergeant who had sat in on Marie's final, futile attempt to convince police the rapist was real. They needed to meet with their counterparts in Colorado, which figured to be humiliating, and to find Marie and tell her about O'Leary.

"One of the worst things that we were ever going to have to do," Rider says.

They went to Colorado first. On March 14 the two men introduced themselves to the two detectives who had caught the rapist. Although the Lynnwood officers reeled at their department's mishandling of the case, their approach to the aftermath left Galbraith with a sense of appreciation. "They were nice. They were nice. You could tell that they had that victim's interest at heart in how they were going to try to fix this for her. They weren't arrogant. There was no wall. There was no feeling of—we're on defense. It is what it is, and now we act." Galbraith and Hendershot gave a briefing on their cases and provided a copy of O'Leary's fingerprints, obtained after his arrest.

In Kirkland, the police had preserved their physical evidence, including the DNA that proved a match with O'Leary. But the Lynnwood police, upon concluding that Marie was a liar, had destroyed the bedding, the hairs, the fibers—even the rape kit, with all that evidence collected at the hospital when Marie did every awful thing asked of her in order to help the police catch the stranger with the knife. Any hope of a DNA match was gone. When they checked to see what was left, all the Lynnwood police found was a single card with some partial fingerprints lifted from the sliding glass door. That card, coupled with this copy of O'Leary's prints, was Lynnwood's only hope of proving O'Leary's guilt through physical traces left behind.

The same day they met with the two Colorado detectives, Rider and Cohnheim went to the Jefferson County jail to see if

O'Leary would talk. But once he heard who they were and what they wanted, he requested an attorney, shutting down any questioning.

The next day the two went to Lakewood, to the offices of the Colorado Bureau of Investigation. Together, in one room, investigators from all the agencies that had captured O'Leary in Colorado—Golden, Westminster, Aurora, Lakewood, the CBI, and the FBI—convened with the police from Lynnwood, the department that might have prevented the Colorado attacks had its detectives worked their case instead of closing it as únfounded. The meeting was not comfortable.

"We sat in a group of outstanding investigators that put together an unbelievably good case, solved this case for us, and we're in the room looking at each other like we don't even deserve to be here, our department screwed this up so bad," Rider says. "They've got to be looking at us like, 'How could you let that happen?'"

The Lynnwood officers were struck by how well the Colorado agencies worked together—"just the spirit of cooperation," Cohnheim says. They shared information. They held routine meetings. "They all knew each other," Cohnheim says. "You could see that communication wasn't forced or new." In Washington State, the police in Lynnwood had scuttled Kirkland's efforts to coordinate, even though the two cities were only sixteen miles apart. Despite Shannon's tip—and her insistence the two cases might connect if only someone would look—detectives from the two departments never met in person. Nor did they write down and file whatever information was passed over the phone. The investigative files for both agencies offer not a word about contact between the two.

In Colorado, Rider and Cohnheim witnessed the power of relationships. They also saw that the police in Colorado had investigative tools the Lynnwood police did not. When the two returned home to Washington, they made sure their department got an automatic license plate reader.

One trial concluded, Rider turned to the next—the one he dreaded most. Now he had to tell Marie.

EXTRAORDINARY AS MARIE'S case was—a victim assaulted, then accused—others like it could be found around the country, reflecting, in some police departments, a dismissiveness toward reports of sexual violence that at times crossed into hostility.

For Marie, vindication came through a photograph—an image, captured and saved by her rapist, confirming the truth of Marie's story. For a thirteen-year-old in White Bear Lake, Minnesota, it took video. In 2001, the thirteen-year-old reported being abducted and sexually molested, then dumped at a shopping mall. "You were never there. You never got dropped off there," a police detective told the girl. He told her he had watched surveillance video from the mall, which failed to back up her story.

"You keep lying and lying and lying and lying," he said.

More than a week later, the girl's parents reviewed the mall's surveillance tape for themselves—and discovered footage showing that their daughter had been telling the truth all along.

In Vallejo, California, Denise Huskins, a physical therapist, disappeared from her home in 2015. When she reappeared two days later, police detectives refused to believe her story of having been kidnapped and sexually assaulted, likening her account to the plotline of the best-selling novel *Gone Girl*. The police called her story a hoax, with one lieutenant saying Huskins "owes this community an apology." Several months later the police discovered that Huskins's account was true. They found video of her being sexually assaulted, along with other evidence. A disbarred lawyer who had gone to Harvard pleaded guilty to kidnapping Huskins and was sentenced to forty years. But even after that,

Huskins continued to encounter abuse online, with one man posting on Facebook:

> You are going to hell for the bullshit u have done. . . . Eat shit, whore.

Huskins, in a Facebook post of her own, wrote:

> All I did was survive, and I was criminalized for it.

In the United States, there's no saying how many women have been accused of making a false claim of rape, only to have the claim later proved true. There's no such statistic kept. But even Marie's case—the extreme example where persecution becomes prosecution, where a victim is not only accused of lying, but criminally charged with it—does not stand alone. At least three other cases like it have surfaced in media reports since the 1990s.

In Madison, Wisconsin, a legally blind woman, known as Patty, reported being raped at knifepoint in 1997. But the police didn't think she acted like a rape victim should, according to *Cry Rape*, a book journalist Bill Lueders wrote about the case. The lead detective interrogated her—and deceived her. He made up a story about how the police had tested for latex residue from the supposed rapist's condom, and the test came back negative. (There was no such test.) He told her the nurse had found no sign of injury. (The nurse had.) He confronted Patty about her history of depression and use of Prozac, and questioned just how blind she was. Patty buckled, saying she'd lied, and was charged with obstructing an officer. "What she's being presented with is a world gone mad," her attorney told a judge. "It is truly a Kafkaesque situation. *I'm blind.* No, you're not. *I was raped.* No, you weren't. *There was physical evidence.* No, there wasn't." Only after Patty was charged did police test her bedsheet—and discover semen, after which the charge against her was dismissed. In 2004 a convicted sex offender was tried and found guilty of Patty's rape. A lawsuit that Patty filed against the police was dismissed. But city officials passed a resolution extending Madison's "heartfelt apology and deepest regrets," along with $35,000.

In 1997, the same year Patty was raped, a teenager in New York City was raped on her sixteenth birthday. Detectives in Queens learned that the teenager, Fancy Figueroa, was two weeks pregnant—and assumed her rape claim was pretext. Figueroa, who has since made her identity public, pleaded guilty to false reporting and was sentenced to three days of picking up garbage. In 2003, a DNA check incriminated Figueroa's attacker—a man who had gone on to rape two other teens. He was convicted in 2004 and sentenced to twenty-two years. In the years before her attacker's arrest, Figueroa battled depression and moved to North Carolina in order to get away. "I felt they hurt me more than the rapist hurt me," she said of the two detectives who accused her of lying. "He just came and left, but for six years nobody believed me. I lost my family. I lost my freedom. I lost a little of my sanity." Figueroa's mother described her conflicting emotions to the *New York Daily News*: "I feel happy that Fancy can close a chapter in her life, but to tell the truth I would have liked it better had it turned out she lied. It would have been better that she had never been raped."

In 2004—the year Patty's rapist was convicted in Wisconsin, the year Figueroa's rapist was convicted in New York—a nineteen-year-old named Sara Reedy worked as a gas-station cashier in Cranberry Township, Pennsylvania. Reedy, who was pregnant, was paying her way through college. One night a man robbed the station of about $600 and, at gunpoint, sexually assaulted Reedy. Afterward, at the hospital, a detective interviewed her. "His first question to me was, 'How many times a day do you use dope?'" Reedy would recall later. He accused her of stealing the money and contriving a story of sexual assault as cover. "And he actually went to the extent of saying, 'Your tears won't save you now,' when I finally started crying. It was like a horrible Lifetime movie." Reedy was arrested on charges of theft and false reporting, and spent five days in jail before bailing out. A month before Reedy was to stand trial, a construction worker was arrested while assaulting a woman in a convenience store in Brookville, Pennsylvania. He subsequently confessed to attacking a series of women across the state, including Reedy. The charges against her were dropped. Reedy, who elected to make her identity public, sued the police and received a settlement for $1.5 million.

The dismissiveness at the heart of these cases has long roots. In her 1975 book *Against Our Will: Men, Women and Rape*, Susan Brownmiller described going to a police station in New York's Greenwich Village and asking for rape statistics. The precinct, she learned, had received thirty-five complaints that month—and made two arrests.

"Not a very impressive record," she told a sergeant.

"You know what these complaints represent?" the sergeant told her. "Prostitutes who didn't get their money."

For Brownmiller, the sergeant's attitude reflected something profoundly troubling in law enforcement: "A police officer who does not believe there is such a crime as rape can arrive at only one determination," she wrote.

Recent parallels also abound, cropping up in media accounts and academic literature in the years since Marie was raped. From 2009 to 2014, the Baltimore County Police Department dismissed 34 percent of rape allegations as false or baseless. The percentage itself was troubling enough. More troubling yet was how it was reached. The department often deep-sixed complaints without even taking the elemental step of having a sex crimes detective interview the alleged victim, a *BuzzFeed News* investigation found.

In 2014, a social work professor in Michigan published a study based on interviews with police in a "midsized city in the Great Lakes region." One officer talked of cheating wives who have "been out all night, you know, blah blah blah, 'Oh, I was raped.'" Another said: "We find that girls utilize the rape card to mess with people. . . . They use it to get back at a boyfriend or they need attention, they're having a bad week, you know, 'If I cry rape my whole family will come to me and I need that.'" In 2016, the sheriff in Bingham County, Idaho, told a local television station: "The majority of our rapes—not to say we don't have rapes, we do—but the majority of our rapes that are called in, are actual consensual sex."

MARIE WAS BACK in Puyallup, south of Seattle. Now twenty, approaching twenty-one, she had moved in with a former foster family, the same one she'd been with that first day of high school, back when everything seemed to be falling into place. But now, as then, something went sideways. Marie and the family got into an argument, so Marie moved in with another of her old foster families, who lived down the street.

It was as though Marie had gone back in time, bouncing from foster home to foster home. She was unsettled as ever. She still didn't have her driver's license. Her employment prospects remained limited, as she drifted from one retail job to another. Her life was on loop.

Days after she moved in with her latest family, Marie saw she had a phone message from the Lynnwood police. They said they were looking for her, that they needed to talk. They didn't say why.

Marie flashed back to the call from Sergeant Mason, three days after she had been raped, saying he needed to talk to her. She had the same question now: *Am I in trouble?*

Maybe I missed some court date, she thought. Whatever it was, Marie didn't want the police feeling agitated at having to hunt her down. She could just see them charging through her door with an arrest warrant. So she called them back and provided her new address.

On March 18, they arrived—two years, seven months, and

one week after Marie had been raped. There were three of them: Commander Rider, Sergeant Cohnheim, and a woman who worked as a domestic-violence coordinator, Lynnwood's closest equivalent to a victim's advocate.

They asked if there was a quiet place to talk. Marie walked them to her room and shut the door.

Rider had prepared for this moment. But when the moment came, he didn't know what to say. How do you say: Now, we believe you. Now, we hope you can trust us and work with us and help us bring to justice the man who raped you. Now we want to treat you as a victim to be helped instead of as a liar. He knew that whatever healing Marie had done, "we were just about to rip that wide open."

Asked years later for the words he used, Rider couldn't remember. But he remembered the look on Marie's face. "Stunned," he says. When his words to her registered, she wept, experiencing, all at once, shock, relief, and anger.

They told Marie her record would be erased.

They handed her a check for $500, a refund of her court costs.

They handed her an envelope with information about counseling for rape victims.

The last time Cohnheim had seen Marie was when she had tried to take back her confession to lying. He had watched as Detective Rittgarn threatened her with jail if she failed a polygraph. Seeing Marie again, Cohnheim understood she had been "victimized twice"—first by a rapist, then by his police department.

How can we ever make her whole? he wondered.

He didn't think it was possible.

I HAVE SOMETHING to tell you, Marie said on the phone.

The police just came by, Marie told Shannon. They said the man who raped me has been arrested in Colorado. Now—they believe me.

For Shannon, there could be no simple reaction to this news, no single emotion. Relief, grief, and guilt—all washed over her. O'Leary's arrest meant Marie had been vindicated. It meant Marie had been raped. It meant Marie had been abandoned—"at the most desperate time of her life," Shannon says.

"It's very complicated," Shannon says. "Knowing they caught him and at the same moment knowing it actually happened. That she was raped and nobody believed her, especially the people in her life that had been supporting her, taking care of her, and trying to mend her, help her. And we didn't believe her. It was horrible."

Shannon asked Marie if they could meet. What Shannon had to say, she wanted to say in person.

As they'd done so often together, the two went for a walk in the woods. About a hundred feet down the trail, they stopped. "I was ready to apologize," Shannon says. Shannon told Marie how sorry she was that she hadn't believed her. She apologized for telling Marie she could no longer spend the night. She said she would understand if Marie never forgave her and never talked to her again.

Marie gave Shannon a hug. She told her it was okay, that she forgave her.

There was no "I told you so," no "Why didn't you believe me?" Marie's absolution was immediate and unconditional. "I was just so shocked that she was willing to forgive me for that," Shannon says. "Because it was such a huge thing. It went on for so long."

"I'm a forgiving person," Marie says. "I was born with that, or something. It might take a while to forgive or trust, but I do forgive."

MARIE CALLED WAYNE, her former case manager at Project Ladder.

I knew you weren't lying, Wayne told Marie.

Wayne's words landed with a jolt. Marie didn't know what to say. She had a rush of thoughts—Then why didn't you say something? Why didn't you stick up for me? You were my *case manager*—but left them unspoken.

For Wayne, perhaps it was easier to remember it this way, or to say as much. But his words were belied by what he had written before: His case note, typed one week after the attack, said he didn't believe that Marie had been raped.

MARIE CALLED JORDAN.

Jordan told Marie how sorry he was that all of this had happened to her.

Talking to Jordan, Marie had never wavered, never taken back her account of being raped. And Jordan had never wavered in believing her. Yes, he had considered the possibility she was lying. But he had just as quickly dismissed it. She wasn't that kind of person. Sometimes you just know. "And on top of that, I knew who she was before and I knew who she became after. And they weren't the same, because she was hurt."

But in addition to threatening Marie's freedom, the police had damaged her friendships. They left her believing that Jordan had distrusted her. Jordan told her that wasn't so. Still, she had wondered, nursing doubts about all that had been said outside of her hearing. In the years after, Marie and Jordan had drifted apart.

Marie hadn't read the police's reports, so she didn't know that they made no mention of Jordan doubting her story. Jordan had told Marie the truth: He had not branded her a liar.

MARIE CALLED PEGGY.

"She said she was sorry," Marie says. "She didn't seem like she was in that much of a shock when I said it—like when someone shrugs their shoulders or something."

The muted response disappointed Marie. Marie wanted something more from Peggy, but Peggy—initially, at least—was unable to give it. She didn't want to reflect on her role, knowing where her thoughts would lead. Marie's settlement with Shannon had been clean: Both Shannon's apology and Marie's forgiveness were unreserved. With Peggy, the reckoning would be complicated. Years later Peggy would not remember for sure how she learned of O'Leary's arrest. Maybe Shannon told her, even before Marie called. Or maybe it was Peggy's mom who broke the news. Peggy does remember her mom cutting out an article about O'Leary's capture and giving it to her. "There was still so much guilt attached to it that I sort of put it over here and said, okay, yes, this really did happen. But it's still really painful to acknowledge it.

"I think there was a lot of denial on my part," Peggy says. "It was just so painful. I . . . I knew when I heard all the evidence that it was true. But it was still just horrifying that it really did happen. And that I was involved in not believing her."

In time, Peggy would look back with deep regret on the call she had made, telling the police she doubted Marie's story. "I feel that if I would have shut my mouth, they would have done their job instead of relying on what was just my attempt to be very honest with them," she says.

"I was trying to be a good citizen, actually. You know? I didn't want them to waste their resources on something that might be this personal drama going on.

"I should have known better. You should always believe the victim until proved otherwise. That was a mistake I made. I did make that mistake. And I'm very sorry for it."

Peggy would reach out to Marie—and offer something more than she had in that first phone call, something akin to Shannon's walk in the woods. "Eventually we did have a sit-down dinner and I took her out and I apologized to her for not believing her. We tried to have a heart-to-heart about it. And I know that it took her still a little bit longer to forgive me. We have a decent relationship now, but it took a long time."

MARIE TOLD THE Lynnwood police she wanted an apology—not from the department itself, and not from some higher-up speaking on the department's behalf.

She wanted an apology from the detectives who hadn't believed her.

On the appointed day, Marie went into a conference room at the Lynnwood police station and waited. From Rittgarn, she would receive no apology. He was now in Southern California, working as a private investigator. His LinkedIn profile said he did surveillance for divorce and workers' compensation cases. He also did contract work for the federal government, conducting background employment investigations, according to his profile.

Mason, though, was still there. He came into the conference room, looking "like a lost little puppy," Marie says. "He was rubbing his head and literally looked like he was ashamed about what they had done." He told Marie he was sorry—"deeply sorry," Marie says. To Marie, he seemed sincere.

His apology helped—"a little bit," she says. "You can't go back two and a half years and fix all I had to go through. An apology doesn't really fix that."

Marie could have used this meeting to delve into the reasons Mason hadn't believed her. But she couldn't bring herself to ask—because, she says, "I don't know if I'd want the answer."

15

$327\frac{1}{2}$

Bob Weiner's phone buzzed at seven o'clock one March morning. He was standing on the side of a soccer field in a suburb west of Denver, watching his daughter squeeze in a scrimmage before school. Detective Stacy Galbraith was calling.

"Oh my God, you don't know what we just found," she began. They had discovered another victim of O'Leary's predations. She described how Evans had found the photos of Marie in Washington, bound, gagged, and terrified.

"You will never believe this," she finished. "She was prosecuted for false reporting."

"You're kidding me," Weiner said.

It was the latest twist in a case that Weiner considered one of the most horrific in his fifteen-year career at the Jefferson County district attorney's office. Weiner was one of the most senior prosecutors in the office, which covered two counties west of Denver. Prosecutors and cops don't always get along—to cops, prosecutors can be too picky; to prosecutors, the cops can play fast with the rules. None of that had happened in this case. Galbraith and Weiner had been in contact almost since the beginning. They had talked frequently during the six-week hunt, consulting each other over search warrants and the timing of O'Leary's arrest.

With O'Leary locked up, Weiner had turned his attention to building his case. Galbraith and Hendershot had done what

Weiner called a "fantastic, unbelievable investigation." But O'Leary was facing life in prison. With the stakes so high, it seemed unlikely he would take a plea. The state's case had to withstand every attack the defense could mount and convince a jury to convict. As Weiner reviewed the facts, he saw holes. "It wasn't ready for trial," he said.

At first, he worried about the physical similarities between Marc and Michael. Any good defense attorney would try to raise reasonable doubt by arguing that Michael O'Leary had been the actual rapist. Perhaps Michael had carried out the attacks, while his doppelgänger brother ran his pornographic website empire? "We need to alibi the brother," he told Galbraith and Hendershot. He had Galbraith pull every time card from the furniture store where Michael O'Leary worked as a delivery truck driver, all the way back to August 2008. No luck. Michael hadn't been on the job when most of the incidents took place.

Hendershot and Ellis pitched in to help Weiner, launching what they called "Project Mazda." Hendershot pulled up every registration in Colorado of a 1993 white Mazda pickup. There were seventy-seven. She gathered ten patrol officers from Westminster and began sending them all over the state to take pictures of the trucks. The strategy was simple: If the defense tried to argue that the white Mazda on the videotape from Amber's attack was different from O'Leary's, Weiner would pull up pictures of every Mazda in Colorado. Only O'Leary's truck would match.

But the discovery of the pictures in the memory cards from O'Leary's cameras—of Amber, of Sarah, and now of Marie— brought the officers' travels to a halt. Weiner would view the images in his office, his screen turned away from his door to prevent passersby from seeing them. Although the photos did not show O'Leary's face, they did show his birthmark. Weiner even had a crime scene technician do a comparison of the moles on O'Leary's body with the ones visible on the body of the rapist.

The mole map, with lines and arrows connecting similar marks, showed that Marc and the attacker were the same. Weiner knew he had O'Leary. There was no need to worry about mistaken identity. "Once we found the photographs it was like, 'Okay.'"

Weiner had one more concern about the images. He asked Galbraith and Hendershot to check O'Leary's porn sites, to see whether he had posted any of the photos. One morning, the two women met at the FBI's regional headquarters in Stapleton, a neighborhood built on the site of Denver's old airport. In a long, low room filled with computers, they sat down back to back, each facing a terminal screen. They began to search every website that O'Leary owned, or even that he linked to.

"We looked at porn all day," Galbraith says.

"All day. All day," Hendershot adds. "We literally looked at, honest to God, porn all day long."

"Gross stuff," Galbraith says.

In the end, they did not find any images of the victims. They couldn't rule out that the photos might be posted in some dark corner of the Internet. But at least they could tell the women that they had found no evidence that O'Leary carried out his threats. It brought a measure of peace of mind to the victims—and to Weiner.

The son of an FBI agent, Weiner had been involved in some of the biggest rape and murder cases in the region. In the courtroom, he cut a striking figure, seeming to vibrate with intensity. He was tall, thin, with a high forehead and the ropy build of a long-distance runner—which is exactly what he was. Weiner ran marathons. For practice, he'd jog through the high mountains that surrounded his home in a Denver suburb perched in the Rockies some 7,000 feet above sea level. At forty-two, he'd finished the Boston Marathon at 2:31:20, second in his age division. He was so good that he was sponsored by a running shoe manufacturer.

Running gave him clarity. It helped free his mind from the

haunting images of the victims, and allowed him to focus on the mechanics of the case. And there was much to think about—even with the pictures in hand.

Weiner worried, for instance, about the amount of time that passed during each rape. Each woman had endured three or four hours of abuse. "The typical juror is going to sit there and think, 'Well, she didn't yell. Why didn't you scream? Why didn't you fight? You could have easily gotten away.'" And he worried that O'Leary had such detailed knowledge of each victim. The jurors might wonder: Did she know this guy?

Those kinds of concerns hinder many rape investigations. Researchers call it "downstreaming"—the tendency of each person in the investigative chain to think about how the rape accusation will look to the next person to examine it. It begins with the victim—her fears about whether she might be judged by the cops about the length of her dress, or the number of tequila shots she drank. It next infects the police, who wonder what the prosecutor will think of a case with no physical evidence, only one person's word against another's. And finally it extends to the prosecutor, who must ponder how a juror will perceive a woman's testimony. Doubt afflicted every stage of a rape prosecution.

Weiner believed he could prove the facts of the case—he had actual pictures of the rapist committing the crime, after all. But the skepticism attached to rape victims made a trial no easy thing. He was particularly concerned about the women O'Leary had attacked, who would have to serve as witnesses. How would they hold up? They would face hostile questioning. They would endure having painful, intimate details of the attacks splayed before a courtroom of strangers and written up in the press. They would take the witness stand with O'Leary sitting only a few feet away. In the end, would they agree to testify?

The trial was set for October 2011. Weiner knew he had to prepare. After all, he was not only battling O'Leary's defense. He was also up against hundreds of years of legal history.

MARIE'S CASE CONCERNED one police department, which bungled one investigation, which led one court to hold her a liar. But her experience was no aberration. When it comes to reports of rape, the criminal justice system has long embraced the "cherished male assumption that female persons tend to lie," as Susan Brownmiller once wrote. In courtrooms throughout America, the historical default setting has been doubt.

The jurist with the greatest impact on our legal system's response to rape allegations lived four centuries ago. Sir Matthew Hale, a contemporary of Oliver Cromwell and Charles II, became Lord Chief Justice of England in 1671. He was "by far the most renowned and respected judge of the time," one account says. In legal circles, his name became venerated. A biographer wrote in 1835: "So resplendent, in short, were his excellencies, that, to this day, if an instance of *singular* virtue and uprightness, especially in the legal profession, is to be adduced, the mind turns as instantly to Lord Hale, as the needle to the pole." Language equally fulsome can be found in accounts written since.

Hale, known for his piety, integrity, and sober judgment, wrote a massive, two-volume criminal law treatise, *The History of the Pleas of the Crown.* He called rape "a most detestable crime," then added words quoted many times hence: "It must be remembered, that it is an accusation easy to be made and hard to be proved, and harder to be defended by the party accused, tho never so innocent."

Hale evoked the fear of the false accuser—which has roots even in the Bible, where Potiphar's wife, rejected by Joseph, accuses him of rape—and made for that fear a legal frame. He described two cases of men he believed to have been wrongly accused, one by a fourteen-year-old girl with designs of blackmail. Jurors, Hale wrote, should consider: Is the woman claiming rape of "good fame"—or "evil fame"? Did she cry out? Try to flee?

Make immediate complaint afterward? Does she stand supported by others? Judges and jurors must be vigilant, Hale wrote, lest the crime's heinousness fuel them "with so much indignation, that they are over-hastily carried on to the conviction of the person accused thereof by the confident testimony, sometimes of malicious and false witnesses."

The English judge was full of advice, even beyond the law. He wrote a letter to his young grandchildren, 182 pages long, prescribing counsel for each. For Mary: "If she cannot govern the greatness of her spirit, it will make her proud, imperious, and revengeful . . ." For Frances: "If she be kept in some awe, especially in relation to lying and deceiving, she will make a good woman and a good housewife." As for Ann, he perceived a "soft nature," and therefore forbade plays, ballads, or melancholy books, "for they will make too deep an impression upon her mind."

Hale, in his letter, shudders at the world around: "The whole constitution of the people of this kingdom is corrupted into debauchery, drunkenness, gluttony, whoring, gaming, profuseness, and the most foolish, sottish prodigality imaginable . . ." He especially despises what has become of young women: They "learn to be bold" and "talk loud." They "make it their business to paint or patch their faces, to curl their locks, and to find out the newest and costliest fashions. If they rise in the morning before ten of the clock, the morning is spent between the comb, and the glass, and the box of patches; though they know not how to make provision for it themselves, they must have choice diet provided for them . . ." His complaint continues, with one sentence lasting 160 words. Hale was married twice. There was gossip his first wife cheated; he was mocked as a "great cuckold." He refers to English gentlewomen as "the ruin of families."

"There is . . . evidence that Sir Matthew Hale might have been somewhat below the norm for the times in terms of his views of women," Gilbert Geis and Ivan Bunn write in their book, *A Trial of Witches*. The book details an event that blotted Hale's legacy, "be it only so slightly." In 1662, at Bury St. Edmunds, Hale presided at the trial of two elderly women accused of witchcraft. He instructed the jury that witches were real, saying Scripture had affirmed as much. Upon the jury's verdict of guilty, Hale sentenced Amy Denny and Rose Cullender to hang. (He had condemned another convicted witch four years before.) Thirty years later, Hale's handling of this trial, preserved in written record, served as a model in Massachusetts. "Indeed, the Salem witch-hunts might not have taken place if there had not been a trial at Bury St. Edmunds: the events at Salem notoriously imitated those at Bury," Geis and Bunn write.

Hale's influence upon witchcraft trials would expire as belief in witches waned. But his influence on rape cases would endure. As long as three hundred years after Hale's death in 1676, many a jury in the United States would be cautioned with his words. Courts called it the "Hale Warning": an instruction to jurors in rape trials to be wary of the false accusation, hard to be defended and easily made.

ON DECEMBER 16, 1786, Thomas Jefferson, while away in Paris, penned a letter to James Madison. He complained of a dislocated right wrist—"the swelling does not abate"—permitting him to write only with "great pain." He wrote of setting out soon for the South of France, in hopes the mineral waters there would heal. He wrote of commerce—fish, flour, turpentine, tobacco—between the United States and France. Then, almost in passing, he wrote of his opposition toward harsh punishment for rape, "on account of the temptation women would be under to make it the instrument of vengeance against an inconstant lover, and of disappointment to a rival."

The man who had authored the Declaration of Independence was writing to the man who would author the Bill of Rights—to warn of the woman scorned, crying rape.

Seven years later, a criminal prosecution in New York City captured how the early American legal system used Lord Hale's criteria to undermine a woman's credibility. Henry Bedlow stood trial in 1793, accused of raping Lanah Sawyer. Bedlow was an aristocrat, described in annals as a "libertine" and "rake." Sawyer was a seventeen-year-old seamstress, daughter of a seaman. The two met when Sawyer, taking a summer stroll, was harassed on the street and Bedlow interceded. He gave a false name, telling Sawyer he was a lawyer named Smith. She agreed to accompany him days later on a nighttime walk. On that night, Bedlow pulled her into a brothel and raped her, she said. He said he seduced her.

At trial, five defense lawyers spoke on Bedlow's behalf. One warned the twelve men of the jury that this case put "the life of a citizen in the hands of a woman, to be disposed of almost at her will and pleasure." Another said: "Any woman [who] is not an abandoned prostitute will appear to be averse to what she inwardly desires." A third asked how a "sewing girl" could imagine a lawyer paying her any attention "unless with a view of promoting illicit commerce." She walked with him late into the night. "Is it probable that a girl who had thus abandoned the outworks of her chastity, and left every pass to it unguarded, would be long in surrendering the citadel?"

The defense attorney who spoke the longest was Henry Brockholst Livingston, who would later be named to the US Supreme Court. (He was appointed by Thomas Jefferson.) Addressing the jury, Livingston quoted Hale—"an accusation easy to be made"—and applied Hale's prescribed inquiry to Lanah Sawyer. Was she of good fame? Although "a cloud of witnesses" said she was, "she may have had the art to carry a fair outside, while all was foul within," Livingston told the jury. She said she screamed. But did she also stamp her feet? And why, upon agreeing to stop for ice cream, did she draw the night out? "Instead of taking a single glass of ice cream, and returning, as would a girl jealous of her reputation, she stays with him here a full hour and [a] half." Livingston argued that Sawyer made up the story of being raped upon finding that Bedlow had no further occasion for her. "You all know how strong the passion of revenge exists in a female breast; a deserted woman sets no bounds to her anger."

The trial lasted fifteen hours. The jury deliberated fifteen minutes. The verdict was "not guilty."

THE TWENTIETH CENTURY'S leading expert in the field of evidence was John Henry Wigmore. A mustachioed scholar, accomplished in twelve languages, he helped found the *Harvard Law Review* and served as dean of Northwestern University's law school for twenty-eight years. Law professors and students call his masterwork *Wigmore on Evidence*, which is easier to say than *A Treatise on the Anglo-American System of Evidence in Trials at Common Law: Including the Statutes and Judicial Decisions of All Jurisdictions of the United States and Canada.* A University of Chicago law professor called Wigmore's tome "perhaps the greatest modern legal treatise," saying its analysis forms "the very structure of the law of evidence today."

Wigmore also read up on psychiatry and psychology, becoming "the best legal friend that psychology had." In cases where women alleged rape, he urged psychiatry's merger with the law. In his treatise's third edition—what became his final, authoritative version, published in 1940—Wigmore expanded on some language he had written in the 1930s on women and credibility. He took the notion expressed by Henry Brockholst Livingston a century and a half before—*fair outside, while all was foul within*—and added Sigmund Freud.

Modern psychiatrists have amply studied the behavior of errant young girls and women coming before the courts in all sorts of cases. Their psychic complexes are multifarious, distorted partly by inherent defects, partly by diseased derangements or abnormal instincts, partly by bad social environment, partly by temporary physiological or emotional conditions. One form taken by these complexes is that of contriving false charges of sexual offenses by men. The unchaste (let us call it) mentality finds incidental but direct expression in the narration of imaginary sex incidents of which the narrator is the heroine or the victim. On the surface the narration is straightforward and convincing. The real victim, however, too often in such cases is the innocent man . . .

To summarize: She imagined it.

"No doubt," Wigmore wrote, every judge and prosecutor had seen cases of this.

Henceforth, he wrote: "No judge should ever let a sex offense charge go to the jury unless the female complainant's social history and mental makeup have been examined and testified to by a qualified physician."

Wigmore died in 1943. Forty years later, Leigh Bienen—then a public defender, later a faculty member at Wigmore's Northwestern University—examined the scientific source materials upon which Wigmore built his argument and found them wanting. But despite Wigmore's dubious research and "repressive and misogynist position," his views remained influential with lawyers and judges. "If there is a single source of the law's concern with false reports in sex offense cases, it is the Wigmore doctrine," Bienen wrote.

For women alleging rape, the doctrine's core premise—"she imagined it"—was simply another variation of "she wanted it," a presumption long voiced in courts and legal literature. "Although the woman never said 'yes,' nay, more, although she constantly said 'no,' and kept up a decent show of resistance to the last, it may still be that she more than half consented to the ravishment,"

Greene Carrier Bronson, a New York Supreme Court justice, wrote in 1842. In 1952, a *Yale Law Journal* article said that "many women" require "aggressive overtures by the man. Often their erotic pleasure may be enhanced by, or even depend upon, an accompanying physical struggle."

In the 1970s and '80s, the feminist movement generated powerful pushback, helping reform rape laws around the country. While Marty Goddard and Susan Irion helped institute rape kits and trauma training, legislatures adopted rape-shield statutes—restricting evidence about a rape accuser's sexual history—as courts abandoned jury instructions that used the language of Sir Matthew Hale.

As some legal commentators have noted, the repudiation of Hale was about three centuries late. His words aren't true now: When most rapes go unreported, the accusation cannot be considered "easy to be made." But his words weren't true then, either. The era offered plenty of examples of women made to suffer for coming forward. In 1670, two indentured servants in Virginia accused their master of rape; for this, they were punished with extra years of servitude. In the early 1700s, in trials seven years apart, two women in Maine reported being raped. One received an admonition for public rudeness, the other fifteen strips for lewdness.

And though Hale may have faded, his legacy yet lurks. In 2007—one year before Marie reported being raped—a state legislator in Maryland, a criminal defense attorney who chaired the House Judiciary Committee, invoked Hale's warning during a hearing on whether to deny parental rights to rapists whose victims conceive. The lawmaker, Joseph Vallario Jr., said he quoted Hale as a history lesson. But his words caused "outrage," according to a headline in the *Washington Post*. A Maryland anti-rape advocacy group criticized Vallario for citing "archaic and misogynistic doctrine." The law didn't pass. Ten years later, when state delegate Kathleen Dumais tried for the ninth time to push the measure through, an all-male panel drawn from both houses of the legislature let the bill die, leaving Maryland as one of sixteen states that does not allow a rape victim to terminate the parental rights of her attacker.

ONE MORNING IN July, Weiner got a phone call from O'Leary's public defender, Jeffry Dougan, a young trial lawyer with three years' experience. Dougan brought a message from O'Leary.

"My guy wants to plead guilty. He wants to get it over with. He doesn't want to put the victims through this," Weiner recalled Dougan saying. Dougan had advised O'Leary against taking a plea, but O'Leary was insistent. There was only one condition. Weiner had to drop all of the charges pertaining to kidnapping.

O'Leary's request surprised Weiner. But he figured he knew the reason for it. And it wasn't a sudden change of heart.

Weiner knew that O'Leary was nervous. In a recorded jail phone call, O'Leary had told his mother that he thought the detectives were going to find stuff on his computer. He just wasn't sure how much.

He found out when Weiner had turned over discovery to O'Leary's public defender. Contrary to the gotcha moments in courtroom dramas, the justice system frowns on surprises. To allow for investigation before trial, each side must show the other certain evidence it is prepared to present. Weiner had recently provided Dougan with the photos Evans had recovered, alerting O'Leary for the first time that police had managed to salvage images of him—or at least a person with his exact body marks— raping women. Images that he thought were safely locked behind layers of unbreakable computer encryption.

Now, he was exposed.

Still, Weiner didn't understand what O'Leary would get out of the deal. Even if Weiner dropped the kidnapping charges, O'Leary would still face life in prison. There would be no reduction in his sentence. So what was the point? Why not fight it out, no matter how overwhelming the evidence—what, after all, did you have to lose? "It was unusual," Weiner says. "But it was an unusual case as well." Weiner figured it was something psychologically important. Maybe O'Leary could accept being a rapist. But not a kidnapper.

Whatever the reason, Weiner figured he might have some leverage. Like Evans, Weiner had become obsessed with the Wretch, the encrypted file from O'Leary's computer. Weiner wasn't tech savvy—he called the computer file a "container." But he knew that anybody who'd gone to that much trouble to conceal its contents had something worth hiding. He wasn't sure just what. Could there be other women, other rapes? Or evidence of some kind of secret club of men who raped women and swapped pictures? Was there child pornography?

He needed to know what was inside.

"I'm thinking it's pretty bad," he says.

Weiner called Dougan back with a counteroffer. He would consider a plea deal—but O'Leary had to turn over the password to the Wretch. Dougan got back to him quickly: unequivocally no. The speed and surety of the response heightened Weiner's suspicions. It "told me that there was something pretty significant there," he says. Galbraith shared the news with Hendershot, Burgess, and Hassell in an email on July 7, 2011: "O'Leary WILL NOT give up the encryption code. PERIOD."

Though O'Leary wouldn't give up his secret, Weiner believed he still had the terms of a good deal: Drop the kidnapping charges in return for the guilty plea. Before he signed off, Weiner consulted with the victims, one by one, in his office.

Each woman had a different reaction. Doris was hesitant to drop any charges. She had no fear of a trial. "She's really tough, like, 'I'm not afraid of this guy,'" Weiner recalled. Amber was nervous that news of the case might reach her friends and family.

Sarah was still emotionally blasted, ready to take the deal. And Lilly was distrustful. She was upset at Hassell—if he had investigated her case more thoroughly, he might have stopped the rapes in Golden and Westminster.

Weiner described to the women what the process ahead would entail if the case proceeded to trial. The public testimony. The tough cross-examination. The possibility that O'Leary might try to influence their mental states through words or gestures at trial. "Sex offenders are the biggest manipulators of human beings that there are," he warned.

At times, the law could seem not to care much for victims. In the strictest legal sense, these crimes had been committed against the state, not the four women. Weiner would give great consideration to their concerns, but he was under no obligation to follow their desires—his client was the public. And O'Leary was innocent until proven guilty. The judge and the attorneys would give deference to his right to a fair trial. "Oftentimes, you will be frustrated because it appears that the focus is not on you, but it's on the offender," Weiner told the four women. "Rest assured, it's not lost on us."

Eventually, each of the women agreed: take the plea. Weiner thought it for the best. It would spare them the indignities of trial. And O'Leary would still face a long time in prison—his ultimate sentence to be determined by a judge.

Before Weiner signed off on the deal, he asked once more. Would O'Leary give him the password?

Once more, the answer came back: no.

O'LEARY'S SENTENCING WAS held on a freezing day in early December at the towering, curvilinear Jefferson County district courthouse. You could see its sparkling glass dome from the apartment complex where O'Leary had raped Amber almost a year earlier. It was easy to imagine that O'Leary had glanced at it, looming against snow-covered Rockies, during the hundreds of hours he stalked the graduate student.

The small gray-and-brown courtroom brimmed with people. Galbraith, Hendershot, Burgess, and Grusing were there. So were Ellis and Shimamoto. Lilly and Doris sat on one side. O'Leary's mother, stepfather, and sister sat on the other. O'Leary sat up front, at a long, shiny table directly in front of the judge. He had close-cropped hair, a black shirt, and a thick brown security belt. His long, pale face contorted violently every few minutes—a nervous tic that had the effect of squeezing all his facial features together toward his nose.

Judge Philip McNulty sat up front. White hair framed his bald pate. In fifteen years on the bench, he had earned a reputation for fairness, compassion, and a preternaturally calm demeanor. He would one day be appointed the district court's chief judge. McNulty called the court to order. *The People of the State of Colorado v. Marc O'Leary* had begun.

Weiner spoke first. He painted a picture of a cool, methodical sociopath bent on increasing violence. He described how O'Leary had started with Doris in Aurora. How he failed with Lilly in Lakewood. How he bought a gun after stealing cash from Sarah's Westminster apartment. How he threatened Amber with a similar-looking gun in Golden. This was a man who treated rape as a job—a job he said he loved. This was a man who should be put away forever. The way Weiner figured it, O'Leary deserved a minimum of 294 years.

The night before, Weiner had provided the judge with blown-up photos of the victims, partially redacted to protect their privacy. "Look at the faces of those victims, the pain and the torture that they went through. What he took from these women and the manner in which he took them can never, ever be replaced," he told McNulty.

At the time of his arrest, O'Leary had been planning another attack in another Denver suburb, Weiner told the judge. Investigators had found his surveillance notes. "Like a wolf, he was a predator," Weiner said.

O'Leary's victims went next. Galbraith and Hendershot read statements from Amber and Sarah.

The rape changed her, Amber's statement said. She installed three locks on her door. She fastened them the moment she came home. She used to sleep with her windows open to catch the summer breeze. Now they were always closed. Holidays churned up terrible memories. Colors she once loved—the colors she had decorated her bedroom with—now reminded her of the rape. "I'm still in the process of forgetting this incident and moving on, but I am lucky to a point that the person who did this has been found," she wrote. "I don't need to live in fear anymore."

Sarah had just been getting back on her feet when the attack happened. Her husband had died. She had moved into a new apartment. The rape stole even more from her. She thought her phone was tapped. She believed hackers had infiltrated her email. She became frightened when she saw an upstairs neighbor with a similar build to the man who raped her. She called them the "losses in her life"—loss of freedom and safety, loss of trust, loss of a sense of peace. "This event has not defeated me. I was knocked down temporarily, but I'm back on my feet again. I may not do all of the things that I like to do. I'm much more vigilant, but I'm still alive and I'm living my life."

When Hendershot finished reading Sarah's statement, she turned to McNulty. She had an unusual request, one she'd made only a few times in her career. Could she offer a comment of her own? The judge said yes.

Hendershot turned to the bench, but kept her gaze on O'Leary, hoping to catch his eye. "Sir, this crime has had a profound impact on my life, both personally and professionally," she said. "Mr. O'Leary demonstrated a level of arrogance and disdain that is incomprehensible. With each assault there was no recognition of society's values and no ethical or moral compass." Hendershot asked the judge to put O'Leary away for life.

The women O'Leary had attacked in Lakewood and Aurora rose to speak. Lilly told the judge that she was a spiritual person, dedicated to prayer and worship and service to all of creation. But after the attack, she struggled to find that self. She couldn't be alone in her home. She had violent thoughts. She withdrew from friends. She hired armed guards to protect her home. She racked up medical bills for tens of thousands of dollars. She had no insurance. Collection agencies called constantly. People showed up at her door in search of payment. "I had trouble sleeping. I had a lot of nightmares. I had a lot of trauma," she said.

She told the judge that she believed O'Leary needed help. She called him a "confused human being." But she also thought he needed to go to prison for life. By speaking for justice, the women he had attacked were triumphing over his savagery, Lilly told McNulty. "I'm recovering, everyone is recovering. It has—you know, it's created changes. We're doing the best to reinvent our lives."

Doris, now sixty-seven, stood next. The fraternity house-mother recounted the terror she felt during the attack. Afterward, she purchased a security system. She armed the alarm each time she showered. She described repeated trips to her doctor's office to take tests to make sure she hadn't been infected with HIV. "Each time the wait for the results brought a scary, anxious, uneasy feeling." Outwardly, she had resumed a normal life. But her psyche still needed repair. "No one would come out of this emotionally unscathed," she told the court.

Near the end of her statement, Doris turned to O'Leary—and asked him, directly, how he had found her. "Why were you in Aurora? Do you have a friend or relative in my neighborhood that I should be worried about? Is there any reason I should still be afraid?

"How did I make myself so vulnerable?" she asked the man who had raped her.

FOR THE DEFENSE, the first to speak was Marc O'Leary.

"I'm standing here because I need to be in prison," he began. "I know that probably more than any person in this room. I've known it for a while.

"I am a sexually violent predator and I'm out of control."

He wanted to apologize, O'Leary told the court. And he wanted to explain.

He described suffering periodic, uncontrollable urges to attack women. He had struggled against them ever since childhood. He had a loving family, a lucky existence. "I was, for lack of a better word, enslaved to something I've detested my entire life; and yet I was, you know, unable to disobey in the end, and in the end, I lost. And I lost more than my own life in the process. I've destroyed many others.

"I don't know what caused it," he said. O'Leary didn't cite Jung. He didn't cite the duality theosophy in his books on the occult. He kept it simple. "It sounds cliché, I guess, but it's really kind of an actual Dr. Jekyll and Mr. Hyde in real life."

O'Leary told McNulty he didn't expect pity. But he hoped people could understand—if not him, then others like him. "A lot of people would describe me as a monster," he said. "Things are a lot more complicated than that."

O'Leary turned to Doris, to answer her questions. He found her name on a social-networking site, he said. That was it. She had no reason to be afraid of anyone in her neighborhood. "The terrible reality of it is that, you know, it was—for me it was just an opportunity, which is disgusting, and I know that, but that's—you know, that's the truth.

"You didn't do anything to me."

As O'Leary spoke, his mother sat and listened. She believed

that Marc was guilty. But she had never heard him talk about the secret tortures of his childhood. Never heard him say he felt like two people. Never heard him describe hunting women.

Sheri Shimamoto sat just behind O'Leary's mother. She noticed that the mother held several sheets of paper. Shimamoto assumed it was the statement she planned to give, extolling his good qualities and asking for mercy. As O'Leary described his crimes, Shimamoto watched his mother crumple the paper into a ball.

When she stood to address the courtroom, O'Leary's mother said she had been stunned by her eldest son's arrest. Marc had been a happy kid—talkative, playful, an animal lover. "Had I known or had any clue at all over the years that he was suffering inside and needed help, there's nothing we wouldn't have done to get him help. . . . But, you know, we just didn't see anything." Perhaps it had to do with his time in the military. He seemed a different person after his discharge, she said, darker and more withdrawn. She thought he might have a mental illness and hoped he would get help in prison.

She shared with the court pain from her own past. She herself was a rape victim, attacked at a party when she was fifteen. It was 1963. Nobody talked about sex. Nobody talked about rape. She had discussed the incident with her daughter, but never Michael nor Marc. She regretted it now. Perhaps it would have opened a discussion. She told the victims she understood what they had suffered. She asked for mercy for her son. And for herself. "As a mother, I've heard people say, 'You can't blame yourself for this.' Why, why can't I blame myself? I'm his mother, I raised him; if it wasn't something I did, then it was probably something I didn't do."

Dougan, O'Leary's attorney, addressed the judge. By Dougan's calculation, McNulty could sentence O'Leary to a minimum of twenty-six years. He, too, asked for mercy.

Now, it was the judge's turn.

"Mr. O'Leary, let me address you first," McNulty began. "You indicated that people might hate you, consider you a monster. It's not my job to vilify you. It's not my job to judge you. It is my job to judge your actions."

McNulty noted that the charges against O'Leary could produce a broad range of sentences. He gave O'Leary credit for his lack of a prior criminal record and for showing remorse. "I believe that you are sincere when you make those statements," McNulty said.

The judge then ticked off the evidence against O'Leary. The stalking. The rape tools. The terror inflicted. "The most damning evidence in this case is the evidence you created," he told O'Leary. "These are pictures of women being raped and you taking those pictures while they're being raped, and I—I looked at those women's faces and I saw anguish and fear, despair and hopelessness. And I thought, if you're looking at that, how can anybody push the button to take the picture?"

To reach an appropriate sentence, McNulty weighed O'Leary's crimes in light of others he had judged. McNulty had never seen anything so abhorrent.

"Sir, you hunted the victims in this case like they were your prey, and then you exercised dominion over them for hours and forced them to do unspeakable acts," he said, his voice low and steady. "Your actions in this case were pure evil."

McNulty told O'Leary that he'd lost his privilege to be in free society. He would assess the maximum possible penalty.

The sentence: 327½ years in prison.

O'Leary would never get out.

A FEW DAYS later, back in his cell at the imposing, razor-wired intake center for the Colorado Department of Corrections, O'Leary made an unusual offer. He agreed to discuss his crimes with the investigators, without a lawyer present. He wanted to help the victims get closure, he said. There was one caveat: He would not talk if Galbraith were in attendance. A woman, he said, would make him uncomfortable.

Grusing volunteered for the job. In the ten months since the arrest, cops had turned up evidence of at least one other sexual assault in Washington clearly linked to O'Leary. But they had failed to connect him to any other crimes. The rapes in Kansas had been a dead end—and would remain unsolved. The Wretch stayed sealed. Grusing wasn't sure what he would get out of O'Leary. But an FBI polygrapher had given him a tip once: *The more and longer they talk, the better it is for us.* That was Grusing's goal. Get O'Leary talking.

A week after the sentencing hearing, at 11:15 a.m. on December 15, 2011, Grusing found himself sitting across from O'Leary in a narrow white cinder-block cell lined with black square acoustic tiles. Grusing wore a blue polo shirt, green pants, and hiking shoes. O'Leary was in a red jumpsuit, open at the neck to reveal a white T-shirt beneath. His hair was shaved close to his head. He wore black tennis shoes, the laces removed to prevent him from hanging himself. His face contorted constantly, his features squeezing in, then returning to normal.

O'Leary crossed his arms as Grusing sat down. He was reluctant to talk, he told Grusing. He'd had second thoughts. He'd been treated badly in lockup. A guard had threatened to put him in solitary confinement. "I'm not in a talkative mood right now," he said.

Once again, Grusing had come prepared. He had studied how O'Leary had learned from every attack. How meticulous he had been. How hard he worked to conceal his trail. Here, thought Grusing, was a man with pride in his work. A man who would be flattered by the opportunity to demonstrate his expertise. "You're a very important person, you're a very accomplished rapist weirdo and we would like to study you," was how Grusing had conceived of his pitch. He made O'Leary an offer. Perhaps he would welcome the chance to talk with a profiler from the agency's famed Behavioral Analysis Unit?

O'Leary shifted in his seat. "There's a lot to talk about," he said.

Over the next four hours, O'Leary went on nonstop, a scholar monologuing on rape tactics to a single, seemingly rapt pupil. Grusing would lean forward, scribble on a legal pad at times, and occasionally share tidbits of the cops' investigation. It didn't take much to keep O'Leary going.

"It was like I'd just eaten Thanksgiving dinner," he said of one attack, kicking back in his chair.

As he described each rape, he lingered on details. Doris had chastened him. "I left before I think I normally would have left, because [she] had said a couple of things that sort of hit me." He downplayed his talk about wolves and bravos with Amber as "bullshit." "The conversation and stuff was basically just to fill in the gaps" between his attacks, he said. "In a different situation, had we met on different terms, we might have gotten along." He expressed his deepest regret about Sarah. He attacked her after failing with Lilly. "She got me at my worst," he said.

He admired Lilly's split-second decision to flee. "I was kind of pissed. But at the same time, I was cracking up. Smart girl. She had one chance and she took it." O'Leary told Grusing a story about something that happened before he attacked Lilly, back when he was still doing surveillance. One night he had been standing on a chair, peeking into her window, when he heard a noise. What the hell is that? he wondered. He looked up. On the roof, just above him, a gray fox was staring at him. O'Leary gestured at the fox to scare it away. The fox didn't move. O'Leary decided to retreat. As he walked toward his truck, though, the fox followed him. It waited while he got in, and didn't leave until he began to drive off. He thought Lilly might actually have an animal protector. "There's a lot more to this world than most of us realize," O'Leary told Grusing.

O'Leary let spill lessons for law enforcement. He described the countermeasures he'd taken to avoid the police. He knew that the Army had a sample of his DNA. He worried that the cops might be able to access that record and identify him. So he took steps to avoid leaving genetic traces. He told Grusing that he knew, in the end, it was an impossible task. "You can't beat the technology," he said.

He brought up the moment when Grusing and another cop had knocked on the door of 65 Harlan Street and found him home. Grusing had handed him a sketch of a dummy burglary suspect. O'Leary had thought it was a subterfuge to collect his fingerprints. He grabbed the laminated paper anyway. He felt safe. He always wore gloves. "There's no way I left prints," he had thought to himself.

He realized that police departments often did not communicate. And so he deliberately committed each rape in a different jurisdiction. "It's basically to kind of, you know, keep you guys off of my trail, I guess, for as long as possible." It had worked well in Washington. The cops in Lynnwood had missed their chance, he said. "If Washington had just paid attention a little bit more, I probably would have been a person of interest earlier on."

He urged cops to track the geography of suspicious-persons reports. By the time a rape happened, it was too late to go search for a predator. His cycle would have ramped down. "It's almost like you guys, as soon as you go on full alert, it's when I go into hiding, that's when I'm a normal person," O'Leary said. He leaned back in his chair and laughed. "We're on the wrong schedule basically."

"Wrong for us," Grusing said.

"Yeah," O'Leary agreed.

Then, without preamble, O'Leary launched into a jeremiad. He had struggled alone his entire life. Struggled and lost. And it wasn't just him. There were other men, too, men who had spent their lives in futile combat to destroy the monster inside them. It was a waste.

"The only way they can stop is some guy like you is going to show up at their doorstep," he told Grusing. "From then on, they're just a specimen. That's all they are. They get paraded in front of the media. Their family life is ruined. And they get locked up in a hole and the world takes them out whenever they want to poke them and prod them." O'Leary flung his hands above him. "They have all these shows and shit, *Criminal Minds* and *Dexter* and *Law & Order: SVU*. As long as it's not happening to them, everybody wants to look at it. As long as the train wreck is not in their neighborhood, then it's fascinating and everybody loves it. They eat it up. People want to sell books."

O'Leary suddenly stopped. He seemed to sink into himself. He stared at the floor.

"We all have predispositions," Grusing said. "Yours, it's what keeps me employed."

Grusing stood up to leave. O'Leary looked up. He gestured to the two-way mirror on a wall in back of the interview room.

"There's a whole gang back there, huh?" he asked.

"Just us and Stacy Galbraith," Grusing replied.

O'Leary dropped his head into his hands. "I knew you were gonna do that," he said.

O'Leary looked directly at the mirror. On the other side, Galbraith looked back.

"Hi, Stacy Galbraith," O'Leary crooned. "I bet you wish you could have shot me."

Grusing interjected.

"We can't bring our guns in here anyway," he said.

"No, I mean when she was at my door and had her gun pointed at me."

Grusing shook his head.

"Well, that's a lot of paperwork."

On the other side of the mirror, Galbraith could not help but feel chilled. That night, for the first time in the entire case, she had trouble sleeping.

Epilogue

EIGHTEEN WHEELS

2011–

SHAKEN AS HE WAS, SERGEANT MASON ELECTED NOT TO quit the police force. "The decision was, I'm not going to let this define me as who I am. I'll learn from it and be a better investigator."

We met Mason at the Lynnwood police station in December of 2015; we interviewed him in the same room where he had interviewed Marie seven years before—across the same table Marie had pounded with her fist, insisting she had been raped. Mason traced his doubts back—the Project Ladder manager's mention of Marie wanting a different apartment, the skepticism Peggy voiced the day after the rape. "Those were people who knew her a heck of a lot better than I did," Mason said.

Mason wasn't disciplined over Marie's case. In the years after, his police record would be commendable.

"I think anybody that's been in this job for any length of time—there's a lot of stuff they see over their career that tends to have an effect on them. Harden a person or whatever," Mason told us. He took from Marie's case the need to be more open-minded, freer with the benefit of the doubt. "Nobody goes into law enforcement thinking they're going to end up victimizing somebody further," Mason said.

We asked Mason about Peggy. "She was relaying information that she thought was important," Mason said. She was being the good citizen she thought she was being. Mason was grateful she called. That he used what she said in the way that he did is on him: "I got it wrong."

We asked about Marie. We told Mason that she wonders about her role in all that happened, if there's some misstep she could have avoided.

"She didn't misstep. It was—me. So that's—just that," Mason said.

"It wasn't her job to try to convince me. In hindsight, it was my job to get to the bottom of it—and I didn't."

"When you look back on this, what haunts you most about this case?" we asked.

"There's several aspects"—he sighed—"that do, but probably the most is . . . what Marie had to endure by reporting this. Yeah . . ."

"Do you think about her a lot?"

For five seconds, ten, fifteen, Mason said nothing. He let the question sit, collecting himself. Half a minute passed before he spoke.

"Can we . . . ?"

"Sure."

"I just need to grab some water."

He left the room.

When Mason came back, he said: "Yeah, I do." He thinks of Marie often. "It's pretty random. Just at different times. Over the course of my day, visiting family out of state—it just depends.

"When I think of Marie, it's more of how she is doing now.

"I hope that she's okay."

THE COURT RECORDS for Marie's false-reporting charge were expunged in the spring of 2011. The file was sealed, its traces eliminated. But Marie knew that erasing history wouldn't prevent its repeating. So in June of 2013, she filed a civil rights lawsuit against Lynnwood in US District Court. "Maybe they could change the way they do things so another woman won't get treated as I did," she says.

The defendants included the city; the two police detectives, Mason and Rittgarn; Cocoon House, a nonprofit that managed the Project Ladder program; and the Project Ladder managers, Jana and Wayne. The lawsuit alleged that the police interrogated Marie without reading her her rights; that the department failed to provide proper training for dealing with rape victims; and that Cocoon House acted in concert with police by not helping Marie get a lawyer. Defense lawyers responded that when the police drove Marie in for questioning, she wasn't under arrest. Marie was free to leave, so the detectives were free to bypass the Miranda warning. Meanwhile, Cocoon House conceded that Jana and Wayne didn't help Marie get an attorney. But they had no duty to, the lawyers said.

One defense argument hovered above the rest. If it succeeded, just about every other argument fell away. Marie waited too long to sue, the defense lawyers contended. They said that the statute of limitations for a federal civil rights claim is three years—and that the clock started ticking for Marie in August of 2008, back when she was questioned and charged with false reporting. They moved to have her lawsuit tossed.

To Marie, the argument was confounding. "You can't file a lawsuit when they don't believe you," she says. Was she expected to sue before O'Leary's arrest validated her basis for suing? Nonetheless, the motion to dismiss posed a challenge for her attorney, H. Richmond Fisher. He likened Marie's situation to a patient who learns, years later, that doctors left a sponge behind during surgery. The law doesn't punish that patient for the time between operation and discovery. Nor, he argued, should the law punish Marie for the time between her arrest and O'Leary's.

In December of 2013, Marie and Lynnwood agreed to mediation, in hopes of settling before trial. Both sides wrote the mediator beforehand. Fisher said Marie wanted $5 million. Lynnwood's lawyers said she was unlikely to see an award "anywhere near the mid-six-figure range, let alone seven figures." Two weeks before Christmas, the mediator called the two sides together, to hash this out in person. The police and Marie stayed in separate rooms while attorneys made their cases. Then Marie was summoned. Asked to tell her story to two higher-ups from Lynnwood's police department, she described what she had been through. She invited them to imagine a daughter of theirs being treated the way she had been treated. The two apologized, acknowledged the department's errors, and pledged to do better.

Marie did not get $5 million. She settled with Lynnwood for $150,000. "A risk management decision was made," one of Lynnwood's lawyers told a newspaper reporter. Marie settled separately with Cocoon House, for an undisclosed amount.

She never heard anything from Rittgarn, the detective who had threatened to book her into jail and had since moved to Southern California. But after Marie's lawsuit was filed, a reporter for the *Seattle Times* reached Rittgarn by telephone. "Rittgarn . . . said he was unaware of the lawsuit," the newspaper reported. "At first he could not recall the case, except that he thought it involved 'that guy from Colorado.'"

Although Lynnwood agreed to settle for $150,000, the city's insurance picked up most of that, leaving Lynnwood to foot only its deductible.

In the end, the city paid $25,000.

"WE HAD A major failing," Lynnwood police commander Steve Rider told us.

"A drastic mistake," he called it. "A reality check. . . . Wrong turn . . . wrong assumptions . . . wrong calls.

"Knowing that she went through that brutal attack—and then we told her she lied?"

Facing fallout, many police departments resort to damage control: foul up, hole up. Get a big case wrong and they go full bunker, refusing to acknowledge, much less apologize. But the Lynnwood police proved an exception. In 2011, after Marc O'Leary's arrest, the city's police chief ordered two reviews—one internal, one external—to determine how Lynnwood's investigation went sideways. The department chose to own its mistakes, and to learn from them.

The internal review, seven pages long, was conducted by a Lynnwood police commander and a sergeant. Neither had worked the initial case. Their report used understated language— saying, for example, that the investigation reached an "incorrect resolution"—but their analysis was pointed enough. The detectives attached too much weight to small disparities in Marie's statements and to Peggy's doubts. Once doubt set in, they interrogated Marie instead of interviewing her. Once Marie confessed, "there was a self-imposed rush to file charges" and close the case. When Marie tried to take back her confession, Detective Rittgarn greeted her with threats.

The external review covered much the same ground, but with language that blistered. This peer review was conducted by Snohomish County sheriff's sergeant Gregg Rinta, who, unlike Mason, had substantial experience with rape cases. For five years he had supervised the sheriff's Special Investigations Unit, which handled up to seven hundred cases a year involving adult sex crimes and child abuse.

"In most respects, there simply was no investigation in this case," Rinta wrote in his fourteen-page report. "For reasons that I cannot explain, [Marie's credibility] became the focus of the investigation and all of the strong evidence that pointed to a serious felony crime, was completely ignored." Rinta recounted all the times the first day that Marie, on one hour's sleep, described being raped. To have Mason then request a written account was unnecessary and even cruel: "What you are asking her to do is tell her story for the FIFTH time." Multiple statements in hand, Mason elevated "minor inconsistencies"—common among traumatized victims—into major discrepancies. As for Peggy's doubts, Mason had no business even mentioning them in a report. Someone's opinion, with no supporting evidence, has "absolutely no relevance in an investigation," Rinta wrote.

In his review, Rinta makes clear how incredulous he is—at both the missteps and the mindset. He cannot fathom the detectives' lack of regard for the trauma Marie reported. He cannot understand their lack of compassion. Referring to the day the detectives first confronted Marie and accused her of lying, Rinta wrote:

> The manner in which she was treated by Sgt. Mason and Det. Rittgarn can only [be] labeled as bullying and coercive. It is painful to read, and difficult to understand how this type of behavior on the part of experienced police officers can happen in a professional police department. If this hadn't been documented in their reports, I would have been skeptical that this actually happened.

The way they hounded Marie, it's not surprising she confessed to lying, innocent though she was, Rinta wrote.

And what happened four days later—when Rittgarn threatened to book Marie into jail and recommend that she lose her housing—was worse. "These statements are coercive, cruel, and unbelievably unprofessional. I can't imagine ANY justification for making these statements."

Rinta recapped what happened afterward: the police escorting Marie down the stairs and handing her off to the two Project Ladder managers; the managers asking Marie, in the presence of the two officers, if she'd been raped; Marie saying no.

"I can only presume that this was orchestrated for the purpose of putting pressure on the victim to tell the 'truth,'" Rinta wrote.

It "is painful to imagine how the victim felt."

At the Lynnwood Police Department, Marie's case led to changes in practices and culture, Rider says. Detectives receive additional training about rape victims and trauma. They learn the protocols of the International Association of Chiefs of Police—the guidelines written by Joanne Archambault—to build trust with victims, to show respect and reserve judgment, to give victims a say over when and where they are interviewed. Rape victims get immediate assistance from advocates at a local healthcare center. Investigators must have "definitive proof" of lying before doubting a rape report. A charge of false reporting must now be reviewed with higher-ups. "We learned a great deal from this," Rider says. "And we don't want to see this happen to anybody ever again."

In 2008, Marie's case was one of four labeled unfounded by the Lynnwood police, according to statistics reported to the FBI. In the five years from 2008 to 2012, the department determined that ten of forty-seven reported rapes were unfounded: 21.3 percent. That's five times the national average of 4.3 percent for agencies covering similar-sized populations during that same period. Rider says his agency has become more cautious about labeling a case unfounded since Marie.

"I would venture to say we investigate our cases a lot more vigorously than many departments do," he says. "Now, we're extra careful that we get the right closure on it.

"Each one of us," Rider says, "will remember this case forever."

ON A NOVEMBER DAY—a blizzard was forecast, but didn't hit—we drove from Denver to Colorado's upper-right corner, where Nebraska lies to the north and east. At the Sterling Correctional Facility, a prison that looks pretty much like any other—

low and long, with concertina wire—we were led through three sets of sliding doors that locked behind us, down a long corridor and into the visiting room.

Marc O'Leary wore green prison scrubs with a ball cap. Stubble lined his jaw. His face looked jowly compared to his intake photo. He blinked in spasms, as though his eyelids were hooked to a motor drive. His hands stayed mostly in his lap, his left thumb bouncing.

"I do a lot of reading," he told us of his days in prison. Philosophy, science, psychology, "or I'll read metaphysical stuff like Taoism. . . . Lately I've been doing meditation. . . . I try not to let my thoughts carry me. . . . I actually took up sewing."

His family visits maybe a couple of times a month. They didn't know about him—not this part of him—until the day he spoke at sentencing. "I spent decades, a long time, learning how to hide this. So I was good at it." We asked if he committed other crimes the police don't know about. "Nothing more serious than breaking and entering," he said. Ever had a formal psychological diagnosis? we asked. No, he told us. "The court assumes because I can speak coherently and I'm not writing crazy stuff in a notebook somewhere that I must be perfectly sane. But if running around breaking into homes and playing out rape theater is not mental illness, then I think the definition is completely lost."

O'Leary wonders if he could have been stopped, years ago, if there had been a program to intervene with young boys suffering deviant fantasies. "There's no safe haven for a person that is on the edge or knows that they're going down the wrong path to really go to and say, 'Look, I need help.'" A program's success would depend on counselors who understand the urge to rape—people like him, O'Leary said. "I don't care if you had twenty PhDs on your wall or were an expert in criminology or psychology or whatever—there's no way I would have opened up completely." O'Leary told us he is "infinitely more qualified" to counsel potential rapists.

One of the biggest questions that brought us here concerns Lynnwood. Back when he saw the news—that the police had closed their investigation, that they had concluded there had been no rape—how did he react? Was he dumbfounded?

"I didn't know until after I was arrested," O'Leary said. "I was told by my public defender in Colorado."

After committing a rape he didn't read or watch the news, or go online to track the investigation's progress. He didn't see the need. "I thought about it sometimes, but I just never followed up. I was—living two lives is a lot of work. I wasn't sleeping. I was literally living two lives. And I was just not focused on that.

"I just kind of assumed that police were looking."

DURING OUR MONTHS of reporting, we spent many hours talking to rape experts—prosecutors, cops, researchers, advocates. To Joanne Archambault, the retired sergeant who has authored guidelines on investigating allegations of rape, Marie's case shows how police skepticism can become a self-fulfilling prophecy. "Unfortunately, interrogating victims and challenging them about inconsistencies just shuts them down or causes them to recant, which reinforces law enforcement's belief that so many of these cases are unfounded."

The Lynnwood detectives not only interrogated Marie, they used the Reid Technique, typically reserved for someone like a robbery suspect. They provoked. They deceived. They studied her physical reactions. Using this approach on Marie was "inappropriate," Sergeant Rinta wrote in his peer review. He added: "Interpreting body language is an inexact science, and should not be used as a conclusive tool in determining the truth, unless one has expertise in this area. Mason and Rittgarn certainly did not." The Reid Technique has come under scrutiny generally, as DNA testing has exposed scores of cases in which innocent people confessed to detectives. Wicklander-Zulawski & Associates, a police consulting firm, announced in 2017 that it would no longer teach the method because of the risk of false confessions. "This was a big move for us, but it's a decision that's been coming for quite some time," the company's president said. John Reid, the technique's namesake, built his reputation in part on a 1955 Nebraska murder case in which he elicited a confession from a young forester named Darrel Parker. Twenty-three years later, a death row inmate named Wesley Peery admitted he was the real killer. Parker was formally exonerated in 2012, the year after Marie's record was expunged.

Marie's case is an object lesson in other ways, too. Archambault warns that a rape victim's recall can be disorganized, inconsistent, or simply wrong. Marie described the rapist's eyes as blue. O'Leary's eyes are hazel. Marie described the rapist as five feet six to five feet nine. O'Leary is six feet two.

Her case shows the risk of the abbreviated investigation and discarded rape kit. Once the police suspected Marie of lying, they stopped investigating. Once they concluded she was lying, they had her rape kit destroyed. Around the country, examples abound of similar neglect, only on a grander scale. In 2007, the year before Marie was raped, a task force comprising state and county investigators raided the Harvey, Illinois, police department and found two hundred unprocessed rape kits. Two years later, in Detroit, an assistant prosecutor discovered a cache of 11,341 untested rape kits in a warehouse, "furred with dust." In 2015, a *USA Today* investigation tallied seventy thousand untested kits nationwide while noting that it was likely a fraction of the true total. The White House that year estimated the backlog at four hundred thousand.

"That's tragic. That's really tragic," says Susan Irion, a principal figure in the adoption of rape kits back in the late 1970s.

But in some ways—culturally and politically—we've also seen a shift. When she was on the police force, Archambault saw how people avoided discussions of rape, how the public wanted police resources devoted to other kinds of crime. But in 2015 the US Department of Justice and the Manhattan district attorney's office dedicated nearly $80 million to clearing the national rape-kit backlog. A key partner in that push was the Joyful Heart Foundation, a nonprofit founded by actress Mariska Hargitay from the popular television show *Law & Order: Special Victims Unit*. In 2016, at the Academy Awards ceremony, Vice President Joe Biden said "Let's change the culture" while introducing Lady Gaga, who sang while surrounded by survivors of sexual assault. A few months later there was a public backlash when Brock Turner, a former Stanford University swimmer, received a sentence of only six months in jail for sexually assaulting an unconscious woman. More than a million people signed an online petition to remove the case's judge from the bench.

Meanwhile, sex crimes police have become more receptive to new approaches. Many detectives receive training in "trauma-informed interviewing," in which they learn about neurological impacts on rape victims. They learn to ask for sensory memories, which can aid recall of other details. (What sounds do you remember? What did you smell?) They learn to let the victim talk without interruption, understanding that a description may not be linear. They learn to ask open-ended questions while avoiding any hint of interrogation.

In Ashland, Oregon, a straight shot south from Lynnwood on Interstate 5, a police detective named Carrie Hull pioneered a program called You Have Options. Launched in 2013, the program aims to increase reporting by sexual assault victims—and thereby increase the chances of identifying serial rapists. Hull knew that many victims have a wish for confidentiality and a fear of not being believed. So her program gives victims a say in how, and even whether, the police proceed. Victims can remain anonymous. If a victim balks at charges being filed, the police honor that decision. In the program's first year, the Ashland Police Department saw a 106 percent increase in reporting. More than a dozen other law enforcement agencies have since adopted the program in states that include Virginia, Missouri, Colorado, and Washington.

The program's approach doesn't sit well with some cops. Their take is that they're being told not to investigate a crime. Hull sees it another way. The victim's information could help solve other cases down the road. It's like the advice Grusing got: Just get them talking.

WE PULLED THE files for the O'Leary investigation from police departments in Aurora, Lakewood, Westminster, and Golden. The records fill volumes. They tell a story of a case with no loose ends—except one.

After resurrecting the photos of O'Leary's victims, John Evans devoted himself to one final task: breaking the Wretch. He dedicated one of the seven high-performance computers on his desk at the Rocky Mountain Regional Computer Forensics Laboratory to cracking the encrypted, seventy-five-gigabyte file where O'Leary kept his most private secrets. For twenty-four hours a day, seven days a week, Evans ran specialized hacking software that hurled passwords at the file. Some of the passwords were scraps of O'Leary's life turned up in the search of 65 Harlan Street. Old passwords. Email addresses. The names of family and friends. But mostly, the software served as a sledgehammer, deploying brute-force computing power to send lists of thousands of words and passcodes at the encryption program. Nothing worked.

"It bugged the hell out of me," Evans says. "I thought he had evidence of a lot more crimes in there. It was something that he didn't want anybody to see."

At the end of six months of constant battering, Evans decided he needed a bigger hammer. He sent the file to the FBI's geek squad, the Cryptologic and Electronic Analysis Unit of the Operational Technology Division. One of the most secretive branches of the agency, the cryptology unit had helped the National Security Administration comb through millions of emails. And its scientists, agents, and coders had helped numerous local law enforcement agencies with tough computer cases. But even the cryptologists could not break open the Wretch.

Evans stored the hard drive containing the original file at the Golden Police Department. The unassuming silver box was stashed on a shelf in the evidence locker, model number WD3200AAKS, serial number WMAWF0029012, case number 1-11-000108.

On some days, when he is running a route high in the mountains, Bob Weiner's thoughts will unexpectedly drift back to the Wretch. It has been years since O'Leary pleaded guilty. He is in prison for the rest of his life. He has never revealed the password. Weiner wonders what it could contain.

"Maybe there's information in there of a murder. I don't know," Weiner says. "My mind, periodically, reverts back to 'What's going on, what is in there?'

"I still think about it."

AFTER MARIE WAS RAPED, people expected her to be hysterical or broken. Marie didn't want to let go of normal, even if that meant pretending. Normal is what she craved before. It's what she craved after. "I basically acted like nothing happened," she says, looking back. "I turned everything off." So the day of, she seemed detached. *Like she was telling me she made a sandwich.* The day after, she rolled around on the grass. As for the giggling, that's something she does when nervous.

We first interviewed Marie in the spring of 2015—close to seven years after she was raped. She was pregnant with her second child. Her husband was at work.

What others found peculiar in Marie's behavior after the attack, Marie traced to her past. "When I was little and living with my mom, I never told anyone about that stuff that happened to me," Marie said. She never told anyone about being sexually assaulted as a child. "I held it all in. I don't know if that guy got away or ended up hurting other people. But I didn't want this time to be like that." That's why she told so many people—the calling around afterward that seemed so inexplicable to Shannon and Peggy. That's also why she told the police, however many times they asked. Most rape victims don't come forward. Marie did. "So nobody else would get hurt," she said. "They'd be out there searching for this person who had done this to me."

She's still shocked at how the police brushed away the evidence. "The marks on my wrists weren't lies," she said. "The next day it hurt even if someone tried to shake my hand. Made me want to cry." That was the same day Peggy called Mason—and doubt set in, and the police began seizing on any variation in Marie's story, which is another thing that gets her. "Little details might have been inconsistent. But in every story there was a person who came in my house and raped me."

When the police told her that Peggy and Jordan didn't believe her—"it broke me," Marie said. She began to doubt herself, at times wondering if she had made the story up: Maybe the rape *had* been a dream. And when she confessed to lying? "I lost everything." She lost herself. Gone was the eager eighteen-year-old starting out. Depression consumed her.

Afterward, she feared going outside. She stayed in and watched a lot of television. Nights were the worst. "Really bad," she said. "One night I did try to walk to the store by myself and felt like I hallucinated someone following me. It freaked me out. I didn't even get a half mile from my house. I ran home—like, running— because I thought I saw someone following me." She stopped going out after dark. At home, in her apartment, she avoided the bedroom. She slept on the couch, the lights on.

The day she learned of O'Leary's arrest, Marie asked the Lynnwood police how many other women he had hurt. She couldn't help but think: If I hadn't recanted, perhaps they would have been spared. It was something else to carry, however unjust the load.

O'Leary pleaded guilty in both of the Washington cases. When he was brought to Washington for sentencing, Marie stayed away. "I didn't want to face him," she said. "That wasn't something I could handle or do."

The grandmother in Kirkland did attend O'Leary's sentencing. "It was very important to me to see that it was him," she says. "It was justice for him, it was justice for me." She spoke at the hearing, but avoided recounting details of the attack. "I didn't want him to relive it," she says. She didn't want to give him that satisfaction. After the assault, she suffered post-traumatic stress. Her heart raced. She kept her blinds closed. She remained on high alert to every noise. Nights were hard, she says. It was especially hard taking a shower, because she couldn't hear anything else, leaving her imagination to fill the void.

O'Leary received forty years for the attack in Kirkland. He received twenty-eight and a half years for the rape of Marie.

When Marie had received counseling as ordered by the court, she told the counselor the truth. She said she had been raped. After O'Leary's arrest in Colorado, Marie wanted to call the counselor—to tell her, when I told you I was raped, I was telling you the truth—but she couldn't find her. Marie knows there may be people who don't know her story's afterword. Her peers from Project Ladder—the teens gathered around that day to hear her confess to lying—do they now know the truth? Elisabeth does. She was the girl to Marie's right, the one Marie sensed sympathy from. They later became friends. Marie learned Elisabeth had also been sexually assaulted—but hadn't said anything, for fear of not being believed. But as for the others in that circle, it's unlikely they all know the postscript. People move on, misconceptions in tow.

Online, the "international timeline of false rape allegations," kept by a man in London, still includes Marie's case in Lynnwood.

She remains an exhibit in the compiler's argument. The truth has yet to catch up to the lie.

We asked Marie to walk us forward from the time she learned of O'Leary's arrest.

With the $500 she received that day, Marie bought a new phone, because her old one was broken. She bought clothes. She gave some money to a friend.

With Shannon's help, Marie got her driver's license—and the day she passed that test, she signed up for another: She enrolled in school to become a truck driver. Being on the road appealed to her. So did getting away from Washington. So did a job that showed she wouldn't be defined by her past: "I just didn't want to be hating life and living in fear."

She passed the commercial driver's test on her first try. The day the license arrived, she boarded a plane. She flew east for a job interview and got the job, which required not just driving but swinging an eight-pound hammer in coveralls, safety glasses, and hard hat. Her next job was driving only: She hauled fresh water to fracking sites. After that she hauled pipe to drilling rigs.

She met a man online, his first message arriving as she sat in her truck, waiting to drop off a load of pipe. "It was so easy to talk to him when I first met him." For Marie, he was also easy to trust. "He was the first guy that ever bought my dinner," she said. They got married and had a child. A few months after our first interview with Marie, they had another. The family now lives somewhere in the middle of the country.

In the fall of 2016, Marie made a phone call from the road. She was in Pennsylvania, on her way to make a delivery in Maine. When Stacy Galbraith answered, Marie introduced herself. She used her full name. She told Galbraith who she was—the woman in the photograph. I want to thank you for all your work, Marie told the detective, and as she spoke, her voice began to break. Galbraith asked Marie how she was. Marie said she was married with two kids. Galbraith said she had two kids of her own. They didn't talk for long, fifteen minutes maybe, but all Marie wanted, all she really needed, was to tell Galbraith how much her work had meant. Before O'Leary's arrest, Marie had been stuck, unable even to get her driver's license.

"She let me move on," Marie says.

In her eighteen-wheeler, Marie left Pennsylvania and made for New England, knocking off her trip's last five hundred miles. When she reached the country's northeast corner, she unloaded her haul, picked up a new one, and headed west for California.

A Note from the Authors

We—"we" being T. Christian Miller and Ken Armstrong—came into this story from separate entrances, then stumbled upon one another in the middle.

Miller was working for ProPublica, a news organization devoted to investigative reporting. In 2015 he was working on a series of stories about police missteps in rape investigations. He wrote about ViCAP, the database the FBI built and then pretty much ignored. He wrote about the police's failure to stop Darren Sharper, a former pro football star who was eventually convicted of raping or attempting to rape nine women in four states. While reporting these other stories, he heard about a serial rapist, Marc O'Leary, who had been captured in Colorado thanks to stellar work by agencies working together across jurisdictional lines. Miller began reporting in the outskirts of Denver, in order to profile an investigation done right.

Meanwhile, Armstrong was living in Seattle and working for the Marshall Project, a nonprofit journalism outlet that covers criminal justice. He knew about Marie's case because her lawsuit had been written about in local newspapers. But Marie had never agreed to be interviewed by the media. Like Sergeant Rinta—the sex crimes investigator who conducted the peer review of Lynnwood's investigation—Armstrong could only imagine what Marie must have felt when she was accused of lying. He reached out to see if she would be willing to share her story, and after seven months of emails and telephone calls, Marie agreed. Beginning in the spring of 2015, Armstrong and Robyn Semien, a producer for the radio show *This American Life*, interviewed Marie, Peggy, Shannon, Sergeant Mason, and others. Armstrong also gathered records from the Lynnwood police, in order to reconstruct an investigation gone wrong.

In the summer of 2015, Miller began reporting the Washington piece of the O'Leary case and reached out to Marie's attorney, H. Richmond Fisher. Fisher told him something no journalist ever wants to hear: another reporter was already working on the story. News shops can be even more turf conscious than police departments, so this discovery elicited some cussing from our employers. But we chose to work together. We knitted our two halves into one—an investigation gone wrong tethered to one done right. In December 2015 we published a twelve-thousand-word story, "An Unbelievable Story of Rape," that contrasted the police investigations in Washington and Colorado and depicted the emotional toll on Marie. In February 2016 *This American Life* aired "Anatomy of Doubt," an exploration into how the suspicions concerning Marie's story started and spread. "People exercising empathy—and getting it wrong," is how Ira Glass put it in the introduction. But even after completing those two stories, we felt there was more to tell. We wanted to trace the historical roots of the skepticism that often confronts rape victims and the misguided assumptions that can lead some detectives astray. We wanted to profile Marc O'Leary and the array of law enforcement officials behind his capture. We wanted to place Marie's case in national context—to show that as awful as her ordeal was, other victims have suffered much the same.

Hence, this book.

As we reported the story out, we came to admire the resolve of those willing to talk to us about something so painful. Marie agreed to be interviewed because she believed that the more her experience was known, the less likely it was to be repeated. Peggy and Shannon agreed to talk in the hopes others could learn from their mistakes. The same went for the Lynnwood police, including Commander Rider, Sergeant Cohnheim, and the case's lead detective, Sergeant Mason.

We tried, without success, to interview Jerry Rittgarn, the former Lynnwood police detective. He replied in an email that he was perturbed at having the Lynnwood police portrayed as bullying Marie ("bullying" was the word used in Sergeant Rinta's report), saying any such depiction was "far from the truth. When you have victims who lie to the police and then seek out attention in the form of a biased story written by the media you sensationalize the case and don't tell the complete truth. If you want a complete truthful account of what occurred, to include interview, evidence, etc., I will do it only under monetary compensation contract." We informed him that we don't pay for interviews.

In writing about rape, we often found ourselves balancing competing objectives. While describing the assaults, for example, we tried to use enough detail to convey the horror of what O'Leary put his victims through. At the same time, however, we wanted to stop short of being gratuitous. In writing about O'Leary's victims, we strove to withhold details that could be used to identify them. (So we say Sarah sang in a church choir, without saying which church.) At the same time, it was important to us to write about the women he attacked as real, distinguishable people instead of as caricatures; doing so required some level of detail. Another challenge concerned language. In this paragraph and elsewhere in the book we've used the word "victim" to refer to Marie and other women attacked by O'Leary. Some who have been hurt—but by no means all—prefer the word "survivor" or "victor." We opted to use "victim," the most common term, as a general descriptor. But we knew that one woman attacked by O'Leary does not identify with that term, so we avoided using it in specific, individual reference to her. In describing O'Leary's assaults we also tried to avoid language that might be associated with consensual sex—changing, for example, the word "fondle" to "grope."

As is common practice to protect the anonymity of victims of sexual assault, we've changed some names in this book. We refer to the people in Marie's life—friends, family, and others—by using first names only. For victims and for suspects who were subsequently cleared, we generally chose pseudonyms or, in Marie's case, her real middle name (which she does not go by). We disclosed a victim's real name if she chose to be identified publicly. We also used full names for police officers, prosecutors, judges, and other public officials, and, of course, for Marc O'Leary.

Throughout the writing and reporting of this book, we tried to be mindful of potential blind spots. Perhaps one of the biggest in this project is gender: while the vast majority of sexual assault victims are women, we are both men. Fortunately, we were able to turn to the women involved in this project and in our lives. Rachel Klayman and Emma Berry were our editors. The head of Crown is Molly Stern. We also sought out other women readers (including our wives) to review

Notes

This book is based on interviews, documents, and data.

The people we interviewed for the Washington thread of this story included Marie; her foster mothers Peggy and Shannon; her friend Jordan; James Feldman, Marie's public defender when she was charged with filing a false police report; H. Richmond Fisher, Marie's attorney in her civil suit against Lynnwood; Sergeant Jeffrey Mason, Sergeant Rodney Cohnheim, and Commander Steve Rider from the Lynnwood Police Department; Corporal Jack Keesee and Detective Audra Weber from the Kirkland Police Department; and the grandmother in Kirkland who was sexually assaulted.

For the Colorado thread, we interviewed, among others, Detective Stacy Galbraith and computer analyst John Evans from the Golden Police Department; Sergeant Edna Hendershot, Officer David Galbraith, Sergeant Trevor Materasso, crime analyst Laura Carroll, crime scene investigator Katherine Ellis, and victim's advocate Amy Christensen from the Westminster Police Department; Detective Aaron Hassell, crime analyst Danelle DiGiosio, and criminalist Sheri Shimamoto from the Lakewood Police Department; Detective Scott Burgess and crime analyst Dawn Tollakson from the Aurora Police Department; Chief Deputy District Attorney Robert Weiner and Public Information Officer Pam Russell from the Jefferson County district attorney's office; Special Agent Jonathan Grusing and Public Affairs Specialist Deborah Sherman from the Federal Bureau of Investigation; Sharon Whelan, the neighbor who made note of the white pickup truck parked across the street; and Melinda Wilding, Marc O'Leary's philosophy professor.

Some of these interviews were conducted while the authors were doing reporting for "An Unbelievable Story of Rape," published by ProPublica and the Marshall Project on December 16, 2015.

For insight into investigations of sexual assault, we interviewed current and former police officers, detectives, prosecutors, victim's advocates, and academics, including Cassia Spohn, director of the School of Criminology and Criminal Justice at Arizona State University; Rebecca Campbell, a professor and researcher at Michigan State University; Jennifer Gentile Long, chief executive officer of AEquitas, a prosecutors' organization focused on violence against women; former sergeant Jim Markey and crime analyst Jeff Jensen from the Phoenix, Arizona, police department; Major J. R. Burton, commander of the special investigations division for the sheriff's office in Hillsborough County, Florida; Ritchie Martinez, former president of the International Association of Law Enforcement Intelligence Analysts; Anne Munch, a consultant and former prosecutor for the Denver district attorney's office; Detective Carrie Hull from the Ashland, Oregon, police department; Sergeant Liz Donegan from the Austin, Texas, police department; and Lisa Avalos, a law professor at the University of Arkansas.

We interviewed Marc O'Leary at the Sterling Correctional Facility in Colorado.

We also interviewed people with expertise in rape investigations or a historical role in the development of investigative tools, including Joanne Archambault, Kimberly Lonsway, and Susan Irion.

For reporting on the FBI's ViCAP program, we interviewed, from ViCAP, Art Meister, former unit chief; Timothy Burke, acting unit chief; Nathan Graham, crime analyst; Kenneth Gross, supervisory special agent and chief division counsel; Kevin Fitzsimmons, supervisory crime analyst; and Mark A. Nichols, assistant section chief. We also interviewed Patricia Cornwell, a novelist, for information on ViCAP.

We received more than ten thousand pages of documents through public-records requests filed with the police departments in Lynnwood and Kirkland, Washington; the police departments in Golden, Westminster, Aurora, and Lakewood, Colorado; the prosecuting attorney's offices in Snohomish County and King County, Washington; the prosecuting attorney's office in Jefferson County, Colorado; the City of Lynnwood; and the FBI.

These documents (and additional records found in municipal, county, and federal court) included crime scene photographs; surveillance footage collected by law enforcement agencies; medical and psychological records; a videotaped interview of O'Leary conducted by the FBI; O'Leary's military records; police personnel files; Project Ladder case notes; police interviews with victims and witnesses, either summarized or transcribed; a record of O'Leary's debit-card spending; and internal and external reviews conducted of the Lynnwood Police Department investigation of Marie's case. On occasion, we had documents specially created—for example, ordering a transcription of O'Leary's sentencing hearing in Colorado.

With the help of the Marshall Project and ProPublica, we conducted our own analysis of the FBI's Uniform Crime Reporting data, allowing us to place Lynnwood's number of "unfounded" rape reports into national context.

Chapter 1: The Bridge

Documents: Lynnwood police reports filed by Rittgarn, Mason, and others; Project Ladder case notes for Aug. 18, 2008; Marie's written statements to the police; and written transcripts of newscasts about Marie's recantation, along with video of the Aug. 15, 2008, KING 5 newscast.

3   **"A western Washington woman has confessed . . ."** *Northwest Cable News*, Aug. 16, 2008, 10:30 a.m. and 4:30 p.m. newscasts.

3   **"Police in Lynnwood now say . . ."** *KING 5 News*, Aug. 15, 2008, 6:30 p.m. newscast.

3   **"Another in a seemingly endless cavalcade . . ."** "Another Motiveless False Rape Claim Exposed," *Community of the Wrongly Accused*, Aug. 21, 2008, falserapesociety.blogspot.com/2008/08 /another-motiveless-false-rape-claim.html.

3   **following a Georgia teenager** "An International Timeline of False Rape Allegations 1674–2015: Compiled and Annotated by Alexander Baron," accessed on Feb. 5, 2017, infotextmanuscripts .org/falserape/a-false-rape-timeline.html.

3   **"As will be seen from this database . . ."** Alexander Baron, "An International Timeline of False Rape Allegations 1674–2015: Introduction," accessed on Feb. 5, 2017, infotextmanuscripts.org /falserape/a-false-rape-timeline-intro.html.

4   **a bitch and a whore.** "Anatomy of Doubt," *This American Life*, episode 581, Feb. 26, 2016.

Chapter 2: Hunters

Documents: Public records from the Golden, Westminster, and Aurora police departments and the FBI. Readers interested in more information about police investigations of sexual assault may consult the training modules for End Violence Against Women International, a comprehensive collection of best practices; John O. Savino and Brent E. Turvey, eds., *Rape Investigation Handbook*, 2nd ed. (San Diego: Elsevier Science, 2011); Cassia Spohn and Katharine Tellis, *Policing and Prosecuting Sexual Assault: Inside the Criminal Justice System* (Boulder: Lynne Rienner Publishers, 2014); and Rebecca Campbell, Hannah Feeney, Giannina Fehler-Cabral, Jessica Shaw, and Sheena Horsford, "The National Problem of Untested Sexual Assault Kits (SAKs): Scope, Causes, and Future Directions for Research, Policy, and Practice," *Trauma, Violence & Abuse* (Dec. 23, 2015): 1–14.

12   **A national government survey found** Jennifer L. Truman and Lynn Langton, "Criminal Victimization, 2014," published by the US Department of Justice, Bureau of Justice Statistics.

13   **"Not every complaint is founded . . ."** Savino and Turvey, *Rape Investigation Handbook*, p. 25.

14   **"Start by Believing" was the slogan** "Start by Believing: Ending the Cycle of Silence in Sexual Assault," End Violence Against Women International, accessed Feb. 22, 2017, startbybelieving .org/home.

17   **Golden was best known** "Coors Brewery Tour," MillerCoors, accessed April 22, 2017, millercoors.com/breweries/coors-brewing -company/tours.

17   **About nineteen thousand people lived** "Golden History," City of Golden, accessed April 22, 2017, cityofgolden.net/live/golden -history/.

17   **Galbraith's first call** "CDOT Encourages Public to Comment on I-70 East Supplemental Draft Environmental Impact Statement," Colorado Department of Transportation, Aug. 27, 2014, codot

.gov/projects/i70east/assets/sdeis-i-70-release-082614. CDOT describes the average daily traffic as up to 205,000 vehicles per day, which works out to 8,541 per hour.

Chapter 3: Waves and Peaks

Documents: "Disclosure of Expert Opinion," an evaluation of Marie by Dr. Jon R. Conte, dated Oct. 18, 2013, filed as a lawsuit exhibit; Lynnwood police reports filed by Mason; and Snohomish County grant documents regarding Project Ladder.

28   **the program sought to reduce homelessness** "Homeless Grant Assistance Program (HGAP) 2007 Project Summary," a three-page Snohomish County document generated in October 2007.

28   **"financial literacy"** "Homeless Grant Assistance Program (HGAP) 2006–7 Project Documentation," a four-page Snohomish County document that provides context, anticipated outcomes, and a timeline for the project.

28   **"laid end to end . . ."** Judith M. Broom, *Lynnwood: The Land, the People, the City* (Seattle: Peanut Butter Publishing, 1990), p. 49.

Chapter 4: A Violent Alchemy

Documents: Public records from the Westminster and Aurora police departments, the Boulder County sheriff's office, and the FBI. For a thorough discussion of false reporting of sexual assault, please see Cassia Spohn and Katharine Tellis, *Policing and Prosecuting Sexual Assault: Inside the Criminal Justice System* (Boulder: Lynne Rienner Publishers, 2014).

34   **She spent her childhood in Arvada** "Fun Facts about Arvada," City of Arvada, accessed April 22, 2017, arvada.org/about/our-community/arvada-fun-facts.

38   **A police surgeon in England** Philip N. S. Rumney, "False Allegations of Rape," *Cambridge Law Journal* 65 (March 2006): 125–58.

38   **The feminist Susan Brownmiller** Susan Brownmiller, *Against*

Our Will: Men, Women and Rape (New York: Fawcett Columbine, 1975), p. 387.

38 **Researchers who specialized in sexual assault** Kimberly Lonsway, Joanne Archambault, and David Lisak, "False Reports: Moving Beyond the Issue to Successfully Investigate and Prosecute Non-Stranger Sexual Assault," *The Voice*, published by the National Center for the Prosecution of Violence Against Women, 2009.

39 **she set the bar high.** Edna Hendershot, Alverd C. Stutson, and Thomas W. Adair, "A Case of Extreme Sexual Self-Mutilation," *Journal of Forensic Sciences* 55 (Jan. 2010): 245–47.

43 **Many could no longer recall events in chronological order.** Rebecca Campbell, "The Neurobiology of Sexual Assault," a Dec. 3, 2012, seminar presentation sponsored by the National Institute of Justice, transcript accessed on June 13, 2017, nij.gov /multimedia/presenter/presenter-campbell/Pages/presenter-campbell -transcript.aspx. Some scholars have questioned whether women's advocates are overstating trauma's effects on the brain in an effort to reduce investigators' skepticism about rape victims' memories. See, for instance, Emily Yoffe, "The Bad Science Behind Campus Response to Sexual Assault," *The Atlantic*, Sept. 8, 2017.

44 **Psychologists have documented the role** Dorthe Berntsen, "Tunnel Memories for Autobiographical Events: Central Details Are Remembered More Frequently from Shocking Than from Happy Experiences," *Memory & Cognition* 30, no. 7 (Oct. 2002): 1010–20.

Chapter 5: A Losing Battle

Documents: Public records from the Golden Police Department, the FBI, and prosecutor's offices in Jefferson County (Colorado), Snohomish County (Washington), and King County (Washington).

56 **He was an alpha.** "Understanding the ASVAB Test," US Army, accessed April 22, 2017, goarmy.com/learn/understanding-the -asvab.html.

57   Their name derived from the unit's "9th Infantry Regiment (United States)," *Wikipedia*, accessed April 22, 2017, en.wikipedia .org/wiki/9th_Infantry_Regiment_(United_States).

59   The most notorious of these Jon Rabiroff and Hwang Hae-Rym, " 'Juicy Bars' Said to Be Havens for Prostitution Aimed at US Military," *Stars and Stripes*, Sept. 9, 2009.

CHAPTER 6: WHITE MAN, BLUE EYES, GRAY SWEATER

Documents: Lynnwood police reports written by Miles, Nelson, Kelsey, Mason, and Rittgarn; Mason's personnel file with the Lynnwood police; Rittgarn's profile on LinkedIn; crime scene photographs taken by Miles; and medical records from Marie's rape exam, attached as an exhibit in her lawsuit against Lynnwood. The quotations of Marty Goddard—as well as many of the details about the earliest rape kits—come from an oral history taken by the University of Akron; Goddard was interviewed on Feb. 26, 2003, in Sacramento, California. The transcript can be found at vroh.uakron.edu/transcripts/Goddard.php. In researching the history of rape kits, other sources that were helpful included: Bonita Brodt, "Vitullo Kit Helps Police Build Case Against Rapists," *Chicago Tribune*, July 31, 1980; Jessica Ravitz, "The Story Behind the First Rape Kit," CNN, updated Nov. 21, 2015; and Chris Fusco, "Crime Lab Expert Developed Rape Kits," *Chicago Sun-Times*, Jan. 12, 2006.

71   Chicago made him nervous Ravitz, "The Story Behind the First Rape Kit."

72   twenty-six hospitals in the Chicago area Brodt, "Vitullo Kit Helps Police."

72   "I remember doing some strange things Ann Wolbert Burgess and Lynda Lytle Holmstrom, *Rape: Crisis and Recovery* (West Newton, MA: Awab, 1979), p. 36.

73   "I am so sore under my ribs," Burgess and Holmstrom, *Rape: Crisis and Recovery*, p. 36.

73   215 hospitals in Illinois Brodt, "Vitullo Kit Helps Police."

75   produced a comprehensive online course Kimberly A. Lonsway, Joanne Archambault, and Alan Berkowitz, "False Reports:

Moving Beyond the Issue to Successfully Investigate and Prosecute Non-Stranger Sexual Assault," End Violence Against
Women International, May 2007.

76   **While investigating child-abuse cases** Joanne Archambault,
T. Christian Miller, and Ken Armstrong, "How Not to Handle
a Rape Investigation," *Digg*, Dec. 17, 2015, digg.com/dialog/how
-not-to-handle-a-rape-investigation#comments.

76   **The public wanted the police** Archambault et al., "How Not to
Handle a Rape Investigation."

77   **During training she plays a 911 tape** Ronnie Garrett, "A New
Look at Sexual Violence," a Q&A with Joanne Archambault, *Law
Enforcement Technology*, Sept. 2005.

77   **"Research shows the more intimate** Garrett, "A New Look at
Sexual Violence."

77   **"The victim's response to the trauma** "Investigating Sexual Assaults," Model Policy, IACP National Law Enforcement Policy
Center, May 2005.

Chapter 7: Sisters

Documents: Public records from Golden, Westminster, and Aurora po-
lice departments and the FBI. Those interested in further reading on the
ViCAP program may be interested in Richard H. Walton, *Cold Case
Homicides: Practical Investigative Techniques* (Boca Raton, FL: CRC/
Taylor & Francis, 2006); and Don DeNevi and John H. Campbell, *Into
the Minds of Madmen: How the FBI's Behavioral Science Unit Revolu-
tionized Crime Investigation* (Amherst, NY: Prometheus Books, 2004).
There is a crime fiction series based on ViCAP, beginning with Michael
Newton, *Blood Sport* (Clinton, MT: Wolfpack Publishing, 1990).

87   **The Federal Bureau of Investigation runs** "Frequently Asked
Questions on CODIS and NDIS," Federal Bureau of Investigation, accessed April 22, 2017, fbi.gov/services/laboratory
/biometric-analysis/codis/codis-and-ndis-fact-sheet.

89   **best known for its Herculean labor** Matt Sebastian, "JonBenét
Investigation the CBI's Largest Ever," *Daily Camera*, Feb. 3, 1999.

89   **Lewis had been forced** Joanne Archambault, Kimberly A. Lonsway, Patrick O'Donnell, and Lauren Ware, "Laboratory Analysis of Biological Evidence and the Role of DNA in Sexual Assault Investigations," End Violence Against Women International, Nov. 2015.

91   **female cops have been building** "Alice Stebbins Wells," International Association of Women Police, accessed April 22, 2017, iawp.org/history/wells/alice_stebbins_wells.htm.

91   **Wells's argument that women brought** Penny E. Harrington, *Recruiting & Retaining Women: A Self-Assessment Guide for Law Enforcement,* National Center for Women & Policing, a Division of the Feminist Majority Foundation, 2000.

92   **a 1985 study found** Robert J. Homant and Daniel B. Kennedy, "Police Perceptions of Spouse Abuse: A Comparison of Male and Female Officers," *Journal of Criminal Justice* 13 (Dec. 1985): 29–47.

92   **A 1998 study of a nationally representative** Carole Kennedy Chaney and Grace Hall Saltzstein, "Democratic Control and Bureaucratic Responsiveness: The Police and Domestic Violence," *American Journal of Political Science* 42, no. 3 (July 1998): 745–68.

92   **And a 2006 study** Kenneth J. Meier and Jill Nicholson-Crotty, "Gender, Representative Bureaucracy, and Law Enforcement: The Case of Sexual Assault," *Public Administration Review* 66, no. 6 (Nov.–Dec. 2006): 850–60.

92   **"What *is* absolutely clear** Joanne Archambault and Kimberly A. Lonsway, "Training Bulletin: Should Sexual Assault Victims Be Interviewed by Female Officers and Detectives?," End Violence Against Women International, Feb. 2015.

92   **Despite the benefits of gender diversity** Harrington, *Recruiting & Retaining Women.*

93   **The result is that no police** Lynn Langton, "Women in Law Enforcement, 1987–2008," Crime Data Brief, Bureau of Justice Statistics, June 2010.

98   **In the late 1950s, Brooks** United States Congress, "Serial Murders: Hearing Before the Subcommittee on Juvenile Justice of the Committee on the Judiciary, United States Senate, Ninety-Eighth

Congress, First Session, on Patterns of Murders Committed by One Person, in Large Numbers with No Apparent Rhyme, Reason, or Motivation," July 12, 1983.

98   **Brooks told a rapt Senate Judiciary Committee** United States Congress, "Serial Murders: Hearing Before the Subcommittee on Juvenile Justice of the Committee on the Judiciary."

99   **They referred to the oddball collection** Don DeNevi and John H. Campbell, *Into the Minds of Madmen*.

99   **The basement was a dark** Stanley A. Pimentel, "Interview of Former Special Agent of the FBI Roger L. Depue (1968–1989)," Society of Former Special Agents of the FBI, nleomf.org/assets/pdfs/nlem/oral-histories/FBI_Depue_interview.pdf.

99   **Research had shown that rapists** Robert J. Morton, ed., "Serial Murder: Multi-disciplinary Perspectives for Investigators," Federal Bureau of Investigation (Behavioral Analysis Unit-2, National Center for the Analysis of Violent Crime), fbi.gov/stats-services/publications/serial-murder.

99   **Studies had found that between one-fourth** Kevin M. Swartout, Mary P. Koss, Jacquelyn W. White, Martie P. Thompson, Antonia Abbey, and Alexandra L. Bellis, "Trajectory Analysis of the Campus Serial Rapist Assumption," *JAMA Pediatrics* 169, no. 12 (Dec. 2015): 1148–54.

99   **two-thirds of rapists** David Lisak and Paul M. Miller, "Repeat Rape and Multiple Offending Among Undetected Rapists," *Violence and Victims* 17, no. 1 (2002): 73–84.

99   **Only about 1 percent of murderers** Morton, "Serial Murder: Multi-disciplinary Perspectives for Investigators."

100   **database was a tragically unfulfilled promise.** T. Christian Miller, "The FBI Built a Database That Can Catch Rapists—Almost Nobody Uses It," ProPublica, July 30, 2015.

Chapter 8: "Something About How She Said It"

Documents: Lynnwood police reports filed by Mason and Rittgarn; Marie's written statements—the one turned in on Aug. 13 and the two on Aug. 14; Mason's personnel file; Rittgarn's LinkedIn profile; external and internal reviews of the Lynnwood police investigation; Project Ladder case notes for Aug. 15 and Aug. 18; and correspondence between the Lynnwood police and state Crime Victims Compensation Program. The Mason and Rittgarn reports described in detail the back-and-forth between detectives and Marie when she was questioned on Aug. 14 and Aug. 18. The part about Marie being confronted with doubts attributed to Jordan and Peggy comes from our interview with Marie. (Jordan also said Marie called him afterward to say the police told her he didn't believe her.) Researching the Reid Technique, the following sources proved helpful: Fred E. Inbau, John E. Reid, Joseph P. Buckley, and Brian C. Jayne, *Criminal Interrogation and Confessions*, 5th ed. (Burlington, MA: Jones & Bartlett Learning, 2013); Fred E. Inbau, John E. Reid, Joseph P. Buckley, and Brian C. Jayne, *Essentials of the Reid Technique: Criminal Interrogation and Confessions*, 2nd ed. (Burlington, MA: Jones & Bartlett Learning, 2015); Douglas Starr, "The Interview," *New Yorker*, Dec. 9, 2013; Robert Kolker, "A Severed Head, Two Cops, and the Radical Future of Interrogation," *Wired*, May 24, 2016 (published in partnership with the Marshall Project); Robert Kolker, " 'I Did It,' " *New York*, Oct. 3, 2010.

111   "**across the United States, Canada, Mexico . . .**" Inbau, *Essentials of the Reid Technique*, p. viii.

111   "**a kind of powerful folk wisdom . . .**" Kolker, "A Severed Head, Two Cops, and the Radical Future of Interrogation."

111   "**Never allow them to give you denials . . .**" Starr, "The Interview."

112   "**An interrogation is conducted only when . . .**" Inbau, *Essentials of the Reid Technique*, p. 5.

112   "**Deceptive suspects generally do not . . .**" Ibid., p. 83.

112   "**In this case, the subject, literally . . .**" Ibid., p. 83.

112   "**The more often a guilty suspect denies . . .**" Ibid., p. 138.

113   "**It is psychologically improper to mention . . .**" Ibid., p. 21.

CHAPTER 9: THE SHADOW WITHIN

Documents: Public records from Golden, Westminster, and Aurora police departments and the FBI. For a discussion of the concept of the shadow in C. G. Jung's writing, please see Stephen A. Diamond,

"Essential Secrets of Psychotherapy: What Is the 'Shadow'?," *Psychology Today*, April 20, 2012.

126 **Jung described the shadow** C. G. Jung, *Psychology and Religion: West and East (The Collected Works of C.G. Jung, Volume 11)*, 2nd ed. (Princeton, NJ: Princeton University Press, 1975), p. 76.

130 **There was the Tic Tac routine** Neil Strauss, *The Game: Penetrating the Secret Society of Pickup Artists* (New York: HarperCollins, 2005), p. 80.

130 **women are "targets."** Mystery and Chris Odom, *The Mystery Method: How to Get Beautiful Women into Bed* (New York: St. Martin's Press, 2007), p. 96.

132 **scanning OkCupid one day** "Marc O'Leary's Ex-Girlfriend: 'Something Was Off Between Us,'" *48 Hours*, Nov. 19, 2016. This segment extra can be found online at cbsnews.com/news/marc-patrick-oleary-48-hours-hunted-the-search-colorado-serial-rapist/.

CHAPTER 10: GOOD NEIGHBORS

Documents: Public records from Golden, Westminster, Aurora, and Lakewood police departments; the King County, Washington, prosecuting attorney's office; the FBI; and Jefferson County, Colorado, district court case no. 11CR430.

146 **He'd gone to Cedarville College** "Why Cedarville," Cedarville University, accessed May 3, 2017, cedarville.edu/About.aspx.

147 **Antioch College was the quintessential** "About" page, Antioch College, accessed May 3, 2017, antiochcollege.edu/about.

147– **"serious psychological and emotional problems . . ."** Kimberly
48   Lonsway, Joanne Archambault, and David Lisak, "False Reports: Moving Beyond the Issue to Successfully Investigate and Prosecute Non-Stranger Sexual Assault," *The Voice*, published by the National Center for the Prosecution of Violence Against Women, 2009.

Chapter 11: A Gross Misdemeanor

Documents: False-reporting citation issued to Marie; the case's court docket in Lynnwood Municipal Court (the file itself has been sealed, but the docket was saved and submitted as a lawsuit exhibit); Lynnwood police reports; FBI Uniform Crime Reporting data; Kirkland police records regarding the Oct. 6, 2008, sexual assault, including Keesee's transcribed interview with the victim; and Washington State 2008 annual caseload report for courts of limited jurisdiction. For more on how false reporting is prosecuted, see: Lisa Avalos, "Prosecuting Rape Victims While Rapists Run Free: The Consequences of Police Failure to Investigate Sex Crimes in Britain and the United States," *Michigan Journal of Gender and Law* 23, no. 1 (2016): 1–64. See, too: Lisa R. Avalos, "Policing Rape Complainants: When Reporting Rape Becomes a Crime," *The Journal of Gender, Race & Justice* 20, no. 3 (2017): 459–508.

156   **shows that while forty-two states** Lisa Avalos, Alexandra Filippova, Cynthia Reed, and Matthew Siegel, "False Reports of Sexual Assault: Findings on Police Practices, Laws, and Advocacy Options," draft report of an advocacy paper prepared for Women Against Rape, Sept. 23, 2013, p. 9. This report can be found online at womenagainstrape.net/sites/default/files/final_paper_for_war_9-23.pdf.

157   **There, the crime, called "perverting the course of justice . . ."** Avalos, "False Reports of Sexual Assault," pp. 8, 57–58. Avalos's research did not turn up any instances of the Crown levying the maximum, but she tallied thirteen women in the United Kingdom who had received two or three years for falsely claiming to have been raped.

157–   **One journalism institute named** Craig Silverman, "The Year
58   in Media Errors and Corrections 2014," Poynter Institute, Dec. 18, 2014, poynter.org/2014/the-year-in-media-errors-and-corrections-2014/306801/.

158   **lawsuits filed by both the fraternity** T. Rees Shapiro, "Fraternity Chapter at U-Va. to Settle Suit Against *Rolling Stone* for $1.65 Million," *Washington Post*, June 13, 2017.

158 **"into the face of institutional indifference . . ."** T. Rees Shapiro and Emma Brown, "*Rolling Stone* Settles with Former U-Va. Dean in Defamation Case," *Washington Post*, April 11, 2017.

158 **been sentenced to eight days in jail** Peyton Whitely, "Woman Pleads Guilty to False Rape Report," *Seattle Times*, March 19, 2008.

CHAPTER 12: MARKS

Documents: Public records from Golden, Westminster, Aurora, and Lakewood police departments and the FBI. For more information on the debate over abandoned DNA, see Elizabeth E. Joh, "Reclaiming 'Abandoned' DNA: The Fourth Amendment and Genetic Privacy," *Northwestern University Law Review* 100, no. 2 (2006): 857–84; and the US Supreme Court decision *Maryland v. King*, docket no. 12-207, decided June 3, 2013.

172 **Such remnants were called "abandoned DNA"** Kevin Hartnett, "The DNA in Your Garbage: Up for Grabs," *Boston Globe*, May 12, 2013, bostonglobe.com/ideas/2013/05/11/the-dna-your -garbage-for-grabs/sU12MtVLkoypL1qu2iF6IL/story.html.

CHAPTER 13: LOOKING INTO A FISH TANK

Documents: Videotaped FBI interview with O'Leary; Mountlake Terrace Police Department field notes for the April 3, 2007, stop of O'Leary as a suspicious person; police reports from Golden and other Colorado law enforcement agencies; US Army records for O'Leary, for both active and reserve duty; and Lynnwood police records. The law enforcement records included an accounting of O'Leary's debit card purchases; these showed where he shopped and ate, and allowed us to reconstruct his trip from Washington to Colorado.

CHAPTER 14: A CHECK FOR $500

Documents: Correspondence between Golden and Lynnwood police; Golden police reports written by Galbraith; Kirkland police reports;

court records for the Kirkland case filed in King County Superior Court; email correspondence between Galbraith and a King County senior deputy prosecuting attorney on Sept. 8, 2011; Mason's personnel file, which includes his academic transcripts; Lynnwood police reports filed by Cohnheim; and Project Ladder case notes.

202 **In 2004, the NCIS created** *Law Enforcement Information Exchange (LInX) Information Brief*, prepared by the Naval Criminal Investigative Service, Oct. 29, 2009.

205 **"You were never there . . ."** Mika Brzezinski, "Child Who Was the Victim of a Kidnapping Is Further Victimized by Police Detective in Minnesota," *CBS Evening News*, Feb. 23, 2004.

205 **"owes this community an apology."** Catie L'Heureux, "Police Thought This *Gone Girl*–Like Kidnapping Was a Hoax Because the Woman 'Didn't Act Like a Victim,'" *The Cut*, Aug. 3, 2016.

206 **"You are going to hell . . ."** Gabriella Paiella, "Woman Falsely Accused of Faking Her *Gone Girl*–Like Kidnapping in 2015 Says She's Still Being Harassed Online," *The Cut*, Jan. 4, 2017.

206 **"All I did was survive . . ."** Paiella, "Woman Falsely Accused of Faking Her *Gone Girl*–Like Kidnapping in 2015 Says She's Still Being Harassed Online."

206 **He made up a story about** Bill Lueders, *Cry Rape: The True Story of One Woman's Harrowing Quest for Justice* (Madison, WI: Terrace Books, 2006), pp. 59–60, 123–25.

206 **"What she's being presented with . . ."** Lueders, *Cry Rape*, p. 126.

207 **"I felt they hurt me:** Scott Shifrel, "Victim's Vindication: Con Admits Raping Queens Girl," *New York Daily News*, March 19, 2004.

207 **"I feel happy that Fancy . . ."** Scott Shifrel and Leo Standora, "Rape Strains Family Bond; Mom's Doubts Scarred Teen," *New York Daily News*, March 20, 2004.

207 **"His first question to me was . . ."** Natalie Elliott (Q&A with Sara Reedy), "I Was Raped—and the Police Told Me I Made It Up," *VICE*, Jan. 8, 2013.

207 **"And he actually went to the extent . . ."** Elliott, "I Was Raped—and the Police Told Me I Made It Up."

208 **"Not a very impressive record,"** Susan Brownmiller, *Against Our*

Will: Men, Women and Rape (New York: Fawcett Columbine, 1975), pp. 365–66.

208 **"A police officer who does not believe . . ."** Brownmiller, *Against Our Will*, p. 366.

208 **a *BuzzFeed News* investigation found** Alex Campbell and Katie J. M. Baker, "Unfounded: When Detectives Dismiss Rape Reports Before Investigating Them," *BuzzFeed News*, Sept. 8, 2016.

208 **a social work professor in Michigan published** Rachel M. Venema, "Police Officer Schema of Sexual Assault Reports: Real Rape, Ambiguous Cases, and False Reports," *Journal of Interpersonal Violence* 31, no. 5 (2016): 872–99. This article was first published online in 2014.

209 **told a local television station** Natalie Shaver, "Local Sheriff Reacts to Rape Kit Legislation," *KIFI* (LocalNews8.com), posted March 17, 2016. See, too: Salvador Hernandez, "Idaho Sheriff Says 'Majority' of Rape Accusations in His County Are False," *BuzzFeed News*, March 16, 2016.

CHAPTER 15: 327½

Documents: Public records from Golden, Westminster, Aurora, and Lakewood police departments and the FBI; Jefferson County, Colorado, district court case no. 11CR430. For an in-depth examination of the factors affecting prosecutors' decisions to file charges in sexual assault cases, please see Cassia Spohn and David Holleran, "Prosecuting Sexual Assault: A Comparison of Charging Decisions in Sexual Assault Cases Involving Strangers, Acquaintances, and Intimate Partners," National Criminal Justice Reference Service, 2004. The quotations in the Bedlow case come from a trial transcript with a rather unwieldy title: "Report of the Trial of Henry Bedlow, for Committing a Rape on Lanah Sawyer: With the Arguments of the Counsel on Each Side: At a Court of Oyer and Terminer, and Gaol Delivery for the City and County of New-York, Held 8th October, 1793 / Impartially Taken by a Gentleman of the Profession." It can be found online at tei.it.ox.ac.uk/tcp/Texts-HTML/free/N20/N20224.html.

217 **The son of an FBI agent** John Meyer, "A Balance of Career, Fitness—on the Run," *Denver Post,* April 30, 2007.

217 **At forty-two, he'd finished** "Boston Marathon Race Results 2007," Boston Marathon (plug the name Robert Weiner into the search box), accessed April 24, 2017, marathonguide.com/results /browse.cfm?MIDD=15070416.

218 **Researchers call it "downstreaming"** Cassia Spohn and David Holleran, "Prosecuting Sexual Assault: A Comparison of Charging Decisions in Sexual Assault Cases Involving Strangers, Acquaintances, and Intimate Partners."

219 **the "cherished male assumption . . ."** Susan Brownmiller, *Against Our Will: Men, Women and Rape* (New York: Fawcett Columbine, 1975), p. 369.

219 **"by far the most renowned . . ."** Gilbert Geis and Ivan Bunn, *A Trial of Witches: A Seventeenth-Century Witchcraft Prosecution* (London: Routledge, 1997), p. 3.

219 **"So resplendent, in short . . ."** John Bickerton Williams, *Memoirs of the Life, Character, and Writings, of Sir Matthew Hale, Knight, Lord Chief Justice of England* (London: Jackson and Walford, 1835), p. viii.

219 **"It must be remembered, that . . ."** Sir Matthew Hale, *Historia Placitorum Coronae: The History of the Pleas of the Crown,* ed. Sollom Emlyn (London: Printed by E. and R. Nutt, and R. Gosling, assigns of Edward Sayer, Esq., 1736), vol. I, p. 635.

220 **"with so much indignation . . ."** Hale, *Historia Placitorum Coronae,* p. 636.

220 **"If she cannot govern . . ."** Matthew Hale, *Letter of Advice to His Grand-Children, Matthew, Gabriel, Anne, Mary, and Frances Hale* (London: Taylor and Hessey, 1816), pp. 30–31.

220 **"If she be kept in some awe . . ."** Hale, *Letter of Advice,* p. 31.

220 **"for they will make too deep** Ibid., p. 30.

220 **"The whole constitution of the people . . ."** Ibid., p. 15.

220 **"make it their business to paint . . ."** Ibid., p. 116.

220 **"great cuckold."** Alan Cromartie, *Sir Matthew Hale 1609–1676: Law, Religion and Natural Philosophy* (Cambridge, England: Cambridge University Press, 1995), p. 5.

220 **"the ruin of families."** Hale, *Letter of Advice*, p. 119.

220 **"There is . . . evidence that Sir Matthew Hale . . ."** Geis, *A Trial of Witches*, p. 119.

221 **"Indeed, the Salem witch-hunts . . ."** Ibid., p. 7.

221 **only with "great pain."** *The Papers of Thomas Jefferson*, vol. 10, Julian P. Boyd, ed. (Princeton, NJ: Princeton University Press, 1954), p. 602.

221 **"on account of the temptation . . ."** Ibid., p. 604.

223 **accomplished in twelve languages** William R. Roalfe, *John Henry Wigmore: Scholar and Reformer* (Evanston, IL: Northwestern University Press, 1977), p. ix.

223 **"perhaps the greatest modern legal treatise,"** George F. James, "The Contribution of Wigmore to the Law of Evidence," *University of Chicago Law Review* 8 (1940–41), p. 78.

223 **"the best legal friend that psychology had."** James M. Doyle, "Ready for the Psychologists: Learning from Eyewitness Errors," *Court Review: The Journal of the American Judges Association* 48, no. 1–2 (2012), p. 4.

223 **"Modern psychiatrists have amply studied . . ."** John Henry Wigmore, *Wigmore on Evidence*, 3d ed., rev. by James H. Chadbourn, vol. 3A (Boston: Little, Brown and Company, 1970), p. 736.

224 **"No judge should ever let . . ."** Wigmore, *Wigmore on Evidence*, p. 737.

224 **"repressive and misogynist position,"** Leigh B. Bienen, "A Question of Credibility: John Henry Wigmore's Use of Scientific Authority in Section 924a of the Treatise on Evidence," *California Western Law Review* 19, no. 2 (1983): 236.

224 **"If there is a single source . . ."** Bienen, "A Question of Credibility," 241.

224 **"Although the woman never said 'yes,'** *People v. Hulse*, 3 Hill (NY), 316.

225 **"aggressive overtures by the man . . ."** Quoted in Peggy Reeves Sanday, *A Woman Scorned: Acquaintance Rape on Trial* (Berkeley: University of California Press, 1996), p. 158.

225 **In 1670, two indentured servants** Estelle B. Freedman, *Rede-*

fining Rape: Sexual Violence in the Era of Suffrage and Segregation (Cambridge, MA: Harvard University Press, 2013), p. 15.

225 **two women in Maine reported** Sharon Block, *Rape and Sexual Power in Early America* (Chapel Hill: University of North Carolina Press, 2006), pp. 38, 92.

225 **"archaic and misogynistic doctrine."** Lisa Rein, "Comments on Rape Law Elicit Outrage," *Washington Post*, April 6, 2007.

225 **Kathleen Dumais tried for the ninth time** Catherine Rentz, "All-Male Panel Ruled on Rape Bill During Maryland's Legislative Session," *Baltimore Sun*, April 17, 2017.

229 **In fifteen years on the bench** "First Judicial District—District Judge," Colorado Office of Judicial Performance Evaluation, accessed April 24, 2017, coloradojudicialperformance.gov/retention .cfm?ret=987.

EPILOGUE: EIGHTEEN WHEELS

Documents: Court records from Marie's lawsuit filed in the US District Court for the Western District of Washington; memos provided by H. Richmond Fisher and Lynnwood's attorneys to the mediator; settlement records for Marie's lawsuit, including an invoice from the insurer; internal review of the Lynnwood Police Department's handling of Marie's case; peer review of the Lynnwood investigation, conducted by Sergeant Rinta; Mason's personnel file; training materials now used by the Lynnwood police; and FBI Uniform Crime Reporting data. For more on the You Have Options program, see: Katie Van Syckle, "The Tiny Police Department in Southern Oregon That Plans to End Campus Rape," *The Cut*, Nov. 9, 2014.

242 **"A risk management decision was made,"** Diana Hefley, "Lynnwood Settles with Rape Victim for $150K," *Daily Herald* (Everett, WA), Jan. 15, 2014.

242 **"Rittgarn ... said he was unaware ..."** Mike Carter, "Woman Sues After Lynnwood Police Didn't Believe She Was Raped," *Seattle Times*, posted June 11, 2013.

247 **"Unfortunately, interrogating victims and challenging them ..."**

Joanne Archambault, T. Christian Miller, and Ken Armstrong, "How Not to Handle a Rape Investigation," *Digg,* Dec. 17, 2015, digg.com/dialog/how-not-to-handle-a-rape-investigation #comments.

248 **"This was a big move . . ."** Eli Hager, "The Seismic Change in Police Interrogations," Marshall Project, March 7, 2017.

248 **John Reid, the technique's namesake** Douglas Starr, "The Interview," *New Yorker,* Dec. 9, 2013.

248 **Parker was formally exonerated** Todd Henrichs and Peter Salter, "State Apologizes, Pays $500K to Man in 1955 Wrongful Conviction," *Lincoln Journal Star,* Aug. 31, 2012.

248 **"furred with dust."** Anna Clark, "11,341 Rape Kits Were Collected and Forgotten in Detroit. This Is the Story of One of Them," *Elle,* June 23, 2016.

248 **investigation tallied seventy thousand untested kits** Steve Reilly, "70,000 Untested Rape Kits *USA Today* Found Is Fraction of Total," *USA Today,* July 16, 2015.

249 **dedicated nearly $80 million** Eliza Gray, "Authorities Invest $80 Million in Ending the Rape Kit Backlog," *Time,* Sept. 10, 2015.

249 **Hull knew that many victims** Avery Lill, "Oregon Detective Pioneers New Sexual Assault Reporting Program," NPR, Sept. 22, 2016.

Acknowledgments

We would like to express our deepest thanks to the many people who helped us on this journey. It began with the editors who encouraged us to pursue the reporting for our piece, "An Unbelievable Story of Rape." Bill Keller and Kirsten Danis at the Marshall Project; Stephen Engelberg, Robin Fields, and Joseph Sexton at ProPublica; and copy editor Amy Zerba shaped the narrative and honed the writing to a fine polish. We were fortunate to have a third partner in the reporting for our original story—*This American Life*, the industry standard for wise, thoughtful radio. Our thanks to the episode's producer, Robyn Semien, and to the show's host, Ira Glass.

Our agent, Mollie Glick, and her colleague at Creative Artists Agency, Michelle Weiner, helped turn our story into a project worthy of a book. They supported us and encouraged us at every step of the way.

Molly Stern, Rachel Klayman, Emma Berry, and Matthew Martin at Penguin Random House's Crown Publishing Group had the vision and courage to take on a difficult topic. They nurtured our efforts from start to end, providing us editing, oversight, and wise counsel. Ayelet Waldman and Michael Chabon consulted with us and shared ideas. Titles can be tough.

We enlisted friends and relations to read early drafts. Our thanks to Ruth Baldwin, Ramona Hattendorf, Lyn Heinman, Anna Ly, Leslie Miller, Maureen O'Hagan, Serene Quinn, and Craig Welch for allowing us to punish them so, and for their invaluable feedback.

We would like to thank the librarians at the Gallagher Law Library at the University of Washington for entrusting us with old and brittle books. Librarians are the best.

Reporting can be expensive. The Fund for Investigative Journalism—which, in its first year, helped pay for Seymour Hersh's work exposing the My Lai massacre—kindly provided us with a grant to defray our research costs for this book. So many journalists owe the FIJ a debt of gratitude. Count us among them.

Index